SPEAKING TRUTHS WITH FILM

Speaking Truths with Film

Evidence, Ethics, Politics in Documentary

BILL NICHOLS

UNIVERSITY OF CALIFORNIA PRESS

University of California Press, one of the most distinguished university presses in the United States, enriches lives around the world by advancing scholarship in the humanities, social sciences, and natural sciences. Its activities are supported by the UC Press Foundation and by philanthropic contributions from individuals and institutions. For more information, visit www.ucpress.edu.

University of California Press
Oakland, California

Library of Congress Cataloging-in-Publication Data

Names: Nichols, Bill, author.
  Title: Speaking truths with film : evidence, ethics, politics in
  documentary / Bill Nichols.
  Description: Oakland, California : University of California Press,
  [2016] | "2016 Includes bibliographical references and index.
  Identifiers: LCCN 2015045232 | ISBN 9780520290396 (cloth : alk. paper)
  | ISBN 9780520290402 (pbk. : alk. paper) | ISBN 9780520964587 (ebook)
  Subjects: LCSH: Documentary films—History and criticism.
  Classification: LCC PN1995.9.D6 N5425 2016 | DDC 070.1/8—dc23
  LC record available at http://lccn.loc.gov/2015045232

Manufactured in the United States of America

25 24 23 22 21 20 19 18 17 16
10 9 8 7 6 5 4 3 2 1

In keeping with a commitment to support environmentally responsible and sustainable printing practices, UC Press has printed this book on Natures Natural, a fiber that contains 30% post-consumer waste and meets the minimum requirements of ANSI/NISO Z39.48–1992 (R 1997) (Permanence of Paper).

For Victoria Costello,
an inspiring presence in my life

Contents

Preface

This book is a selective collection of essays spanning more than forty years of writing about documentary film. It brings together work that arose from a variety of circumstances, most notably graduate seminars on selected topics in documentary and various invitations to present lectures. The essays complement my three books on the documentary film. As a whole they explore issues of documentary form, structure, and aesthetics; the question of ethics and how standards and conventions can be both honored and productively violated; evidence and how it is constructed and used; and politics as a vital dimension to the documentary form. Each Part features two major essays that explore the key issues and stand in a complementary or contrapuntal relation to each other. These issues receive additional elaboration in the Further Reflections segments, which consist of shorter, more occasional pieces that take up more local or specific questions and films.

This book is not designed primarily as a textbook though it certainly can be used as one. It is also not a monograph that systematically examines the topics identified, nor is it a comprehensive treatment of a limited swath of documentary work but, instead, offers a wide-ranging series of explorations into crucial topics, drawing from a wide range of examples both historical and contemporary. Since the essays have been written over an extended period they also possess an internal historical dimension as evidence of the evolution of my thinking (priorities, questions, issues) over the course of my career. The field has changed, and I have as well. Whether the changes are in parallel or at some angle to each other I cannot say, though I am struck, for example, by the radical shift from the 1970s, when a radical filmmaking group struggled to remain solvent (Newsreel, the group discussed in the final part to this book), and the number of social-justice-minded filmmakers who gain financial support for their work today. Over the course of time I have taken a commitment to political change for granted, leavened by a deepening appreciation for the formal complexities of the documentary, an evolution that leaves me distressed by what would seem a godsend: an emphasis on social impact as a frequent condition for funding. But social impact, measured empirically, is not the same as social justice, achieved broadly. The former may, in fact, hinder the latter. There is a fly in the metrics ointment, and the final essay here attempts to say what it is.

I've made no attempt to preserve the essays in their original form. I've taken liberties. These amount mainly to factual corrections and the inclusion of further thoughts or more recent examples. The original essays remain available elsewhere, of course, but to reprint them with flaws that I can now see, from the grammatical to the conceptual, does not strike me as a useful service. My ultimate goal in assembling the work here is to increase their use value for those who share my enthusiasm and dedication to the documentary film.

Acknowledgments

Without the determined, persistent effort of my editor, Mary Francis, to pull these essays together, they would have remained tucked into a variety of journals or lingered on my computer's hard drive. I am extremely grateful for the consistent encouragement, occasional prodding, and astute feedback that I have received from Mary over the time it has taken to make this book a reality.

Mary sustains the great tradition of film-book publishing that the late Chick Callenbach began when he edited both film books and *Film Quarterly* for the University of California Press. He published my first major article on film and was the press's editor for my first book, *Movies and Methods.* Chick wrote several provocative books of his own and was a constant source of infectious enthusiasm and fundamental encouragement. I owe him an enormous debt of gratitude.

Many of the essays grew out of graduate seminars I have taught, and although the students who participated in those seminars may not realize it, they taught me as much as I them. Their presentations, questions, and papers were a constant source of stimulation and a challenge to rethink old assumptions and pursue new ones. Some of them have begun to publish their own books, and as a result I have continued to learn from them well after our seminars concluded. Other essays began as presentations at conferences or other events. Such occasions allow for valuable dialogue and feedback that has only helped to strengthen the talks and facilitate their conversion to print. I thank the organizers of these events at Cal Humanities, San Francisco; Film and Media Studies, Indiana University; the Getty Research Institute, Los Angeles; The Humanities Institute, Scripps College, Claremont; It's All True Film Festival, Rio de Janeiro; School of Image Arts, Ryerson University, Toronto; the Visible Evidence Conference, Stockholm; and Yamagata Film Festival, Japan.

The anonymous readers of the manuscript I first sent to the press offered extremely valuable suggestions about structure and content. They helped me reframe the essays into complementary pairs, eliminate some stray dogs that had wandered into the mix, and urged me to provide the introductory, contextual essays that begin the book as a whole and open each of the major parts.

Over the years since *Representing Reality* appeared, to be followed by so many other terrific books, articles, and conferences on documentary film, I have found myself in the company of a truly wonderful group of scholars, filmmakers, conference organizers, and friends. I cannot name them all, but I can try to mention a few of the people who have been most influential: Tamas Almasi, Pat Aufderheide, Ib Bondebjerg, Christina Burnett, Lucien Castaing-Taylor, John Corner, Tim Corrigan, Martijn de Pas, Ally Dierks, Pat Ferrero, Arild Fetveit, Péter Forgács, Jane Gaines, Jill Godmilow, Chris Holmlund, Chuck Kleinhans, Amir Labaki, Julia Lesage, John Lightfoot, Irina Leimbacher, David and Judith MacDougall, Toney Merritt, Raya Morag, Maria Dora Morão, Clarice Peixoto, Natalie Rachlin, Fernão Ramos, Michael Renov, Ruby Rich, Daniel Robin, Bob Rosen, Oksana Sarkisova, Steve Seid, Amos Vogel, Malin Wahlberg, Patricia Rebello, Rafael Sampaio, Gilberto Sobrinho, Janet Walker, Tom Waugh, Linda Williams, Brian Winston, and Patty Zimmerman. The Visible Evidence conferences, which have become a global event, bringing together scholars, filmmakers, and others who share a passion for this extraordinary form, have given the entire field a great opportunity to meet and exchange ideas on an annual basis. The founding figures of Visible Evidence—Michel Renov, Jane Gaines, and Faye Ginsburg—deserve special thanks for creating this forum and for complementing it with the Visible Evidence series of books that have provided some of the most seminal texts in our field.

Many of the essays here appear for the first time in print. In other cases I have extensively modified essays that first appeared elsewhere. I do not see any virtue in reprinting essays as they first appeared if improvements can be made. The willingness of different journals to publish my work has been a constant source of encouragement to continue since it is the use value of the essays for others that matters most to me.

And to those who take up the challenge of making the films that look at the world around us, and who thereby prompt others to reflect and comment of these achievements, I say, Thank you for all you have given us. Your contributions have led to the golden age of documentary we now enjoy and to a future of abundant possibility.

Introduction

More than forty years ago, in 1972, when I submitted my master's thesis on Newsreel, two years before a PhD program existed at UCLA, and when I thought I might well become a screenwriter, the thesis served, in my mind, as a political gesture of support toward the New Left rather than a contribution to film studies as such. Film studies was in its infancy, with only a smattering of doctoral programs available around the country, and to the extent that the academic study of film existed, it was largely oriented toward national cinemas and auteur and genre criticism, drawing inspiration from figures like James Agee, Béla Belász, Raymond Durgnat, Manny Farber, Peter Harcourt, Pauline Kael, Jim Kitses, Siegfried Kracauer, Jay Leyda, Dwight MacDonald, Hugo Münsterberg, Andrew Sarris, Susan Sontag, Parker Tyler, Robin Wood, and, of course, the bold assertions and theoretical claims of the Russian pioneers of the 1920s. Even today, this remains a pretty good group of writers for anyone's introduction to film, but it is also a far cry from the thousands of academicians now constituting the film studies scene and the standard-issue textbooks that describe but don't exclaim. The waves of European film theory that *Screen* magazine would introduce were still some years in the future, and mentions of Christian Metz, Umberto Eco, Laura Mulvey, Jacques Lacan, Raymond Bellour, Julia Kristeva, Stephen Heath, Jean-Pierre Oudart, Roland Barthes, and the increasingly vanguard work in *Cahiers du cinéma* remained rare.

Documentary film criticism in the 1970s remained a minor area of interest among those with any serious interest in film at all, with little of substance to give weight to its examination. Writing on documentary consisted largely of essays on individual films, historical surveys, collections of interviews, and the writings of figures like John Grierson and Paul Rotha. Unlike the more arcane and formalist commentary that swirled around the avant-garde, notably at *Artforum*, later at *October*, the writing about documentaries was clear, direct, and straightforward, with little conceptual ambition but much political enthusiasm. The sharp disparity in the intellectual tone of engagement between the two forms of criticism no doubt contributed to the misguided sense that these variants of nonfiction film had little in common.

Documentary was a form for the left-leaning filmmaker, then and now, and both the Soviet and British examples, along with the instigations of the Communist Party in the 1930s—mainly through the various Film and Photo leagues that cropped up around the world—gave a sense of urgency and purpose to the form that made it seem sharply removed from both Hollywood entertainment and avant-garde formalism. It felt fully worthy of a 327-page master's thesis, "Newsreel: Film and Revolution" (rules and guidelines for theses were few and far between in those early days at UCLA; that I may have written a dissertation never occurred to me).[1]

What motivated me to write the thesis also motivated my interest in fiction film. Social themes held great interest for me, and an early (also excessively long) term paper on the outsider in film, from *La guerre est finie* to *Easy Rider*, captured much of my interest in art cinema, independent film, sociological concepts, and their visual representation. The question of the visual began to loom as a central preoccupation as the works of European filmmakers who first drew me to film (Antonioni, Godard, Truffaut, Fellini, Bergman) became amplified by the heavy emphasis on Hollywood auteurism that permeated UCLA in the early 1970s. B-movie directors like Sam Fuller, Phil Karlson, Jacques Tourneur, Robert Aldrich, Nicholas Ray, and Edgar G. Ulmer, along with the more celebrated directors Ford, Hawks, Hitchcock, Minnelli, and Welles, suddenly appeared to be individual auteurs with distinct thematic preoccupations and visual styles rather than repetitious practitioners of generic formulas. A seminar on film noir with Professor Howard Suber confirmed my impression at the time that the key to understanding cinema lay in visual analysis. Social themes and political issues need to be understood in relation to the cinematic means of representation. *How* something got said came to matter as much or more than *what* got said. These considerations led to my first major article to appear in print: "Style, Grammar and the Movies," *Film Quarterly* 28, no. 3 (1975): 33-49. A mix of systems theory, semiotics, sociology, and close analysis, it also seemed at some remove from my initial interest in documentary.

Yet the centrality of *what* got said never disappeared. I joined the first cohort of film-studies doctoral students at UCLA in 1974 and became more fully immersed in the surge of theoretical issues and political concerns that psychoanalysis, structuralism, poststructuralism, semiotics, feminism, and Marxism all stimulated. The essays collected in volume 1 of *Movies and Methods* in 1976 exemplified the balance between close analysis and social context that held my attention during that period. And when it came time to choose a topic for my dissertation, returning to Newsreel and the question of how to use film as an agent for social change seemed an obvious choice. The dissertation wound up as a book published in a modest and short-lived series of dissertations from Arno Press in 1980: *Newsreel: Documentary Filmmaking on the American Left.*[2] Meanwhile, I had also managed to infiltrate *Screen* with two essays on documentary, despite the journal's heavy emphasis on continental film theory and the feature fiction film: "American Documentary Film History," a discussion revolving around the Workers Film and Photo League, based heavily on my master's thesis; and "Documentary: Theory and Practice," an early attempt to theorize the formal organization of the documentary in relation to the work of Christian Metz.[3]

In 1974, after completing course work but with my dissertation yet to be written, I accepted my first full-time teaching appointment, a one-year job as an assistant professor at Queen's University in Kingston, Ontario. What seemed a stopgap measure transformed, through a variety of unforeseeable circumstances, into a thirteen-year tenure in a small but extremely productive and successful department. Meanwhile, I became heavily involved for more than ten years in teaching Film 101, the university's first-year introduction to film, while serving as department head for most of that time (it was a Queen's tradition for senior faculty to conduct the introductory courses, and, unexpectedly, I had become head and tenured within my first five years at Queen's). This spurred me to write *Ideology and the Image*, with chapters drawn from lecture material used in the introductory course.[4] It contained chapters on documentary film theory, Fred Wiseman's films, and ethnographic film, but this apparent imbalance relative to what a book based on introductory course material might be expected to contain did not strike me as particularly unusual. My combined interest in the how and the what made it seem like a natural way to approach the study of film.

As other topics drew my attention, a full-blown examination of documentary film remained on the back burner or, perhaps more properly, lay dormant until the appearance of David Bordwell's *Narration in the Fiction Film.*[5] (Well, not entirely dormant. In 1983 I published an article, "The Voice of Documentary," inspired by a spate of strongly political documentaries released at that time; it has proven to be my widely anthologized contribution to the field for reasons that, to this day, remain a bit unclear to me.)[6]

David Bordwell had always seemed a formalist maverick, openly hostile to the prevailing currents of poststructural, psychoanalytic, Marxist, and feminist film theory but an avid and brilliant champion of formal analysis. *Narration in the Fiction Film* added cognitive science to his repertoire. Its analysis of classical (Hollywood) and art cinema narration remains a standard reference point for me. It introduced extremely useful concepts but sequestered them in a strictly formal context. The mix was maddening to me, and I wound up responding in two ways. On the one hand, I wrote a sustained critical analysis of Bordwell's concept of the human as an entity devoted to cognitive processing outside of almost any social context,[7] and, on the other, I asked myself, Wouldn't a similarly rigorous but radically different approach to documentary film be of genuine value? Ironically, one of the most formal studies of fiction film yet written prompted me to return to documentary and attempt to formulate some basic concepts that might govern it.

The result was *Representing Reality*.[8] Its appearance predated the beginnings of the annual Visible Evidence conferences (first held at Duke University in 1993) and offered the first sustained, theoretical formulations regarding documentary film as a whole. Suddenly, and unpredictably, work that I had been doing for almost twenty years took on a pioneering aspect as this field blossomed into the rich, vibrant form of serious, engaged commentary that it has been ever since. I became, without ever seeking the designation, a documentary film scholar and was soon but one of many in a still-expanding field. (The first Visible Evidence conference may have had several dozen participants. The more recent ones have had several hundred in venues around the world from Stockholm to New Delhi.) Numerous essays followed in various publications as I came to focus more heavily on documentary. Two more books also resulted: *Blurred Boundaries* and *Introduction to Documentary;* and a collection of essays on the work of Péter Forgács, coedited with Michael Renov, *Cinema's Alchemist*.[9]

A selection from the essays that I've written since the 1970s constitutes this book. Most arose as a result of an invitation to give a public talk or a desire to conduct a graduate seminar to pursue a research interest. I have always resisted the temptation to teach the same course repeatedly, despite the apparent savings of precious mental energy. Instead, I have sought to offer courses and seminars on areas of new interest or on topics that I believed were unresolved. In that way seminars on reenactments, encounter, evidence, and alternative sexuality gave me opportunities to explore aspects of documentary that I might not have otherwise done, certainly not with the stimulation and challenge of doing so in the company of smart, motivated students.

The essays chosen for this volume cover a range of topics and issues and are arranged into five parts. Each part contains two major essays followed (with the exception of part 5) by "Further Reflections" on the same general topic. Each of the two major articles approaches the topic from a different angle. The two essays serve less to launch a comprehensive analysis of a specific topic than to investigate it from different but complementary perspectives. These essays, coupled with the shorter pieces that follow, are designed to pose as many questions and suggest as many possibilities as they resolve. The dialogue we have with documentary film, as with the rest of our social and cultural landscape, evolves as the object of our study evolves. These essays stand as one contribution to that dialogue.

PART I

Documentary Meets the Neighbors

The Avant-Garde and Fiction Film

WHAT DISTINGUISHES DOCUMENTARY FILMS THAT REPRESENT our shared reality from fiction films that imagine elaborations of it or alternatives to it? And if documentary and the avant-garde are commonly regarded as polar opposites, pursuing content over form or form over content, respectively, how can they share much in the way of common purpose? One gives priority to the world around us, the other to the vision of a filmmaker. Or so it seems.

More doggedly than I realized at the time, I pursued these questions in *Representing Reality* and *Blurred Boundaries.* Can we distinguish documentary from its neighbors in any consistent way? What makes a documentary a documentary? Is it internal to the film or a question of framing and context? Three questions taken up in *Representing Reality* remain pertinent: (1) How does storytelling relate to the examination of historical events (a problem familiar to historians, anthropologists, and others but less often addressed among most film critics whose focus is mainly on fiction films)? (2) What is the role of rhetoric in making persuasive arguments in documentaries? and (3) How does objectivity function as a (rhetorical) mantle all the better to shroud the subjective, persuasive, and ideological dimensions to documentary films? In each case something feels different about the uses of storytelling, rhetoric, and objectivity, but it is not easy to say what that is in a conclusive way.

The essays here continue this investigation into intriguing aspects of the complex overlap between documentary and its neighbors. "Documentary Film and the Modernist Avant-Garde" returns to the question of how documentary came to be considered a distinct form of cinema in the late 1920s. Prior to that, the word *documentary* did not designate any particular type of film even though most documentary historians assign its origin to much earlier times, often to the quotidian events captured by the Lumière brothers at the end of the nineteenth century in films like *Workers Leaving the Lumière Factory* (1895). I argue that earlier works like these are best understood in other ways that locate them in a different moment of social history and a different period of film history. By the 1920s, however, documentary and avant-garde efforts were closely aligned, sharing the same fertile soil of experimentation and differentiation from the mainstream fiction film. The differentiation was gradual, and incomplete, but the result was that a new form of filmmaking achieved recognition around the world.

Here's another question: how do documentaries incorporate a fantasmatic dimension despite their realist predilections? By *fantasmatic* I mean an entire mise-en-scène that possesses more of a psychic reality than a historical one, more an imaginary basis than a factual one. Although documentary is often seen as a sober enterprise, it clearly contains elements that are removed from the usual forms of factual representation, most notably but not exclusively in reenactments. "Documentary Reenactment and the Fantasmatic Subject" explores this idea at length and proposes a possible typology for reenactments from highly realistic ones to extremely stylized, even Brechtian ones.

Part I also introduces "Further Reflections," shorter, more sharply focused pieces, often in different formats such as the letter, book review, or online post. As a whole, these pieces serve to instigate reflection rather than exhaust a topic. They suggest ways in which the overall topic—the relation of documentary to its closest neighbors in this case—can be further explored. They also provide examples of how forms of critical writing other than the standard essay form can contribute to our understanding of an underlying issue or question.

The "Letter to Lynn Sachs on *Investigation of a Flame*" provides a personal response to Sachs's quite experimental documentary on the Catonsville Nine. I relate my viewing of the film to what I was doing at the time of the original event and how her formal choices generated a particular form of recall, one better discussed in a letter than an essay. The letter was prompted by an invitation to contribute to a book of letters to independent and experimental filmmakers—a superb idea, I thought—but the book never materialized in that form.

The concluding piece in this part, "*Breaking the Frame*: Gender, Violation, and the Avant-Garde," began as a post on my website. I edited and amplified it for the book, but it remains primarily an indication of how I responded to Marielle Nitoslawska's poetic, highly experimental account of Carolee Schneemann's career as a filmmaker and artist. The blog does not fully review the film or probe any particular aspect of it in depth, but it does clearly point to the blurred boundaries that make any attempt to differentiate or define documentary from its neighbors a most vexing matter.

**Documentary Film and the
Modernist Avant-Garde**

OVERTURE

How is it that the most formal and, often, most abstract of films and the
most political, and sometimes, didactic of films arise, fruitfully intermingle,
and then separate in a common historical moment? What motivated this
separation and to what extent did it both succeed and fail? Our understanding of the relationship between documentary film and the modernist avant-
garde requires revision. Specifically, we need to reconsider the prevalent
story of documentary's "birth" in early cinema (1895–1905). How does this
account, inscribed in almost all of our film histories, disguise this act of
separation? What alternative account does it prevent?

Ostensibly, the origin of documentary film has long been settled. Louis
Lumière's first films of 1895 demonstrated film's capacity to document the
world around us. Here, at the start of cinema, is the birth of a documentary
tradition. Robert Flaherty's *Nanook of the North* (1922) added plot development, suspense, and more fully delineated characters to recordings of the
historical world. He gave the documentary impulse fresh vitality. And in
1929 John Grierson, the documentary film movement's greatest champion,
used his own film portrait of North Sea fishing, *Drifters*, to convince the
British government to establish a filmmaking unit within the Empire
Marketing Board, an agency charged with the circulation of food products
and the promotion of "empire" as, in Grierson's words, not the "command
of peoples" but "a co-operative effort in the tilling of soil, the reaping of
harvests, and the organization of a world economy."[1] Grierson presided
over an institutional base for documentary film production; thus, it was on
his watch that documentary film practice reached maturity. It was not until
I had the opportunity to prepare a paper comparing and contrasting the
careers of Dutch avant-garde and documentary filmmaker Joris Ivens and

Russian suprematist painter Kazimir Malevich that I began to wonder if this story of documentary's beginnings did not belong more to myth than to history.[2]

The established story of documentary's beginnings continues to perpetuate a false division between the avant-garde and documentary that obscures their necessary proximity. Rather than the story of a very early birth and gradual maturation, I suggest that documentary film only takes form as an actual practice in the 1920s and early 1930s. Earlier efforts are less nascent documentaries than works organized according to different principles, both formal and social. The appearance of documentary involves the combination of three preexisting elements—photographic realism, narrative structure, and modernist fragmentation—along with a new emphasis on the rhetoric of social persuasion. This combination of elements itself became a source of contention. The most dangerous element, the one with the greatest disruptive potential—modernist fragmentation—required the most careful treatment. Grierson was greatly concerned by its linkage to the radical shifts in subjectivity promoted by the European avant-garde and to the radical shifts in political power promoted by the constructivist artists and Soviet filmmakers. He, in short, adapted film's radical potential to far less disturbing ends.

Modernist techniques of fragmentation and juxtaposition lent an artistic aura to documentary that helped distinguish it from the cruder form of early actualités or newsreels. These techniques contributed to documentary's good name, but they also threatened to distract from documentary's activist goals. The proximity and persistence of a modernist aesthetic in actual documentary film practice encouraged, most notably in the writings and speeches of John Grierson, a repression of the role of the 1920s avant-garde in the rise of documentary. Modernist elitism and textual difficulty were qualities to be avoided. The historical linkage of modernist technique and documentary oratory, evident since the early 1920s in much Soviet and some European work, failed to enter into Grierson's own writings. The same blind spot persists in subsequent histories of documentary film.

But even though the contribution of the avant-garde underwent repression in the public discourse of figures like Grierson, it returned in the actual form and style of early documentary itself. Repression conveys the force of a denial, and what documentary film history sought to deny was not simply an overly aesthetic lineage but the radically transformative potential of film pursued by a large segment of the international avant-garde. In its stead a more moderate rhetoric prevailed, tempered to the practical issues of the day. For advocates like Grierson the value of cinema lay in its capacity to document, demonstrate, or, at most, enact the proper, or improper, terms of individual citizenship and state responsibility.

My primary thesis is that a wave of documentary activity takes shape at the point when cinema comes into the direct service of various, already active, efforts to build national identity during the 1920s and 1930s. Documentary film affirms, or contests, the power of the state; that is, it addresses issues of public importance and affirms or contests the role of the state in confronting these issues. These acts of contestation, more than affirmation, were what initially drew me to the documentary tradition that ran from the work of the Film and Photo League in the 1930s to Newsreel in the 1970s.[3] The radical potential of film to contest the state and its law, as well as to affirm it, made documentary an unruly ally of those in power. Documentary, like avant-garde film, casts the familiar in a new light, not always that desired by the existing governments. The formation of a documentary film movement required the discipline that figures like Grierson in Great Britain, Pare Lorentz in the United States, Joseph Goebbels in Germany, and Anatoly Lunacharsky and Andrei Zhdanov in the Soviet Union provided for it to serve the political and ideological agenda of the existing nation-state.

The modernist avant-garde of Man Ray, Rene Clair, Hans Richter, Louis Delluc, Jean Vigo, Alberto Cavalcanti, Luis Buñuel, Sergei Eisenstein, Dziga Vertov, and the Russian constructivists, among others, exceeded the terms of this binary opposition of affirmation and contestation centered on the bourgeois-democratic state. It proposed alternative subjects and subjectivities until the consolidation of socialist realism, the rise of fascism and Stalinism, the necessities of exile, and the exigencies of the Great Depression depleted its resources. From the vantage point of the avant-garde, the state and issues of citizenship were obscured by questions of perception and consciousness, aesthetics, the unconscious, actions, and desire. These questions were more challenging imperatives than those that preoccupied the custodians of state power.

THE STORY OF ORIGINS AND A QUESTION OF MODELS

By 1930, with the adoption of sound in the cinema and the onset of a global depression, documentary had gained recognition as a distinct form of filmmaking. What brought it into being? The standard histories assume the existence of a documentary tradition, or impulse, that long precedes the formation of a documentary movement or institutional practice. This ancestral pedigree guarantees documentary's birthright, but, as we will see, it also poses a problem. If the documentary form was latent in cinema from the outset, why did it take some thirty years before Grierson would bestow the name *documentary* on it?

In the familiar story of documentary's ancestral origins it all begins with cinema's primal love for the surface of things, its uncanny ability to capture life as it is. Documentary represents the maturation of what was already manifest in early cinema with its immense catalogue of people, places, and things culled from around the world. British documentary filmmaker and historian Paul Rotha wrote in 1939 that documentary left the confines of fiction for "wider fields of actuality, where the spontaneity of natural behaviour has been recognized as a cinematic quality and sound is used creatively rather than reproductively. This attitude is, of course, the technical basis of the documentary film."[4]

Film historian Jack Ellis followed a similar line some fifty years later. Documentary "could be said to have begun with the birth of film itself. The filmed recordings of actuality in the experiments of technicians at the Edison laboratory in West Orange, N.J., might qualify."[5] Erik Barnouw, author of the most widely used history of documentary film, opens his account with a reference to the early pioneers of the 1890s, who "felt a compelling need to document some phenomenon or action, and contrived a way to do it. In their work the documentary film had prenatal stirrings."[6]

In these origin stories Rotha, Ellis, and Barnouw associate nascent documentary film production with the photographic, or indexical, documentation of preexisting phenomena.[7] The passage from document to documentary, then, follows an evolutionary progression. Prenatal stirrings become adult strides once we add an infusion of mature narrative stock in the form of Flaherty's *Nanook of the North* and Grierson's robust organizing skills. According to Thompson and Bordwell, Grierson, like a Promethean hero, animates this slumbering giant all by himself: "The burgeoning of the documentary mode resulted largely from the efforts of Scottish-born John Grierson."[8] As Grierson himself puts it, "There is money for films which will make box-office profits, and there is money for films which will create propaganda results. These only. They are the strict limits within which cinema has had to develop and will continue to develop."[9] Documentary film form thus brings to life the cinema's unfulfilled propagandistic (or oratorical) potential. Put differently, this origin myth begs the question: if photography and film possessed the capacity to document from the outset, why must we wait three decades after the beginnings of cinema for an actual documentary film movement to appear? Is this not necessarily a decisive historical act rather than a natural evolutionary progression?[10]

The alternative history presented here underscores how the appearance of documentary film involves conditions peculiar to the moment of its inception after World War I rather than its purported ancestry. Well-established elements of cinema are brought into play. They only take documentary form in specific historical circumstances that function as "innovative spurs, movements that launch new energies."[11] Apart from such circumstances, potentialities would remain dormant or contribute to quite different waves or genres.[12] Origin myths of distant ancestors and elaborate pedigree legitimate a new genre by equipping it with a distinctive lineage traceable to the birth of cinema itself. Not coincidentally, such myths deflect scrutiny from the similarity and overlap between 1920s documentary and the avant-garde. They also rationalize the enforcement of boundaries to separate documentary from "obviously" unrelated alternatives like the avant-garde.

In fact, of the four elements that contribute to the formation of a documentary film wave, only one had been in place since 1895: the capacity of cinema to record visible phenomena with great fidelity. To this capacity we must add three elements: (1) the gradual elaboration of narrative codes and conventions distinct to cinema (1905–15) that allow any film to utilize a storytelling structure capable of inspiring belief in its representational gestures, largely through emphasis on vivid characters, linear actions, and the cinematic organization of time and space via continuity, parallel, and point-of-view editing; (2) the least acknowledged element: a wide array of modernist, avant-garde filmmaking practices that flourish throughout the 1920s; and (3) a range of techniques intended to achieve persuasive, rhetorical engagement.

None of these elements alone leads to the appearance of documentary film. Each leads elsewhere as well. Rather than tracing a line of descent for documentary, it will be more profitable to describe each element briefly and to indicate how it came to contribute to the appearance of a documentary film form in the period between the wars.

PHOTOGRAPHIC REALISM

Like scientific documentation, the "cinema of attractions," described by Tom Gunning as the prevalent pre-1906 mode of representation, relies on the authenticating effect of camera optics and photographic emulsions to generate images that bear a precise set of relations to that which they represent. Both scientific evidence and carnival-like attractions exhibit noteworthy aspects of the world with indexical precision. Such images readily serve as documents but not documentaries.[13] In science they offer proofs or record phenomena beyond what the eye can see. As "attractions" they solicit "spectator attention, inciting visual curiosity, and supplying pleasure through an exciting spectacle—a unique event, whether fictional or documentary, that is of interest in itself."[14]

Unfettered from narrative structure or scientific analysis, a cinema of attractions is a form of excitation, exhibitionism, or spectacle. It engenders an effect comparable to the effect of reality TV shows such as *Cops* or *Survivor*, namely, "Isn't this amazing!"[15] We witness strange, violent, dangerous, or catastrophic events but receive only minimal analysis of them. A program on ABC in January 2000 entitled "Out of Control People" provided a latter-day Mondo Cane–like catalogue of soccer rioting, college-student rampages, prison uprisings, and other examples of its own title with small snippets of commentary from "experts" who make reference to mob behavior and group psychology. The intent of the program was clearly far more sensationalistic than educational. The sensationalism gained immeasurably from the use of "documentary" images of actual events.

As the surrealists were eager to demonstrate, the language of sensationalism could also readily insinuate itself into the protocols of science. Lisa Cartwright has carried this insight into the belly of scientific experimentation to chronicle the misuses of documentary images in work that purports to follow scientific procedure but detours toward issues of morbidity and spectacle.[16] Such an effect underscores a sense of amazement, and sometimes outrage, rather than rational understanding. Allan Sekula notes that documentary work can amass a mountain of evidence, "and yet, in this pictorial presentation of scientific and legalistic 'fact,' the genre has simultaneously contributed much to spectacle, to retinal excitation, to voyeurism, to terror, envy and nostalgia, and only a little to the critical understanding of the social world."[17]

In classic surrealist/dadaist form the pretensions to knowledge that allow exotic travelogues to masquerade as scientific statement became the direct target of Luis Buñuel's unsettling account of poverty in Spain's Las Hurdes region, *Land without Bread* (1932), itself a work with a fascinating precursor in Adrian Brunel's mock travelogue of a trek across the Sahara Desert, *Crossing the Great Sagrada* (1924). Buñuel's film is heavily informed by a written ethnography of a poor region of Spain published a few years earlier, but it turns science on its head to underscore the sensationalism that surrounds "attractions" concocted from elements of everyday Hurdano life. *Land without Bread* condemns the very procedures of fieldwork, detailed description, and objective commentary that would form the backbone for ethnographic encounter in the decades to come.[18]

Spectacle in early cinema, like visual evidence in science, relied on an impression of photographic realism, the better to convince us of the authenticity of remarkable sights. One of the most vivid conjunctions of spectacle and photographic realism occurs in pornography. Markers of authenticity affirm that an actual sex act has occurred, even if this act occurred, like most fiction-based acts, solely for the purpose of being filmed. It is safe to conclude that the documentary potential of the photographic image does not lead directly to a documentary film practice. Neither spectacle and exhibition nor science and documentation guarantee the emergence of a documentary film form. Movements involve historical contingency, not genetic ancestry. Something more than the ability to generate visual documents, however useful this may be, is necessary. Much can be documented, but most documents are not documentaries.

NARRATIVE STRUCTURE

If the indexical image and cinematic document lends itself to multiple purposes, it may well be a necessary if not sufficient condition for the appearance of documentary film. Narrative enters into the equation in a similar fashion. Narrative clearly leads elsewhere, toward fiction, so much so that its value to documentary can be easily underestimated. Few would claim documentary as the evolutionary culmination of cinema's narrative endowment. What narrative does is make time something more than simple duration or sensation. Through the introduction of a temporal axis of actions and events involving characters or, more broadly, agents (animals, cities, invisible forces, collective masses, and so on), narrative imbues time with historical meaning. Narrative allows documentary to endow occurrences with the significance of historical events. Narrative overcomes the fetishizing lure of spectacle and the factual conclusiveness of science. It restores the mystery and power of historical consciousness.[19]

Narrative not only facilitates the representation of historical time; it also supplies techniques by which to introduce the moralizing perspective or social belief of an author and a structure of closure whereby initiating disturbances can receive satisfactory resolution. Such resolution gives an imprimatur of conclusiveness to the arguments, perspectives, and solutions advanced by the film. Typically centered on a main character or hero in classic narrative fiction, such a structure proves detachable from individualized agents or heroes; social issues such as inadequate housing, floods, the isolation of remote regions, or the exploitation of an entire class can establish the story's initiating disturbance. Resolution follows less from a hero's actions than from the documentary's own solution to social problems: slum clearance in *Housing Problems* (Edgar Anstey and Arthur Elton, 1935); the creation of the TVA in *The River* (Pare Lorentz, 1937); railroad construction in *Turksib* (Victor A. Turin, 1929); and a workers' strike in *Misère au Borinage* (Joris Ivens and Henri Storck, 1934).[20] The form of such films takes over the work customarily assigned to the heroic efforts of an individual protagonist.

MODERNIST PRACTICES

The modernist avant-garde of the 1920s introduces a third contribution to the appearance of a documentary film form. It is this milieu, with its own formal conventions and social purpose; its own amalgam of advocates and practitioners, institutions, and discourses; and its own array of assumptions and expectations on the part of audience and artists, that provides both representational techniques and a social context conducive to a documentary movement.

Individuals such as Buñuel, Vigo, Vertov, Richter, Delluc, and Ivens moved readily between an emphasis on the effects of form itself, in keeping with the modernist tradition, and an emphasis on social impact, in keeping with a documentary impulse.[21] Films that shared an avant-garde emphasis such as Laszlo Moholy-Nagy's unrealized plan for a "city symphony film," *Dynamics of a Great City* (1921–22),[22] *Fievre* (Delluc, 1921), *Retour à la maison* (Man Ray, 1923), *Ballet mécanique* (Fernand Léger, 1924), *Mechanics of the Brain* (Vsevolod Pudovkin, 1926), *Rien que les heures* (Cavalcanti, 1926), *A Sixth of the World* (Vertov, 1926), *The Bridge* (Ivens, 1927), *Emak-Bakia* (Ray, 1927), *Ghosts before Breakfast* (Richter, 1927), *Berlin: Symphony of a City* (Walter Ruttmann, 1927), *Un chien andalou* (Buñuel and Salvador Dali, 1928), *Inflation* (Richter, 1928), *Man with a Movie Camera* (Vertov, 1929), *Rain* (Ivens, 1929), *À Propos de Nice* (Vigo, 1929), *L'Age d'or* (Buñuel, 1930), *Salt for Svanetia* (Mikhail Kalatozov, 1930), and *Land without Bread* (Buñuel, 1932) affirmed the close proximity of modernist exploration and documentary address.

Such a fusion of interests was particularly evident in Soviet Russia throughout the 1920s and into the early 1930s before socialist realism gained dominance. Figures such as Aleksandr Rodchenko, Vladimir Tatlin, Vera Stepanova, Kazimir Malevich (in his late paintings), El Lissitzky, Alexei Gan, Lyubov Popova, Alexander and Victor Vesnin, the Stenberg brothers, and Vladimir Mayakovsky were among the many artists who contributed to a constructivist movement that combined formal innovation with social application.

Without the capacity to disrupt and make new, documentary filmmaking would not have been possible as a discrete rhetorical practice. It is the modernist avant-garde that fulfills Grierson's own call for the "creative treatment of actuality" most relentlessly.[23] The explosive power of avant-garde practices subverts and shatters the coherence, stability, and naturalness of the dominant world of realist representation. Documentaries from the interwar period cobble images together with remarkable abandon, fully in accord with the pioneering spirit of the avant-garde. (Voice-over commentary, poetic or expository, lends them a purposefulness the avant-garde typically eschewed.) Raul Ruiz reminds us of the fabulous heterogeneity of documentary images in *De grands événements et des gens ordinaires* (*Of Great Events and Ordinary* People, 1979) when his voice-over commentary describes this peculiar feature of the world presented by documentary as we witness a collage of isolated objects from everyday life cascade before us.

The "creative treatment of actuality" is authored, not recorded or registered. Creative treatment turns fact to fiction in the root sense of the Latin *fictio*, to shape or fashion. The concept of making, or authorship, moves us away from indexical documents of preexisting fact to the semiotics of constructed meaning and the address of the authorial I. As Ivens asserted, "It is the personality of the artist alone which distinguishes him from both reality and simple recording."[24] Or as Dziga Vertov, a figure claimed by documentary historians but himself rooted deeply in the theory and practice of the constructivist avant-garde, proclaimed in 1923, "My road is toward the creation of a fresh perception of the world. Thus, I decipher in a new way the world unknown to you."[25]

In a similar spirit Rodchenko attacked the tradition of the painted portrait as a romantic mystification compared to the documentary power of the photograph or, preferably, a series of photographs: "Art has no place in modern life. . . . With the appearance of photographs, there can be no question of a single, immutable portrait. . . . The photograph presents a precise moment documentarily. . . . Crystallize man not by a single 'synthetic' portrait, but by a whole lot of snapshots taken at different times and in different conditions."[26]

Modernist elements of fragmentation, defamiliarization (ostranenie, Verfremdungseffekt), collage, abstraction, relativity, anti-illusionism, and a general rejection of the transparency of realist representation all find their way into acts of documentary filmmaking. As Vertov wrote, "I am eye. I have created a man more perfect than Adam. . . . I take the most agile hands of one, the fastest and most graceful legs of another . . . and, by editing, I create an entirely new, perfect man."[27] Such techniques and aspirations speak less to a flight from the social world into aesthetic reverie than to a critique of "an ideology of realism" designed to "perpetuate a preconceived notion of some external reality to be imitated, and indeed, to foster a belief in the existence of some such commonsense everyday shared secular reality in the first place."[28] The 1920s avant-garde set out to revise the terms and conditions by which to construct representations of a shared secular reality.

The films mentioned above, from *Dynamics of a Great City* to *Land without Bread*, combine an avant-garde impulse with a documentary orientation. They disabuse their viewers of any commonsense reality. Such work constructs a new order of understanding. In the midst of upheaval, when, as the Russian Revolution seemed to confirm, "the bourgeoisie begins to decay as a class, in a world of social anomie and fragmentation, then that active and conquering mode of the representation of reality which is realism is no longer appropriate."[29] For whom is it no longer appropriate? At the very least, for these filmmakers and other artists and activists who now saw things in a radically new way.

In France, Delluc introduced the concept of photogenie to describe how, in Richard Abel's words, "cinema acted as a transformative, revelatory medium of absorption and de-familiarization."[30] Meanwhile, anthropologists such as Michel Leiris and Marcel Griaule, modernists such as Robert Desnos and Georges Bataille, and scholars such as Carl Einstein and Andre Schaffner joined together at the journal *Documents* to demonstrate, in layout and text, that "to write ethnographies on the model of collage would be to avoid the portrayal of cultures as organic wholes or as unified, realistic worlds subject to a continuous explanatory discourse."[31]

Hannah Höch, John Heartfield, Moholy-Nagy, and Rodchenko drew on the technique of photomontage to subvert, reorder, and transform the face of photographic reality. Instead of the resolution-oriented structure of classic narrative, or the comparable problem-solution pattern of much documentary, modernist experimentation favored an open-ended, ambiguous play with time and space that did less to resolve real issues than to challenge the definition and priority of an issue per se. Modernist strategies remind us of the intractable kernel of potentially traumatic disturbance that makes the experience of history itself so different from its narrative representation. In what could be a justification for the radical transformations of an avant-garde, Slavoj Žižek asserts, "What emerges via distortions of the accurate representation of reality is the real—that is, the trauma around which social reality is structured."[32]

It was precisely the power of the combination of the indexical representations of the documentary image and the radical juxtapositions of time and space allowed by montage that drew the attention of many avant-garde artists to film. Most turned away from conventional narrative structure, but many still chose to "relocate [a film's] subject in 'the image of the object,' in the plastic and rhythmic conjunction or juxtaposition of representational 'documentary' images,"[33] a goal not unlike that of Bertolt Brecht, who challenged the theater director to adopt the new style and perspective of a "great epic and documentary theater."[34] The modernist avant-garde contributed something vital to the appearance of documentary film; it imaginatively reconstructed the look of the world with images, or shots, taken of this world. As in the photographs of Atget, street scenes— from the backstreets of Paris in Ray's *L'étoile de mer* (1928) to the puddles and umbrellas of Amsterdam in Ivens's *Rain*—became a staple of modernist work.

The street, in fact, becomes a site of strange delights and bizarre discoveries: the mysterious box dropped by the woman in *Un chien andalou* and the "barbaric ritual" of tearing heads from chickens that Buñuel finds on the village streets of Los Hurdes in *Land without Bread*. These sights followed even earlier efforts to document life in the street such as the extraordinary footage generated for Albert Kahn's *Archives de la planète*. One example is an extended long take of men entering and leaving a public urinal on a Paris street (*Les grands boulevards, Paris*, October 1913). The exchange of gazes between the camera and the urinal's visitors attests to the surreal and complexly charged nature of this "archival" encounter.[35]

Such images lent historical potential to images of everyday life, even as these images altered our ordinary perception of the world. They only require yoking to the oratorical voice of the filmmaker to make them fit for documentary representation. The street, along with the car, the machine, and the city—with their position halfway between the animate and the inanimate—provide a ready-made subject for the avant-garde as well as the documentarian. From Germaine Dulac's harsh parody of male prerogative in *The Smiling Madame Beudet* (1923) to Vigo's satiric view of the urban bourgeoisie at leisure in *À Propos de Nice*, the avant-garde gave voice to the subversion of social convention. Although some avant-garde films, such as those of Viking Eggeling (*Symphonie diagonale*, 1921–24) or the early work of Richter (*Rhythmus 23*, 1923; *Rhythmus 25*, 1925) moved strongly toward abstraction, or "pure cinema," a great many works began with images of a recognizable reality in order to transform it. On this point constructivist art, Soviet montage theory, and the European avant-garde stood in accord: the world as it offers itself to us provides the starting point for both political and aesthetic acts of transformation.

RHETORICAL STRATEGIES

Documentary took identifiable shape when photographic realism, narrative structure, and modernist fragmentation served the goal of social persuasion. Oration added another element of social consciousness to cinematic representation. It called on the audience to put itself at one with the social perspective of the film and to prepare itself to act accordingly. Rhetorical speech, in the form of editing patterns, intertitles, and voice-over commentary, channels techniques of defamiliarization toward preferred forms of social change. Like the other three elements, rhetoric does not necessarily lead to documentary film. As a persuasive strategy it also supports overt propaganda, all advertising, and some forms of journalism. But from the ecstatic celebration of the completion of the Turkestan-Siberian railroad with titles that shoot toward the viewer with increasing intensity over rapidly cut images of onrushing trains at the conclusion of Victor Turin's *Turksib* to the carefully choreographed images of masses and leaders, followers and their one Fuhrer in Leni Riefenstahl's *Triumph of the Will* (1934), rhetorical strategies allowed documentary expression to achieve a distinctive voice of its own.

DOCUMENTARY'S HISTORICAL MOMENT

Over the course of the 1920s a wave of documentary filmmaking took shape that allowed differentiation between the modernist artist and the social orator. This new movement first took shape, however, not in the as yet unfounded British documentary, where the promotion of documentary film required the derogation of the modernist avant-garde, but in constructivist art and Soviet cinema, where avant-garde and documentary tendencies engaged in a lively interaction.

Grierson, like others, was well aware of the Soviet achievement and of its parallels with his own plans for a new film form. In fact, Grierson contributed the English titles to *Turksib;* he also played a key role in the American distribution of Eisenstein's first film, *Strike* (1925)—a work, like Flaherty's *Moana*, rich in documentary value.[36] The Soviet example, however, like the modernist avant-garde generally, represented a form of excess for Grierson. Its rhetorical exuberance and political radicalism spilled far beyond the bounds of what his government sponsors expected. Grierson's vision of the role of the artist differed from that of the Soviet filmmakers and constructivist artists in the 1920s. In each case two strands of modernist discourse become intertwined but in radical rather than conservative forms. Margaret

Olin describes these two discourses as "one 'documentary,' exhorting the reader to participate in, so as to ameliorate, the conditions it describes [which I have also termed oratorical], and the other 'artistic,' concerning itself with the problematics of selfhood and otherness."[37] Documentary film in the 1920s and 1930s achieves this braiding by assigning amelioration—and all the other modalities of social intervention—to those categories of selfhood and otherness that revolve around issues of citizenship and the nation-state.

The principle of citizenship as self-realization, frequently invoked by constructivists and filmmakers in the Soviet Union in relation to the creation of a "new man," became the singular raison d'être for Grierson's conception of the documentary: not to foment revolution but to preserve the status quo. Grierson's commitment to government and corporate sponsorship as the only viable means of institutional support required an act of separation from the more radical potentialities of the modernist avant-garde and the particular example of the Soviet cinema. Grierson campaigned long and hard for a documentary film practice that persuaded more than informed, guided more than observed. The social orator undertook the task of offering moral and political guidance to the confused masses by means of emotionally (rhetorically) compelling argument. Fulfillment lay in carrying out one's responsibilities to the common goals embodied in the nation-state. Grierson's discussions of meanings and values, virtues and models, never occurred in a realm of timeless contemplation. They played a crucial role in developing what Foucault would call "strategies of domination" in relation to the alternatives posed by the European avant-garde and the Soviet model.[38] How did he accomplish this?

Among other things, Grierson shifted the focus of his search for a model from the rhetorical and organizational example of Soviet cinema to the lone, romantic figure of Robert Flaherty, a semicommercial maverick specializing in heroic tales drawn from exotic locations.[39] Flaherty had the right sense of drama and conflict but the wrong sense of modernity. In a series of written commentaries, Grierson lamented that Flaherty—maker of, under Grierson's sponsorship, *Industrial Britain* (1933), a film more about potters and glassblowers than the assembly line—harnessed his storytelling genius to an outmoded vision of "man against the sky" rather than to the needs of the modern day "documentary value" but not the documentarian's voice of social consciousness. Flaherty gave no guidance to the man on the street; his was an escape to earlier times and distant pleasures. With this critique Grierson fabricated an ostensible issue: how to make Flaherty's romanticism—one step removed from Hollywood escapism—topical and propagandistic. This allowed him to sidestep the actual issue: how to make the Soviet cinema's radicalism palatable to non-radical, bourgeois-democratic ends?

To the extent that Grierson did address the model of Soviet cinema, he invoked the same convenient scapegoat he had already fashioned from Flaherty; he found Soviet films escapist and inadequately pragmatic, just as Flaherty did. Grierson wrote:

> The great Russian directors . . . were begun in propaganda and were made by it. . . . One cannot do less when recording a world revolution than develop a tempo to take it. . . . But the whole effect was hectic and, in the last resort, romantic. . . . After the first flush of exciting cinema, the Russian talent faded. . . .
>
> Russian directors are too bound up—too aesthetically vain—in what they call their "play films" to contribute to Russia's instructional cinema. They have, indeed, suffered greatly from the freedom given to artists in a first uncritical moment of revolutionary enthusiasm, for they have tended to isolate themselves more and more in private impression and private performance. . . . One's impression is that when some of the art and all of the bohemian self-indulgence have been knocked out of them, the Russian cinema will fulfil its high promise of the late twenties.[40]

Grierson thus aligns himself with the advocates of socialist realism, who, by 1932, had the political power to label the politically radical and formally experimental directions in Soviet cinema unproductive trickery. The clear and decisive harnessing of creative energies to a specific form of social purpose took top priority for Grierson. Artistic license must be consistently subordinated to the propagandistic goal of giving citizens their proper orientation to the state.

And what did Grierson have to say of the European avant-garde? Its private, rather than public, sponsorship proved dilettantish, if not decadent. Or in Grierson's own words:

> Documentary was from the beginning—when we first separated our public purpose theories from those of Flaherty [read: Soviet cinema]— an 'anti-aesthetic' movement.[41]

> There has grown up another more independent cinema. I do not mean here the avant garde cinema which for a while flourished in France and has raised its head wherever family fortune and youthful enthusiasm have allowed it. The French avant garde with Rene Clair . . . Cavalcanti, Epstein and Jean Renoir, made its dash for liberty by exploiting its friends. . . . All the requisites of an independent cinema were there except principle, and the loyalty which goes with principle. . . .

Something more solidly founded than the avant garde there has been, and that is the propagandist cinema.[42]

By 1930–32 a documentary film movement existed but with its radical potential harnessed by figures like Grierson to the specific needs of the nation-state. As Grierson put it:

> The State is the machinery by which the best interests of the people are secured. Since the needs of the State come first, understanding of these needs comes first in education. . . . The needs of the State in this great period of revolutionary change are urgent; and the citizen has neither the leisure nor the equipment for the promiscuous exercise of his mental and emotional interests.[43]

> I suggest, in fact, that the problems of education and art, and their inevitable interest today, lie in the realm of the imaginative training for modern citizenship and not anywhere else.[44]

> There it is . . . from the dramatization of modern organization and the new corporate elements in society to the dramatization of social problems: each a step in the attempt to understand the stubborn raw material of our modern citizenship and wake the heart and the will to their mastery.[45]

These remarks expose the tip of Grierson's larger social and aesthetic orientation. Although documentary filmmaking in the 1920s generally shares in the progressive politics of that period and represents one of the prime examples of a turn toward what William Stott called "documentary expression," Grierson's own position more closely resembles neoconservative political theory and the elitist aesthetics of the Bloomsbury group. Grierson's neoconservatism draws from (1) Benedetto Croce's and Graham Wallas's prewar emphasis on intuition and the irrational as vital forces that discredit liberal trust in reason (Grierson himself concluded that the state had to move and persuade rather than inform and explain); (2) a Hegelian idealist view of the state that privileged the technocratic vision of a governing elite over the strategic maneuvering of political parties; and (3) a corporatist model of state organization in which a civil service mandarinate arbitrated conflict and dispensed wisdom rather than awaited the outcome of tedious parliamentary debates. Grierson placed himself among the elite and drew few distinctions between his views and more virulent forms of totalitarianism. In 1942, for example, Grierson opined to a friend that Britain had two choices: make an alliance with Russia or make an alliance with Germany. England "could do a deal with Germany that would save more of England's world privileges than can be saved any other way."[46]

Grierson's affinity with the aesthetics of the Bloomsbury group involved, first, a rejection of realism as a transparent style. To give the impression of observing lived reality mattered less than utilizing more innovative techniques, including those of the avant-garde, to urge preferred solutions to social problems. Second, it evidenced a distrust of the rise of a mass or popular audience since such audiences could not be counted on for reasoned, political judgment. Grierson coupled his neoconservative view of public "service," or propaganda, to an aesthetic of art as a "hammer" to hit nerves and guide actions. Clive Bell's comment—"Society must be permeated and, what is more, continually nourished by the unconscious influence of this civilizing elite. . . . The majority must be told that the world of thought and feeling exists. . . . To point the road is the task of the few"[47]—could easily be Grierson's own. To warrant sponsorship, art must be useful to the needs of an idealist model of the state. Guiding the masses toward the fulfillment of their civic responsibility and national patrimony is paramount. This aesthetic's mechanisms may seem totalitarian, but idealist principles and distrust of the masses justifies it. If we are to locate Grierson's attacks on the modernist avant-garde effectively, his famous definition of documentary as "the creative treatment of actuality" must be coupled with his less-well-known definition of propaganda as "the constructive management of public affairs."[48]

Documentary gains a definition and institutional base as it fulfills its potential to be what Lenin once called it, "the most important art."[49] It is the art most fully equipped to engage a mass audience via the mediations of the new technologies of photographic fidelity and mechanical reproduction. As Peter Galassi notes in his essay for the Museum of Modern Art's Rodchenko catalogue, "the adaptation of the modernist aesthetic to hortatory functions was an international phenomenon of the 1930s, blind to ideological distinctions. . . . [One thing that Stalin, Hitler, and Henry Luce shared] was a talent for persuading a massive audience that life was as good as their picture of it. To achieve this, their artists did not overthrow modernism; they adapted it."[50]

Like newspapers and radio before it, cinema contributed a powerful rhetorical voice to the needs of the modern state, which had to find ways to enact popular, compelling representations of the state's policies and programs. Such enactments would engage its members in ritual, participatory acts of citizenship. Documentary film practice became one such form of ritual participation.

Although shadowed by elitism, and hence vulnerable to critique, the modernist avant-garde's greatest threat was not a failure to pay off but the risk of paying off too well. The very techniques of fragmentation, defamiliarization, suspended belief and activated disbelief, radical heterogeneity and arbitrary closure that characterize avant-garde film destabilized the institutional solidity and civic respectability with which Grierson sought to endow the documentary. The modernist avant-garde provided a way to represent traumatic events in a manner less fetishistic "than any traditional representation of them could ever be."[51] Solutions, not traumas, however, were what Grierson and others like him sought. Richter's inflation, for example, pans across scores of bewildered faces as money loses value and disaster looms. His abstracted, lateral shots of real faces in an unreal space unfurl like a scroll of indefinite length; the traumas of technological modernity defy the fiscal policies of the nation-state. Inflation fetishizes no heroes, no managerial elite, no solution, no story of good cheer.

Griersonian documentary promises the mastery of events through participatory rituals suited to the citizen-subject. Modernism exposes such participatory rituals as just that: rituals. The modernist avant-garde thwarted the illusion of mastery that comes with realism and narrative. Modernism refused to render events such as the Depression, war, political revolution, or, later, the Holocaust "clearly and unambiguously identified as to their meaning" or to liberate us from the shadow they cast over our desire to "envision a future free from their debilitating effects."[52]

From this perspective Grierson's strategy for documentary film production asked of audiences what John F. Kennedy so famously asked of his fellow citizens: "Ask not what your country can do for you; ask what you can do for your country." The orator not only reaches citizens but also contributes to the construction of the sense of identity necessary for citizenship in the first place. Films of ritual participation mark the dominant tradition, be they investitures of monumental fascism in Nazi Germany (*Triumph of the Will*), the "people's" communism of Soviet Russia (*Old and New*, Eisenstein, 1929; *Salt for Svanetia; Three Songs of Lenin*, Vertov, 1934), the Labor-Conservative coalitions of 1930s Britain (*Housing Problems; Coal Face*, Cavalcanti, 1935; *Smoke Menace*, John Taylor, 1937), or the New Deal interventionism of Rooseveltian America (*The Plow That Broke the Plains*, Pare Lorentz, 1936; *The River*).

Not all documentary was state or corporate sponsored. Some filmmakers chose to contest the power of the state, often in alliance with various social-democratic or national communist parties outside the U.S.S.R. The Film and Photo leagues that appeared in numerous countries, with their photo documentation and film newsreels of hunger marches, strikes, and social protests were prime examples of oppositional effort.[53] But rather than return to the radical potentiality of modernist technique, oppositional documentary endorsed the more realist tone of dominant documentary production and the issues of self and other that fell within the circumscribed limits of the citizen in relation to the state. The New York Film and Photo League, for example, allowed a contingent of artistically ambitious members to split off to make more full-blown documentaries on larger issues, such as the background to the Spanish Civil War, while the majority insisted on the primacy of news-oriented topical reports or newsreels. Neither group seriously entertained the stratagems of the avant-garde.

Ivens exemplifies the avant-garde filmmaker turned leftist documentarian who offered relentless opposition to the bourgeois-democratic state.[54] Ivens made films in eight countries between 1927 and 1946 (The Netherlands, Belgium, U.S.S.R., Spain, China, the United States, Canada, and Australia). His alliance with the Soviet Union and the Comintern's shifting policies of militancy and popular-front unity make him a vivid representative of the radical left's combination of attacks on capitalism, on the one hand, and a defense of the Soviet Union, on the other, even when the latter defense called for a suppression of the former attacks.

Ivens also went further than his American counterparts in keeping modernist techniques alive. The gradual shift from the modernist aesthetic of *The Bridge* and *Rain* to the social activism of *The Spanish Earth* (1937), in support of the Republican cause, and *Song of the Rivers* (1953), a tribute to dockworkers and longshoremen around the world, also takes condensed form in Ivens's remake of *Zuiderzee* (1930). *Zuiderzee* is a loving chronicle of the state's reclamation of fertile land from an inland sea. It stresses the remarkable feats of engineering skill and physical labor, however, rather than the role of government. But in *New Earth* (1934), Ivens uses a shortened version of the same footage with a new conclusion: he adds a virulent denunciation of an unregulated, international stock market and the social indifference of rich investors who allow the fruit of the land to go to waste when no profit can be made from its sale. Ivens shows the wholesale dumping of grain into the sea. In *New Earth* a voice-over commentary of moral denunciation replaces *Zuiderzee*'s tone of poetic observation. The state has failed to live up to its responsibilities to regulate markets; ordinary people must pay the price. Ivens employs reenactment and defamiliarizing juxtapositions to make his point. He vividly adopts the modernist strategies Grierson disparaged and undermines the sense of sacrifice Grierson prized. It is, however, precisely the adaptation of modernist technique to a hortatory function still revolving around the nation-state that makes Ivens into Grierson's opponent. They face each other on common ground but from opposite sides of the battle lines.

In the period after 1930, Ivens clearly adopts the perspective of the left with a focus that remains concerned primarily with the role of the state. This perspective leads Ivens to produce work that addresses the failure of the state to ensure decent living conditions *(Misère au Borinage)*; the ability of the Soviet state to develop resources crucial to the well-being of the people *(Komsomol,* 1932); the failure of the world's governments to respond to the cries for aid by the Spanish government in its battle against a military coup *(The Spanish Earth)*; and a failure by his own Dutch government to heed the demands of a colonized people for their independence *(Indonesia Calling,* 1946). Like other members of the great tradition of the oppositional documentary, Joris Ivens remains centrally preoccupied with the power of the state and the rights of its citizens. Rather than join the harassed left-wing opposition to Western governments in the postwar years, however, Ivens moved behind the Iron Curtain, where he remained an active filmmaker until his death in 1989. His later career, however, as a propagandist for the "wrong" side essentially disappears from all Western film history books.[55]

CONCLUSION

Not until the 1970s does an opposition of a different kind displace the state from its central position in documentary rhetoric. Since then, these have been the central issues and debates: (1) the ethical, political, and ideological implications of the different modes of documentary production; (2) the quality and value of individual filmmaking oeuvres; (3) the usefulness of documentary film as a disciplinary (anthropological, sociological) or personal (autobiographical, poetic) form of knowledge and power; (4) the social efficacy of specific films and different modes; and (5) the challenges of historical representation and contemporary observation.

Reacting against the small-scale, observational quality of documentaries in the 1960s that began to shift attention from the state to facets of everyday life and lived experience—be they those of candidates *(Primary,* Drew Associates, 1960) or high school students *(High School,* Frederick Wiseman, 1968)—work in the 1970s returned to the modernist techniques that observational cinema rejected. *The Life and Times of Rosie the Riveter* (Connie Field, 1980) reinvents the intertextual compilation techniques of Esfir Shub. *Union Maids* (Julia Reichert and James Klein, 1976) and *With Babies and Banners* (Lyn Goldfarb, Lorraine Gray, and Ann Bohlen, 1979) revive the use of the interview to recount historical events and personal experience. Staged reenactments return in *David Holzman's Diary* (Jim McBride,

1967) and *Daughter Rite* (Michelle Citron, 1979). Collage techniques gain new currency in Emile de Antonio's *In the Year of the Pig* (1969) and Santiago Alvarez's *The 79 Springtimes of Ho Chi Minh* (1969). Together with works such as *The Woman's Film* (San Francisco Newsreel, 1971), *Word Is Out* (Mariposa Film Group, 1977), *Who Killed Vincent Chin?* (Christine Choy and Renee Tajima, 1988), *I'm British but . . .* (Gurinder Chadha, 1989), *Tongues Untied* (Marlon Riggs, 1989), *Sink or Swim* (Su Friedrich, 1990), *Paris Is Burning* (Jennie Livingston, 1991), *Isle of Flowers* (Jorge Furtado, 1990), *History and Memory* (Rea Tajiri, 1991), *Bontoc Eulogy* (Marlon Fuentes, 1997), and *Free Fall* (Péter Forgács, 1998), these films take up alternative subjectivities and identities involving issues of sex and gender, ethnicity and race, personal memory and public history.

The approach to documentary representation adopted by these works no longer requires a strategic separation from modernist techniques. The power of the state, along with its achievements and failures, is secondary to the development of a heightened sense of solidarity among specific subcultures and minority groups. The perspectives, histories, and initiatives of such previously unheeded groups command attention. Collaboration between filmmakers and their subjects replaces collaboration between filmmakers and government agencies. With this shift the form and style of documentary representations expand to encompass a breadth of perspectives and voices, attitudes and subjectivities, positions and values that exceed the universal subject of an idealized nation-state.

The emergence of a documentary film practice in the 1920s and 1930s drew together various elements of photographic realism, narrative, modernism, and rhetoric at a historical moment when the technology of cinema and the techniques of persuasion could serve the needs of the modern nation-state. In Grierson's hands this involved an act of separation between the self-indulgent avant-garde of modernist expression and a down-to-earth documentary movement of realist persuasion. This separation proved, in fact, partial, if not mythic, however much film histories have perpetuated it.

Vestiges of avant-garde radicalism persisted in some forms of documentary expression throughout the period between the wars, as we can see in Brecht's theater and in films such as Richter's *Inflation*, Turin's *Turksib*, and Ivens's *New Earth*. And as the work of the later 1960s and the 1970s attests, these elements of formal innovation, coupled with social purpose, lend distinction to documentary as an art form capable of envisioning a transformed world. But the myth of separation persists. This myth demands an origin story for documentary film that legitimates its persuasive powers in the objectivity of the photographic image rather than in the aims of the orator. Documentary film histories have perpetuated this origin myth.[56] They continue to circumscribe documentary film within the framework of a sobering ritual of civic participation.

This frame demands enlargement to include a revised sense of ritual that no longer encircles the citizen-subject and nation-state. This revised concept of ritual and performance does away with the traditional center of political power. It dissolves the fixed, central place of the state in favor of a more fluid, affinity-based collectivity of variable needs, shifting alliances, and mutable powers. The newer, post-1970s "wave" of documentary film, like the modernist avant-garde before it, revises our understanding of the subject; it displaces the individual from the stable position of correspondent with the state as suppressed subjectivities claim a voice and image of their own.

Maya Deren, the key figure in the emergence of a postwar American avant-garde, envisioned radical possibilities of these kinds for film form. She championed a vigorous program of ethical engagement and a revised sense of ritual enactment.[57] In her extraordinary publication of 1947, *An Anagram of Ideas on Art, Form and Film*, Deren tries to clear a socially engaged, ethically informed space for a new avant-garde. She restores ethics and the prospect of ritual redemption to the project of the avant-garde, but this restoration comes at the price of stealing back from documentary what all "creative treatments of actuality" share despite the names and limits placed on them. (Deren scorns documentary literalism as much as Grierson mocked avant-garde elitism.) Deren's call for a renewal of the avant-garde, in fact, is of a piece with the post-1970s wave of documentary described here. A rigid sense of separation no longer obtains, and Deren's notion of ritual as a socially transformative act achieves considerable cogency: "The ritualistic form treats the human being not as the source of the dramatic action, but as a somewhat depersonalized element in a dramatic whole. The intent of such depersonalization is not the destruction of the individual; on the contrary, it enlarges him beyond the personal dimension and frees him from the specializations and confines of the personality. He becomes part of a dynamic whole which, like all such creative relationships, in turn, endows its parts with a measure of its larger meaning."[58] I began with historical revisionism, and I conclude with a utopian invocation. I return to the past to change our understanding of it and to make that understanding available to the cinema we have yet to achieve.

2 Documentary Reenactment and the Fantasmatic Subject

"Could you do the kiss again?"

Lonely Boy (*Wolf Koenig and Roman Kroitor, 1962*)

Reenactments, the more or less authentic recreation of prior events, were a staple of documentary representation until they were slain by the "verité boys" of the 1960s (Robert Drew, Ricky Leacock, D.A. Pennebaker, David and Albert Maysles, Frederick Wiseman, and others) who proclaimed everything except what took place in front of the camera without rehearsal or prompting to be a fabrication, inauthentic. Observational or direct cinema generated an honest record of what would have happened had the camera not been there or what does happen as a result of the camera recording people who know they are being filmed. Robert Flaherty's *Nanook of the North* (1922) might be admired for the evidence it provides of Flaherty's patience, exquisite eye, and apparent lack of preconceptions, but his entire salvage anthropology model of coaxing Allakariallak to do what "Nanook" would have done some thirty years earlier, without motorized vehicles, rifles, canned food, wood-frame homes, or filmmakers along for the ride, amounted to one colossal, unacknowledged reenactment and, therefore, fraud.

Times have changed. Reenactments once again play a vital role in documentary, be it of a solidarity movement that cannot be filmed in *Far from Poland* (Jill Godmilow, 1984); a murder for which radically disparate accounts exist in *The Thin Blue Line* (Errol Morris, 1988); the schematic simulation of a harrowing escape from captivity in *Little Dieter Needs to Fly* (Werner Herzog 1997); events during the final days of Salvador Allende's socialist government in *Chile, Obstinate Memory* (Patrizio Guzmán, 1997); or an LSD-inspired drug trip by the drug's inventor in *Dying to Know* (Gay Dillingham, 2014). Apart from the occasional charges of deceit that surround the use of reenactments indistinguishable from actual footage of a historical event, reenactments are once again taken for granted. They pose, however, a number of fascinating questions about the experience of temporality and the presence of fantasy in documentary. Although all aspects of documentary representation possess fantasmatic elements, it is the distinctive quality of these elements in reenacted scenes that provides the primary focus of this discussion.

Reenactments occupy a strange status in which it is crucial that they be recognized as a representation of a prior event while also signaling that they are not a representation of a contemporaneous event. Gregory Bateson argued that when representations take on a meaning that is not their usual meaning, the revised semantics may signify a shift from one discursive frame to another rather than the simple addition of connotations. Such shifts occur when, as he put it in a discussion of how animals distinguish play from fighting, "these actions, in which we now engage do not denote what would be denoted by those actions which these actions denote."[1] A shift in signification changes the name of the game. The reenacted event introduces a fantasmatic element that an initial representation of the same event lacks. Put simply, history does not repeat itself, except in mediated transformations such as memory, representation, reenactment, or fantasy—categories that coil around each other in complex, moiré-like patterns.

When the distinction between reenactment and enactment goes unnoticed or unrecognized, the question of deceit arises. The controversy surrounding the 2004 Academy Award short documentary winner, *Mighty Times: The Children's March* (Robert Houston, 2004), involved charges that reenactments blended imperceptibly with authentic footage of civil rights activity in the 1960s South. Archival footage of visually similar but very different events, such as the Watts Riot in Los Angeles, added to the deception. Viewers must recognize a reenactment as a reenactment even if this recognition also dooms the reenactment to its status as a fictionalized repetition of something that has already occurred. Unlike the contemporaneous representation of an event—the classic documentary image, where an indexical link between image and historical occurrence exists—the reenactment forfeits its indexical bond to the original event. It draws its fantasmatic power from this very fact. The shift of levels engenders an impossible task for the reenactment: to retrieve a lost object in its original form even as the very act of retrieval generates a new object and a new pleasure. The viewer experiences the uncanny sense of a repetition of what remains historically unique. A specter haunts the text.

This specter is a variation on the ghost of the absent subject. Numerous documentaries, outside the observational mode, attempt to resurrect people and lives no longer available to the camera. The person may be unavailable or in hiding (*Waiting for Fidel* [Michael Rubbo, 1974]; *Hotel Terminus: The Life and Times of Klaus Barbie* [Marcel Ophüls, 1988]) or, more often, deceased (*Salvador Allende* [Patrizio Guzmán, 2004]; *Ryan* [Chris Landreth, 2004, on Canadian animator Ryan Larkin]; *Superstar: The Karen Carpenter Story* [Todd Haynes, 1987]; *An Injury to One* [Travis Wilkerson, 2002, on Wobbly organizer Frank Little]; or *Steve Jobs: The Man in the Machine* [Alex Gibney, 2015]). In some cases the person is deceased, but his or her trace remains in the form of footage the subject him- or herself had previously shot. In *Grizzly Man* (Werner Herzog, 2005), *Capturing the Friedmans* (Andrew Jarecki, 2003), *The Maelstrom* (Péter Forgács, 1997), and *Free Fall* (Péter Forgács, 1997), for example, we see home-movie footage of someone who had died prior to the making of the film about them, and in *Rock Hudson's Home Movies* (Mark Rappaport, 1992) and *From the Journals of Jean Seberg* (Mark Rappaport, 1995) we see the feature-film roles and images of stars whose private lives are deciphered from these images. In Adam Curtis's *It Felt like a Kiss* (2009), footage of Rock Hudson playing the suave heterosexual man of distinction again appears, but this time it is used as one of many images to convey the sanitized dream world the United States conjured for itself during its post–World War II ascendancy.

In each case the subject must be reconstituted from available resources. A lost object haunts the film. The attempt to conjure that specter, to make good that loss, or, for Adam Curtis, to identify its fantasmatic dimension signals the mark of desire. What constitutes a lost object is as various as all the objects toward which desire may flow. Such efforts would encompass attempts to make good a trauma, perhaps a death or catastrophe, which Michael Renov sees as the "work of mourning" that documentary can perform for the viewer.[2] But attempts to come to terms with death, catastrophe, and trauma would be an extreme or limit case of the more general desire to come to terms with loss. In other cases the working through of loss need not entail mourning: it can also offer, via what we might call the fantasmatic project, gratification of a highly distinct kind.

A stunning example of this process unfolds in *Capturing the Friedmans*. The film explores the complex web of family relations and submerged desires that lie behind the criminal charges of pedophilia brought against the father, Arnold Friedman, and his teenage son, Jesse. They are alleged to have fondled, seduced, abused, and sodomized dozens of young boys who took computer classes in the family's home. Andrew Jarecki draws on home movies, shot over the course of the family's lifetime; video diaries, shot mainly during the period of tumult precipitated by Arnold and Jesse's arrest; television news reports; and Jarecki's own interviews with most of the involved parties. If the trial of Arnold and Jesse sought to achieve the either/or clarity of guilt or innocence, Jarecki is far more concerned to capture the ambiguity, confusion, and anger that this very process produces within one family.

A fantasmatic power radiates from some of the family's video diaries. These are scenes shot by Jesse or David, two of the sons, as they attempt, with their father, to reenact the form of spontaneous family togetherness that has become the lost object captured in the old 8 mm home movies. This film footage has shown the boys and their father in moments of carefree bliss, dancing, singing, and generally cavorting together with a casual acceptance of the camera as both documenting device and prosthetic extension of another family member. The video or digital footage— distinguishable from the home movies by its absence of film grain, lack of color fading, higher degree of contrast, presence of sync sound, and evidence of the filmed subjects' clear awareness of the recording process as a form of confession or testimonial—however, demonstrates the impossibility of stepping into a temporal river for the first time twice. The boys and their father are markedly older, their dancing and clowning slightly forced, the father visibly burdened by the weight of his arrest and trial, and their mother emphatically excluded rather than simply absent.

The video footage represents the sons' attempt to reenact their own past. They are clearly aware of their attempt as a reenactment rather than a genuine return to a lost object and irretrievable moment: the video footage stands as a sign that describes both the lost object (the unqualified pleasure of physical cavorting that once was theirs) and its absence (the effort that must now be made to reenact what was once spontaneous exuberance). This is nowhere more evident than in the refusal of Arnold's sons to recognize the depressed, inexpressive, nearly stunned expression that haunts their father, an expression that, if acknowledged, would thwart their desire to go through the motions that will generate the compensatory pleasures they desire.

These extraordinary moments, in which the participants attempt to will themselves back to the past and yet know very well that the effort must fail, border on the work of mourning that cinema, and video, makes possible. They compound that semiacknowledged work with the production of a fantasmatic pleasure, for the sons at least, that lessens the sting of that which is lost and cannot be retrieved. They go through the motions that locate them within a mise-en-scène of desire, a *fantasmatique* their mother can no longer share. (She feels profoundly betrayed by Arnold's deceptions, stemming back to the time of the original home-movie footage but never fully admitted before the trial.) The sons and father do, once again, now, what they once did, then, and derive from this act not the original satisfaction of a need but the gratification of a desire that stems from the sequence of images, or signifiers, they fabricate for themselves.

Jean Laplanche and Jean-Bertrand Pontalis stress the importance of the temporal convolution that weaves past and present together. Fantasy is not the mere retrieval of something past, not the recovery of a real object, or, as in the example they adopt, not the milk a baby may have ingested but "the breast as a *signifier*" (my italics).[3] What was once an external object transforms into an image or signifier. The signifier bears an emotional weight. What fantasy restores in this example is not the act of actually obtaining the mother's milk, "not the act of sucking, but the enjoyment of going through the motions of sucking."[4] Such motions, separated from the substance they once yielded (milk), but coupled to the object as signifier ("breast"), produce, when successful, a distinct pleasure.

This pleasure is entirely real. It derives from the corporeal activity of going through the necessary motions, but it is also entirely psychic. Like the reenactment, it involves a pleasure associated with a past event that is transposed into a distinctly different, fantasmatic domain. Pleasure flows from an act of imaginary engagement in which the subject knows that this act stands for a prior act, or event, with which it is not one. A separation that entails a shift from physical needs and their pacification to psychical desires and their gratification, from before to after, from then to now, from object to subject is as integral to the fantasmatic experience as it is to the efficacy of ideology.

A telling moment of this sort occurs in *Chile, Obstinate Memory* when four of President Allende's bodyguards reenact their role in a presidential motorcade prior to the military coup d'état that toppled his government on September 11, 1973. Guzmán cuts between the footage of the men reenacting what they used to do and shots of them actually guarding Allende some thirty-five years ago. Then, Allende and others sit inside a large, black convertible limousine, crowds line the way, and the four men trot alongside, eyes scanning the surrounding scene, as each keeps a hand in contact with one of the four fenders of the car. Now, the men walk alongside an economy size, red, hardtop sedan, on a deserted country road, with no crowd in sight, but each with a hand in contact with the car and their eyes once again scanning the surroundings.

At one point Guzmán freezes the image of the motorcade "then" as the guards identify themselves and compatriots from the still image. The authentic image becomes remote, an instigation for memory and identification, whereas the reenacted image allows the men to "go through the motions" of guarding the (absent) president one more time. The reenactment clearly does not fulfill an official state need this time; instead, it gratifies a personal desire, making possible "the enjoyment of going through the motions of guarding," as it were, when guarding itself remains squarely lodged in the past. Nothing captures this temporal knotting of past and present better than a close-up of the hand of one of the guards slowly fluttering up and down on one of the half-open car windows: the rhythm follows from the cadence of his gait beside the car, but the camera's close-up view of his delicate grip, the rise and fall of his fingers, and the overt absence of an engulfing crowd attest to the psychically real but fantasmatic linkage of now and then.

Despite the gulf between now and then, and as a precondition for the gratification reenactment can provide, the subject becomes "caught up in the sequence of images," which, as Laplanche and Pontalis put it, populate the mise-en-scène of desire. This holds for the bodyguards in this striking scene from *Chile, Obstinate Memory*, just as it does for the Friedman boys in their video reenactments, but it is also true of the viewer, immersed in an experience in which she or he knows very well that the reenactment is not that which it represents and yet, all the same, allows it to function as if it were. Above all, however, the filmmaker is the one caught up in the sequence of images; it is his or her fantasy that these images embody. The filmmaker need not be physically present in the image, as she or he is in many participatory documentaries. "The subject, although always present in the fantasy, may be so in a desubjectivized form, that is to say, in the very syntax of the sequence in question."[5]

This desubjectivization is acutely true of the video recordings by David and Jesse Friedman in *Capturing the Friedmans*. Their former selves haunt the footage in the desubjectivized form of syntactical parallelisms their present selves construct in keeping with the home movies of a decade or more before. The camera functions not as an omniscient observer or third person narrator but as a means of reiterating the function of the home-movie camera generally as familial participant and active instigator in scenes, in this case, of camaraderie and high jinks. These same images subsequently double-up to become part of the fantasmatic structured by Andrew Jarecki. In his case psychic pleasure seems to stem from the construction of ambiguity about what happened in the past, what these social actors have said and done, how they understand the actions and how they wish others to understand them. Jarecki complicates the literal linear and binary logic of the judicial system that sets out to determine "what really happened" and who is guilty and who innocent. He reinscribes the ambiguity of perspective, and voice, that separates such judicial determinations from the plain of fantasy.

Patricio Guzmán, too, in his reenactment of guarding the presidential car, inhabits the syntax of a sequence that he causes to flutter between past and present. He restores specificity (names, relationships) to the past and brings fantasmatic gratification to the present as he goes through the motions of reenacting the past to new ends. This makes the subject's presence, in reenactments, and documentaries more generally, a function of what I have described as the documentary voice of the filmmaker rather than his or her corporeal appearance before the camera.[6] The documentary voice speaks through the body of the film: through editing; through subtle and strange juxtapositions; through music, lighting, composition, and mise-en-scène; through dialogue overheard and commentary delivered; through silence, as well as speech; and through sounds and images, as well as words. This dispersed and polymorphous voice possesses an intrinsically desubjectivized form. The workings of a fantasmatic arise through it.

The voice of an orator, or documentarian, enlists and reveals desires and lacks. It charts a path through the stuff of the world that gives body to dreams and substance to principles. Speaking, giving voice to a view of the world, makes possible the necessary conditions of visibility to see things anew, to see as if for the first time what had until now escaped notice. This is not objective sight but seeing in that precarious, fleeting moment of insight when a gestalt clicks into place and meanings arise from what had seemed to lack meaning or to be already filled to capacity with all the meaning that sight could bear.[7] Such insight does not occur, however, until given external shape, the shape provided by the film's voice as it addresses others.[8]

Voicelessness or speechlessness, as the opposite of voice or speech, is hardly equivalent to objectivity. Just as, according to Laplanche and Pontalis, the distinction between subject and object dissolves in fantasy, so voice, like fantasy, dissolves the distinction between subjectivity and objectivity. In this sense, voicelessness is the absence of an *I* that speaks, an *I* that sets out to encounter a *You* in Martin Buber's famous formulation. Voicelessness is an *I* stripped of the desire that brings a fantasmatic into being. Speechlessness is a condition of the disembodied *I*, which may well make use of language but that speaks in and from a place where instrumentality overwhelms the force of desire.

The documentary voice is the embodied speech of the historical person—the filmmaker—caught up in the syntax of enacted or reenacted images through which the past rejoins the present. Voice, given in reenactments partially as an awareness of the gap between that which was and the effort to return to it, also affirms the presence of a gap between the objectivity/subjectivity binary and the workings of the fantasmatic. Subjectivity suggests it is added to something and could also be subtracted. Objectivity implies the suppression of subjectivity. Voice is the means and "grain" with which we speak and can never be added or subtracted from what is said by the embodied self.

Objectivity desires a fixed relation to a determinate past, the type of relation that permits "guilty/not guilty" verdicts or other definitive answers to the question of "what really happened." Voice, in the form of reenactments that embody the "I know very well but all the same" formulation at the heart of psychic reality, imposes recognition of the relentless march of a temporality that makes the dream of both a pure repetition and an omniscient perspective impossible. The very syntax of reenactments affirms the having-been-thereness of what can never, quite, be here again. Facts remain facts, their verification possible, but the iterative effort of going through the motions of reenacting them imbues such facts with the lived stuff of immediate and situated experience.

Reenactments also foil the desire to preserve the past in the amber of an omniscient wholeness, the comprehensive view we like to think we have that accounts for what has come to pass. The partialness and constructed quality of the reenactment can be the source of a sense of dissatisfaction: the view is too incomplete or too cluttered (it may contain a body or bodies too many as contemporary figures fill in for their historical counterparts). Reenactments are clearly *a* view rather than *the* view from which the past yields up its truth. Reenactments produce an iterability to that which belongs to the singularity of historical occurrence. They reconcile this apparent contradiction by acknowledging the adoption of a distinct perspective, point of view, or voice. Such perspectives can proliferate indefinitely, but each of them can also intensify an awareness of the separation between the lost object and its reenactment. Reenactments belong to a situated fantasmatic that nullifies the status of that other fantasmatic of objectivity, omniscience, and finality that haunts the documentary film and its kindred discourses of sobriety.[9]

In Marlon Riggs's extraordinary autobiographical testament and portrait of black, gay culture, *Tongues Untied* (1989), Riggs recounts an incident from his youth. He is attacked by a gang of white youths who beat him and leave him lying in the street. Riggs relies on a reenactment to represent the incident, but unlike other scenes in the film, in this scene Riggs does not play himself. We encounter a body-too-many, the body of another black male who plays the Marlon Riggs who was attacked on this fateful occasion.

I say fateful because, as Riggs tells us, he was rescued by a young white man. "What a blessing," Riggs exclaims. "What a curse," he adds.

The incident invokes not only racism in its rawest form but also a dynamic of identification and desire that Riggs understands as his own internal burden: to revile his own blackness and to be drawn to those whites, who, like his rescuer, offer some respite from the crude brutality of racism. As such the incident is an iteration of the complex patterns of identification and disavowal that Frantz Fanon described in greater detail.[10] The absence of Riggs's own body from the reenactment strengthens the sense in which this representation of the past is a citation, an iteration, a link in a much longer chain of racist acts where the doer gains his power from the power of iteration itself.[11] Riggs addresses this event and this history in his own voice, from his own perspective, one in which his story and the reenactment that embodies it open onto a larger pattern that can be understood neither in the abstract—seen from an omniscient point of view—nor purely in the concrete—represented as simply one man's experience. The body-too-many of the reenactment displaces Riggs's presence and the racism visited upon him from the polarity of subject/object relations into the very syntax of the sequence. Still situated, still embodied, still spoken through the voice of the film, the reenacted incident folds past over present in those fantas-matic terms that make the psychic reverberations of racism not only a con-ceptual problem but a "curse," as Riggs so aptly puts it, as well. Here, too, a specter haunts the text, and it is the reenactment that brings it to visibility.

This reenactment of a traumatic event in *Tongues Untied* functions less to carry out the work of mourning that follows trauma than to register an apprehension of the power of a past event, a power Riggs contests. In a striking contrast, Irene Lusztig's film *Reconstruction* (2002) cites the Romanian government's reenactment of a crime, in which her grandmother was one of four individuals who robbed a state bank, to reaffirm the power of what was at that time a communist state to write and control the past. In this case the fantasmatic quality of the reenactment pursues what is more clearly than usual an ideological issue: the at least temporarily lost object of state power. It seeks the gratification of going through the motions of stag-ing a mise-en-scène within which that power can reconstitute itself. The robbers, once caught, are compelled to reenact their planning, the robbery, their confessions, trial, and sentencing. They must once again go through the motions of their defiance of the state but, this time, with no hope of success: the motions are choreographed by others.

The state-made film, also entitled *Reconstruction,* had apparently been intended to demonstrate the folly of breaking the law, but it was never shown publicly for reasons that remain unclear. Lusztig, however, found the film and includes significant portions of it in her own. In it the suspects exhibit a decidedly despondent manner, a sign that they know the pleasure of this reenactment will not be theirs. It is a look akin to that of the older Arnold Friedman in his sons' videos as they go through the motions associated with their earlier home movies—eyes vacant, gaze unfocused, words slow in coming and stilted in tone. In one scene a prosecutor attempts to pry a confession from one of the men (Lusztig's grandmother was the only woman involved). The suspect resists; he knows nothing of the crime. Then the prosecutor produces a rifle and two pistols. "Do you recognize these?" "You have those too? I see we've been discovered. Until now I've been hiding the truth." The game is up, and the suspect, in the same hopeless tone, promptly admits his guilt and confesses his crime.

As in the racist incident in *Tongues Untied*, the reenactment introduces a sense of the ritualistic quality that often characterizes reenactments of past events. In this ritual the robbery must be represented as an exception and the power of the state affirmed in another iteration of the eternal ritual of justice fulfilled. The culprits' own bodies serve as the surface for a textual rewriting in which agency reverts entirely to the state. The triumph of judicial invulnerability, however, betrays the very condition of its being in the barely animated bodies of the criminals who must go through the motions of a past event in a context where need and pleasure, desire and gratification accrue only to the state. A "curse" continues to haunt the text in the form of a repressive act that Lusztig exposes by recontextualizing the original reenactment from a distinct perspective or voice of her own. Whereas reenactment for Riggs allows for an owning or owning up to the past, in *Reconstruction* the owning of the past takes the more literal form of the state coming into physical control, or ownership, of the bodies and minds of those who defied it.

Reenactment takes another fascinating turn in Werner Herzog's *Little Dieter Needs to Fly*. Shot down on a bombing run over Laos and captured, Dieter Dengler, after a series of extraordinary adventures, escapes his captors and returns to the United States. This is the story he tells to Herzog, but in the course of doing so he decides to reenact what he first recounts. Dengler and Herzog return to Laos, where local villagers play his captors and Dieter plays his former self.

Unlike the bank robbery reenactment in *Reconstruction*, the walrus hunt in *Nanook of the North*, the reenactments of detention at Guantanamo in *The Road to Guantanamo* (Michael Winterbottom and Mat Whitecross, 2006), or the "pre-enactments" of what might happen in the event of nuclear attack in Peter Watkins's *The War Game* (1965)—all of which adopt the performative qualities of suspenseful, dramatic intensity—the reenacted scenes in *Little Dieter* exhibit a Brechtian sense of distanciation. In one scene, for example, recruited Laotian villagers stand listlessly around Dengler as they "go through the motions" of guarding him by wearing uniforms or displaying weapons. Their halfhearted, good-natured performance clearly conjures what Dengler went through without compelling prisoner or guards to reenter the psychic and emotional space of the original event. Neither Dieter nor Herzog seek to render suspense dramatically or verisimilitude perfectly. The necessary awareness of a gap between past event and present reenactment remains altogether vivid, as it gradually does in *The Thin Blue Line*, where the series of reenactments of the original murder of a policeman construct an Escher-like impossible space of conflicting narratives.

Dieter transports himself back to that which now functions as a lost object through the social gests he puts into motion.[12] It allows him to own his past in a corporeal but fantasmatic form that does not require the presumably therapeutic dramaturgy that Charcot inaugurated in his treatment of hysterics and that so many reenactments imitate. The sense of mastery that arises from this iteration in which the outcome is now known allows him to go through the motions of a triumphant passage that he has, in fact, already completed. It is this passage that the film within a film in *Reconstruction* denies to those whose bank robbery attempt failed. Dieter Dengler, the one who survived what once put his survival in question, now occupies a fantasmatic mise-en-scène that affirms his very survival. "Going through the motions" takes on a formal, ritualistic quality that nonetheless spans the moment between before, when need prevailed, and after, when these social gests function as signifiers of what was but is now, at the moment of signification, past. The gests or signifiers both embody the lost object of a former experience and gratify the force of desire. That they can do both is a result of the fact that they no longer signify what the experience to which they refer signified.

These various reenactments begin to suggest some ways in which reenactments tend to cluster into different types. Some are highly affective, some far less so. Some make their status as reenactment obvious; some do not. These differences do not establish hard-and-fast divisions but do suggest different nodal points within a diffuse and overlapping universe of possibilities. Some particularly common variations include the following.

Realist dramatization.   The most contentious, because it is the least distinguishable from both that which it reenacts and the conventional representation of past events in fiction—be it in the form of a historical drama, "true story," docudrama, or flashback—is the suspenseful, dramatic reenactment in a realist style. Such dramatizations have become a staple of reality TV shows that follow in the mold of *Cops* or *America's Unsolved Mysteries*, but their lineage can be traced back to *In the Land of the Head Hunters* (a.k.a. *In the Land of the War Canoes*), Edward Curtis's fascinating attempt to mix ethnographic detail with melodrama among the Kwakiutl in the Pacific Northwest of 1914; *Nanook of the North*; and many early newsreels or *actualités*. An important model for many of the recent uses of this type of reenactment occurs in the powerful documentary about those who disappeared during Argentina's "dirty war," *Las madres de la Plaza de Mayo* (Susana Blaustein Muñoz and Lourdes Portillo, 1985). As one of the mothers who meet every day at the Argentine White House, La Casa Rosada, recounts how armed men abducted her son in the dead of night, the film cuts to a reenactment of this event. The reenactment possesses the surreal tones of a nightmare with its grainy, high-contrast, and slow-motion imagery in which individual figures are unrecognizable. The distortions work to impede realist transparency. These formal devices shift the reenactment toward the fourth category here, stylized reenactment (see below), but Muñoz and Portillo's expressive rendering of what happened underscores its emotional impact on the mother as something that was not part of the event itself but has been part of its affective reverberation ever since.

Typifications.   In this case there is no specific event to which the reenactment refers, and the sense of separation between event and reenactment fades as a sense of typifying past patterns, rituals, and routines increases. Such reenactments characterized many early documentaries, including *Nanook of the North*, where the suspenseful dramatization of events, presented as if they were present-day, reenacted the typical processes of the Inuit's precontact past. The walrus hunt, seal hunt, fur trapping, and igloo building did not reenact specific historical occurrences as much as characteristic ones. To the extent that the viewer recognizes that the claim to authenticity of these scenes resides not in their depiction of present-day activity, carried out despite the presence of the camera, but in their reenactment of precontact activity, staged for the sake of the camera, this very claim of authenticity undergoes erosion. The indexical quality of the image anchors it in the mise-en-scène of the filmmaker's desire, as it does in fiction, but without reference to any specific historical occurrence.

John Grierson adopted this technique wholesale for the British documentary movement of the 1930s. Reenactments, as typifications, proliferated.

Coal Face (Alberto Cavalcanti, 1935) has several sequences of coal miners mining, or taking their lunch break, that possess a similar aura of present-day reality simply observed when they are, in fact, staged. *Night Mail* (Harry Watt and Basil Wright, 1936) is the most famous example, with its scenes of postal workers sorting mail on the Postal Express as it makes its overnight journey from London to Glasgow. These scenes took place on a sound stage. They reenact, cite, or reiterate the typical, and quotidian, quality of this labor and clearly exhibit a desire to idealize the common working man as a vital part of a larger social whole, despite the less fully acknowledged tensions stemming from class hierarchy.

Such scenes in *Coal Face, Night Mail, Listen to Britain* (Humphrey Jennings and Stewart McAllister, 1942), *Fires Were Started* (Humphrey Jennings, 1943), and other films function as "typical particulars" in precisely the way Vivian Sobchack applies this term to film. The specific actions and objects viewed in a fiction may be highly concrete as relayed by indexical images, but they are not usually understood to have a concrete historical referent: "unless something happens to *specifically* particularize these existential entities as in some way singular, they will be engaged as what philosophers call *typical particulars*—a form of generalization in which a single entity is taken as exemplary of an entire class."[13] This displacement from the singular to the exemplary, if recognized as such, forfeits some of the distinctive peculiarities of the documentary reenactment, perhaps most specifically the heightened sense of viewer responsibility that attends to the historical instead of a fictive world.[14]

Brechtian distanciation.   The reenactment of social gests (such as those in the pioneering *Far from Poland* but also abundantly evident in *Little Dieter Needs to Fly*) greatly increases the separation of the reenactment from the specific historical moment it reenacts, creating a greater likelihood that the fantasmatic effect will come into play. Actions reenacted may possess the qualities of a typification, but shorn of their realist dimension, they simultaneously stand out more boldly as social gests in Brecht's sense of the term. The deflection away from realist representation allows, paradoxically, a stronger link to historical specificity to come into play through the filmmaker's choice to go through the motions of gesturing to the historical rather than representing it as illusion. This quality is also true of the remaining categories.

Stylization.   Highly stylized reenactments—such as those in *The Thin Blue Line* of Randall Adams's interrogation or of the Dallas police officer's murder, in which, most memorably, a perfectly lit container of malted milk shake tumbles through the night air in slow motion as if to blatantly over-dramatize one subject's account—also achieve a sense of separation. This need not be in the ironic key so prevalent in Morris's work. For example, Dennis Tupicoff's *His Mother's Voice* (1997), an animated documentary from Australia, couples the radio interview of a bereaved mother as she is asked how she learned of her son's shooting with two different animated versions of the event. In one case the images show her journey to the house where her son had just been shot; in the other they render her now-altered perception of her own family's home. These animated sequences sever any indexical linkage to the actual event but give voice to the acutely selective and pained perspective from which she experienced it. This is akin to the acute pain that haunts Ari Folman as he attempts to grasp his actual role, and individual responsibility, for a massacre during Israel's attack on Lebanon in 1982 in his animated documentary *Waltz with Bashir* (Ari Folman, 2008). These animated works function in their totality in a manner not unlike the scene of abduction or disappearance reenacted in *Las madres de la Plaza de Mayo*, but they carry the elements of stylization much further and diminish the elements of realist dramatization. The viewer remains vividly suspended in that moment between before and after embodied in signifiers that possess an iconic rather than indexical relation to what has already happened.

Parody and irony.   Other reenactments adopt a parodic tone that may call the convention of the reenactment itself into question or treat a past occurrence in a comic light. Errol Morris skirts the edges of this characteristic in *The Thin Blue Line,* but his ironic perspective takes aim more at the subjectivity of his interviewees than at the capacity of the reenactment to capture the authenticity of past events. In *Cane Toads: An Unnatural History* (1988) Mark Lewis parodies the nature documentary's typical representation of other species, in this case the large, ugly toads that threaten to run rampant across Australia, through multiple reenactments that are more melodramatic and humorous than sober.

Caveh Zahedi also adopts the parodic reenactment wholeheartedly in *I Am a Sex Addict* (2005), a semiserious account of his struggles with sex addiction and the confusion it wreaks on his longer-term relationships and attempts at marriage. At one point, speaking to the camera, he tells the viewer that he lacked money to go back to Paris to reenact his first encounters with prostitutes, so "this street" in San Francisco (the street on which he stands) will have to stand for a Parisian street. The film cuts to another view and an evenly spaced line of about eight young prostitutes in front of a red brick wall as Zahedi walks past, asking each of them the same questions about what they will do and how much she will charge, before hesitating, almost ready to take up the offer, but then deciding against it and going on to the next woman.

Superstar: The Karen Carpenter Story, an underground cult favorite that cannot circulate legally because director Todd Haynes failed to secure permission for the sound track of Carpenter songs, tells the story of the titular heroine's eating disorders, dysfunctional family dynamics, addictions, and death by reenacting via Ken and Barbie dolls key scenes from her short life. For the most part these scenes have the quality of typical particulars, exemplifying hypothetically pivotal moments without reference to historically singular events. The posed shots of dolls, however, add a powerfully ironic edge to the representations: as with *His Mother's Voice,* this decision forfeits the impression of indexical authenticity in the image. At the same time, it compels the viewer to assess this tragedy both as something beyond the reach of any reenactment and as something typically reduced to a cautionary tale about the perils of anorexia and bulimia. The parodic edge puts the mass media's penchant for the realist dramatization of tragedy on display as a potentially exploitative trope. The doll figures, by maintaining a clear separation between reenactment and prior event, may actually mobilize a more complex form of understanding of what this tragedy actually entails than more straightforward representations that confuse the boundary between the two.

Similar points might be made about *The Eternal Frame* (1975), the Ant Farm collective's parodic reenactment of the Kennedy assassination. This video documents the reenactment process, including the behind-the-scenes preparations, far more than it purports to be a documentary about the assassination itself. Unlike *JFK* (Oliver Stone, 1991), *The Eternal Frame* calls the very act of reenactment into question. By exaggerating the separation between then and now, before and after, the video functions to bare the device of reenactment itself rather than rely on this peculiar form to present any final answer to the question of what really happened or generate a mise-en-scène in which the desire for a lost object might find gratification. This is acutely true of Joshua Oppenheimer's *The Act of Killing* (2012) as well, where the reenacted executions by members of Indonesian death squads have the ironic quality of being modeled on movie genres, of being reenacted with a triumphant but deeply disturbing sense of moral indifference to these crimes, and of placing killers who show no remorse into the confessional position normally reserved for victims of such events. (I discuss this film further in "Irony, Paradox, and the Documentary: Double Meanings and Double Binds," in part 4 below.)

Reenactments within these overlapping and fuzzy categories do not do what archival footage and other images of illustration do.[15] They do not provide evidentiary images of situations and events in the historical world. If they allow viewers to think that they do, they lay the groundwork for feelings of deception. The indexical bond, which can guarantee evidentiary status—but not the meaning or interpretation of images taken as evidence—no longer joins the reenactment to that for which it stands. Instead, this indexical bond joins the image to the production of the reenactment: it is evidence of an iterative gesture but not evidence of that for which the reenactment stands. It is, in fact, not historical evidence but an artistic interpretation, always offered from a distinct perspective and carrying, embedded within it, further evidence of the voice of the filmmaker.

Although it is possible, especially with realist dramatizations and typifications, to think that reenactments contribute historical evidence, what they more commonly contribute is persuasion. They fulfill an affective function. For documentaries belonging to the rhetorical tradition, reenactments intensify the degree to which a given argument or perspective appears compelling, contributing to the work's emotional appeal, or convincing, contributing to its rational appeal by means of real or apparent proof. (Ironic uses of reenactment may reverse this tendency toward compellingness.)

As pathos or logos, reenactments enhance or amplify affective engagement. Reenactments contribute to a vivification of that for which they stand. They make what it feels like to occupy a certain situation, to perform a certain action, to adopt a particular perspective visible and more vivid. Vivification is neither evidence nor explanation. It is, though, a form of interpretation, an inflection that resurrects the past to reanimate it with the force of a desire.

Inasmuch as reenactments do not stand for that for which they stand would stand, they effect a fold in time. Reenactments vivify the sense of the lived experience, the *vécu*, of others. They take past time and make it present. They take present time and fold it over onto what has already happened. They resurrect a sense of a previous moment that is now seen through a fold that incorporates the embodied perspective of the filmmaker and the emotional investment of the viewer. In this way reenactments effect a temporal vivification in which past and present coexist in the impossible space of a fantasmatic. This form of coexistence revolves around a lost object and the signifiers that serve as resurrected ghosts that both haunt and endow the present with psychic intensity. Reenactments, like other poetic and rhetorical tropes, bring desire itself into being and with it the fantasmatic domain wherein the temporality of lived experience and the efficacy of ideology find embodiment.

3   **Letter to Lynne Sachs on *Investigation
    of a Flame***

Dear Lynne,

It was such a very pleasant surprise to see you again after so
many years at the benefit for the Anthology Film Archives and to
see Philip Glass there as well. Your work has clearly gelled into an
oeuvre of some note since we were both, passingly, at San Francisco
State University in the late eighties. (Is that when it was? So far
away and long ago?)

I am very glad you were able to send me a copy of *Investigation
of a Flame*, your film about the destruction of draft records by
Daniel and Philip Berrigan and seven others in Catonsville,
Maryland. It is quite a compelling work. I think it is extremely
revealing in terms of the motivations for and consequences of what
took place. This was a part of the history of the 1960s that was
mediated to us by newspapers and TV networks that were in a near
hysteria, fueled partly by a fear that the social fabric, and the social
contract, was being torn asunder by people who would not accept
lies and hypocrisy, and partly by a government determined to
impose its will through a relentless rhetoric of fear—the specter of
Communism back then, the specter of terrorism now. The past does
return, doesn't it, but not always as farce.

I was just getting back from two years in Kenya, where I had
gone to teach in a secondary school and to rethink my trajectory
toward a medical career (I had finished one year at Stanford Medical
School), when that and other events occurred. The assassination of
Martin Luther King had taken place just before I was due to leave
Kenya and the May-June '68 events in France were at their height.
I came back partly with the optimistic thought of resuming my

studies, but now in cinema, and partly with the pessimistic dread that my plans would be postponed by the draft. I was due to report for induction soon after returning and a bit clueless about what my options were. I had heard news of draft resisters and had friends in Paris who worked with draft deserters; I knew I could go to Paris instead of being inducted, but I also knew it would alter the rest of my life more than I could imagine and what other options existed were yet to be discovered.

Events like the one you reexamine flickered past on the limited news that reached my remote village just as I was preparing to leave. Their function on an ethical plane of giving witness to an alternative view of community and relationships was not lost on me, not after having followed Martin Luther King's efforts in some detail. But this had to be filtered out from the general hysteria, scapegoating, and demonizing. The model they enacted of ethical resistance helped lead me to the conscientious objector movement in New York City and a Quaker-based information center, in particular, that set me on the road to freedom from the draft and that painful, divisive war in Vietnam.

I never had access to the interiority of the event, certainly not with [the] complexity that you make available through your film. You give a density and delicacy to the representation of what happened that really enlivens memory and enriches history. The sensitivity and strength, together, of these nine individuals emerges quite vividly. They know what they are doing and why, and have given it very careful thought. They possess an intense awareness of what they need to do, of how strongly they wish to cause no physical harm to anyone who may work at the Catonsville draft center, and how crucial it was for the symbolic level of their actions to take concrete and visible form.

You give their thoughts and actions—through the archival footage and the very personal, moving testimony of those who participated—an exemplary power: they come to stand for all those who undertake symbolic and personally costly actions when driven by conscience and a compelling need to give witness to an alternative sense of social responsibility.

I felt at times that *Investigation of a Flame* bears similarity to *The Thin Blue Line* with the poetic, evocative quality Morris instills, but without the haunting somewhat mysterious overtone that his use of Philip Glass's music imparts. You withhold that kind of musical dramatization; your film remains within a realm of historical witness and quotidian action that is not now, as it was not then, embroidered with the richness of musical tapestry. The actuality of the event, which in *The Thin Blue Line* remains invisible since no one saw the murder that is at the heart of the film, takes visible shape once again. The rapid pans of flowers and other objects, in an evocative color that evokes the past more than a photorealist present, have an austere, provocative quality to them. Unlike Glass's music, whose "work" for Morris's film is clear and highly effective, in that context, the images of gardens and flowers challenge us to determine what "work" they do here, for your film. They do not soften the sharpness of a still vital historical past. They may reduce the pleasures that one anticipates upon stepping up to the box office window (vivid reenactments, dramatic music, suspenseful storytelling), but they reward in ways I am still in the process of contemplating.

What I don't need to contemplate but to remember is that the efforts of people like the ones you feature had a profound impact on me. What to do about the draft? With a "Greetings" letter already in hand telling me to report for induction a few weeks hence, in June 1968 I went back to the courses in theology I had taken at Duke and to the questions of a just war that St. Augustine raised so long ago. I wrote an extremely long appeal to my draft board on Long Island. I requested a change of status to conscientious objector. Remarkably (because very few boards paid much heed to such requests), they granted me a hearing, posed some classic questions like what would I do if my mother were attacked by a robber, and then granted my request. Through a series of additional vicissitudes, I was able to resume my studies and continue my opposition to the war in Vietnam without having to enter the Army. People like the Catonsville 9 had a direct influence on the shape of my life, it turns out, and you have now given the shape of their actions and the clarity of their thoughts a brilliant frame. It is a better world now that your film exists within it. Thanks again, so much, for sending it to me.

Best wishes,
Bill

4 *Breaking the Frame*

Gender, Violation, and the Avant-Garde

Most film people know Carolee Schneemann as the creator of a pioneering piece of avant-garde filmmaking: *Fuses* (1967). She used a handheld camera, striking color effects, expressive editing, hand-etched frames, evocative sound, and her own naked body, together with that of her boyfriend at the time, the composer James Tenney, to celebrate sexuality in a direct, sensuous way. Throughout the short film she and Tenney make love, and the film captures the joy more than the graphic physicality of it. Far from pornographic, it is a loving, engaging tribute to the body, the act of making love, and the power of cinema to evoke the sensual and fuel the imagination. James Tenney remained a major part of her life for some time but not without considerable tumult, some of which finds its way into her subsequent work, work that, on the whole, is conceptually complex, intensely personal, and focused on the body (usually her own as in the taboo-shattering performance piece "Interior Scroll," in which she pulls a tape from her vagina and reads its message about female power).

But Carolee Schneemann is not very well known, at least to the average filmgoer. She didn't cultivate a following the way Maya Deren did. She didn't champion the film medium the way Deren and other filmmakers and critics of the 1940s to the 1960s did. And her other art work drew her more into the orbit of the museum and art gallery than the movie theater. But now we have Marielle Nitoslawska's *Breaking the Frame* (2012), a feature-length profile of Schneemann and her massive achievements as a performance and installation artist, painter, and filmmaker over the course of five decades.

Schneemann proves a highly articulate guide to her own work and life. Her own commentary and read statements figure significantly in the film. She has clearly lived a fascinating life. Her primary base has been a farm where her groundbreaking ideas germinate before she then realizes them in various formats and introduces them to the world.

She went further, sooner, more often, and more daringly in her explorations than many of those in the hothouse climate of the great art cities of New York, Berlin, and Paris. She described one performance piece this way: "I wore farmers overalls," she says, "and I had lots of oranges stuffed everywhere. It was about Cézanne, so I showed slides and talked about his influence—and I kept undressing and dressing. I was naked under my overalls and I'd throw these oranges into the audience, like a still life escaping. Then I'd do my overalls back up and continue the lecture."[1]

A close friend of Stan Brakhage and a generation behind Maya Deren, she has been a true pioneer since the 1960s but remains overshadowed by both of them and by the more ironic, wry film and photography of figures like Andy Warhol and Cindy Sherman. She didn't write the kind of personal, insightful commentary that helped make Deren and Brakhage such central figures; she took more pride and pleasure in the doing of her work than in its promotion, and she slipped between media and conventions more freely and iconoclastically than many potential followers could accommodate. Her famous, or infamous, performance piece "Meat Joy"— loved in Paris, reviled in London—featured four couples writhing on the floor amid fresh paint, raw fish, chickens, and sausage and was, for her, a paean to ecstatic transformation but to her detractors was many other, less transcendent things. Like Bataille she treated taboos as something to be violated, and both reaped the reward and paid the price for doing so.

Breaking the Frame will help her gain the recognition she is clearly due, although the film has also enjoyed only marginal circulation and attention. It has an ethereal, mystique-laden air that runs counter to the didacticism that most often passes for informed biography. Some background knowledge definitely helps, and thus armed, the film offers an enriching sense of Schneemann's life and work and how the two so elaborately intertwine.

Films on the rich and famous, however adulatory or critical, fare better than work drawing our attention to the neglected and overlooked. It is an uphill challenge, and this film does not make it as easy as possible, smoothing over the difficulty and disturbance in Schneemann's work, but in the final analysis this is what makes it a challenge well worth accepting.

PART II

The Audio in *Audiovisual*

AS ANYONE WHO HAS MORE THAN A PASSING INTEREST in sound in all its forms will readily attest, often with more than a hint of exasperation, the *audio* half of *audiovisual* has never received the same degree of attention as the *visual* half. Early film was silent, save for live accompaniment, which was common, and although sound film taught us to respect the power of speech, sound effects, and music more fully, this lesson remained subordinate to confronting the power of the image. My own work has followed this familiar path for the most part, but the essays here attempt to provide some compensation aimed at our understanding of the documentary film in particular.

The first essay, "Documentary Film and the Coming of Sound," discusses how voice-over commentary replaced reliance on intertitles in silent documentaries. But voice-over did more than that. It offered viewers a point of identification with the film, a guide to take us through the succession of images, a moralizing center around which a particular view of the world revolved. These qualities, I suggest, established the voice-over as a primary point of identification for the viewer, an alternative to the actor and the star system in particular, which is the locus of emotional engagement for mainstream narrative cinema. Voice-over commentary aligns documentary with epistephilia more than scopophilia (love of knowledge over love of gazing). Voice-over remains extremely common and comes in a wide variety of forms, but its crucial significance may seem overshadowed by the sync sound comments of social actors (people), music, and the dynamic play of power in interviews. This essay traces the rise of voice-over commentary and suggests reasons for its continuing importance.

The second essay, "To See the World Anew: Revisiting the Voice of Documentary," in which I revisit the essay on the voice of documentary that I originally published in 1983,[1] focuses on the sense of address we experience with documentary films. They speak to us. They invite our consent and want us to understand them as part and parcel of the world outside the movie theater, as part of our lives as more than viewers looking at a screen. This distinguishes the documentary not only from documents, which remain inert and unaddressed—until taken up into speech directed to us—but also from most fiction and avant-garde work, where we oversee, overhear, or witness but have less sense of being addressed as living social actors. The sense of address is a basic element of rhetoric (and ideology). This essay reflects on the relation of the documentary voice to classical rhetoric. Voice as discussed here also clearly relates to the role of sound, and voice-over in particular, but expands the notion to include the meaning of voice as the distinctive tone and perspective of a film's maker.

The essay in "Further Reflections," "The Sound of Music," arose as a prefatory essay to a book devoted to music in documentary.[2] It tries to set the stage for further investigation and reflection, less by offering an analysis of any particular quality of music in documentary than by personal testimony to the power I have seen it display in various screenings of specific films. The careful design of a musical score for documentaries remains a great challenge for many filmmakers—many a work clutters the cinematic graveyard of films that failed to survive the test of time owing to an unfortunate choice of musical score. Of course, using preexisting music can quickly become a legal minefield and original compositions can be unpredictable in their fit. Those films that succeed in achieving a resonant, compelling affect as a result of their musical accompaniment offer potent inspiration for films that have yet to come.

5 Documentary Film and the Coming of Sound

Nowhere in the world does the coming of sound to documentary film correspond exactly to the coming of sound to the feature fiction film (1926–28). Like CinemaScope, color, and most optical effects, sound films were a possibility long before they were a reality. If the exact moment when sound comes to the feature fiction film is a matter of technology, financing, aesthetics, marketing, and audience expectations, it is no less a matter of similar issues, resolved differently, for documentary film. The coming of sound is one of the crucial transitions for documentary and belongs to the early 1930s. The 1960s and 1980s bear similar significance for other reasons. The focus here is on the coming of sound in the 1930s, with brief mention of these later dates.

Just as the advent of sound for the feature-film industry in the late 1920s prompted lively debate (principally about synchronous or nonsynchronous uses of sound and about subordinate or contrapuntal relationships between character and image), so the advent of sound in documentary proposed an array of alternatives. These ranged from poetic narratives to evocative portraits and from professional, studio-produced commentary to the actual speech of people recorded in their everyday life. The choices made among these alternatives are part of a larger story of the nature and function of documentary film in the period from the late 1920s to the late 1930s, when a dominant mode—expository documentary—took hold and became the equivalent of the classic Hollywood mode of production.[1]

Two notable features of this period are the extremely fluid boundary between a documentary and an avant-garde impulse and the refusal of documentary filmmakers to rely on the strategy of using synchronous speech, recorded, of necessity, on sound stages, and accompanied by elaborate musical scores, that the Hollywood studios embraced. It would have meant plucking social actors from their environment, rehearsing what they said and did, and forfeiting the huge appeal of filming on location. A fluid mix of surreal/defamiliarizing and anthropological/descriptive tendencies in nonfiction films fostered considerable experimentation with nonsynchronous music and commentary while the rejection of studio-based recording delayed the wholesale adoption of testimony and interviews until the great flowering of sync-sound options in real-world locations, rather than on sound stages, took place in the 1960s.[2]

In the silent film era, documentary as a mode of representation that offers perspectives on the historical world—sustained by an institutional framework and a community of practitioners and armed with specific conventions corresponding to distinct audience expectations—did not yet exist. We now write about this early history with a retrospective knowledge that we cannot deny but that we also cannot project back onto a time that precedes its arrival. Cinema lacked the taxonomic divisions we may now think natural or inevitable. Early cinema casually blended the staged and unstaged, actors and nonactors, fact and fiction. The factual and fictional made easy bedfellows, as did a desire to surprise, amuse, and entertain as much or more than to inform or enlighten. Only as feature fiction films gained a dominant position did all other cinematic forms become relegated to a subordinate or marginal status, which still did not necessarily mean any kind of careful differentiation among these alternative forms.[3]

From the vast array of possibilities that early cinema offered, some have been remembered, others forgotten; some adopted, others ignored; some praised, others ridiculed or suppressed. Every new history opens the possibility of reconstructing this array of the remembered, adopted, and praised, or the lost, forgotten, or suppressed and of deconstructing the histories that have come before. Each must do so, however, on the terrain of what has survived (and very little survives by accident).

Compared to the amount of material that has survived and earned praise in the history of narrative cinema, it is striking how few examples of what we now call documentary are commonly identified from the period before 1930. Jack C. Ellis, in his standard history of documentary, for example, cites only twenty-six titles from the 1920s in America, Europe, and the Soviet Union as significant works,[4] while Lewis Jacobs lists only twenty-two significant titles from the 1920s.[5] Some of these, such as Alberto Cavalcanti's *Rien que les heures* (1926), could easily be classified as part of the early history of experimental cinema, but, given the vague state in which all nonfeature films existed, it can just as properly be considered an early example of the documentary tradition. These lists suggest how severely limited the field of reference has become. It is also noteworthy that not a single one of these films from the 1920s makes use of sound (though some may well have had live musical accompaniment during their theatrical presentations).

When Louis Lumière privately demonstrated his new invention, the *cinématographe,* in March 1895 by showing *La sortie des usines,* the film produced the shock of apparently putting life itself on a screen. Erik Barnouw describes the effect this way: "The familiar, seen anew in this way, brought astonishment."[6] Lumière may have acted out of convenience or from insight when he chose to film his own workers leaving the Lumière factory for his demonstration, but the basic familiarity of the scene astonishes all the more. Viewers could attest that what they now saw on a screen was what they could have already seen in reality. If there was a trick, it was the trick of appearing to duplicate reality. What could have been more overwhelmingly convincing of the powers of the *cinématographe* than to see something already recognizable and familiar re-presented in a totally unfamiliar but remarkably recognizable manner? A similar astonishment accompanied the invention of the phonograph, with its uncanny ability to mechanically reproduce any audible sound.

Clearly, a central aspect of the early fascination with cinema is based on our ability to recognize the world we already inhabit. The extraordinary power of the photographic camera to take slices of reality and freeze them within an illusionistic frame rises exponentially in this breathtaking succession of cinematographic images that restores motion, and life, to the frozen image. The living, seemingly embalmed on a strip of film, suddenly comes back to life, repeating actions and restoring events that had, until that moment, belonged to the domain of the irretrievable: the historical past.

Cinema made possible an archive of reality distinct from any that preceded it. But this was not the same as a documentary tradition. Erik Barnouw devotes his entire first chapter of *Documentary,* his valuable history of the form, to early *actualités* that captured some aspect of the historical world, such as another famous Lumière brothers short, *Arrival of a Train* (1895). To me, however, these are not documentaries in a meaningful sense and are but one contributing factor to the appearance of documentary films in the 1920s and 1930s. Most importantly, they bore traces of the historical world, as scientific images, X-rays, and fiction films (in the bodies and faces of real actors) all do, but they lacked the distinct voice of a filmmaker who brought an illuminating perspective to these traces. Yet they were recognizable traces. This alone, like the sound of a familiar voice, possesses considerable power but does not constitute a distinct form of cinematic expression.

The act of recognition, though, gives this archive of reality a remarkable hold on the viewer. In moving images a viewer distinguishes human figures on three levels: (1) typical inhabitants of a specific historical period (based largely on popular fashions and familiar locations); (2) well-known public figures not personally known to the viewer but familiar from multiple forms of source material, including records of their speech during the twentieth century and after (Roosevelt, Lenin, or Hitler, for example); and (3) individuals already personally known to the viewer but never seen in the form of moving pictures before, a vital aspect of home movies, and of the discovery of familiar faces in otherwise impersonal crowds and gatherings.[7]

The impression of reality that film conveys depends heavily on these levels of recognition. They give early cinema a distinctiveness that would remain at the heart of the documentary tradition thereafter. Sound—be it speech, sound effects, or music—enhances this distinctiveness, especially when the sound appears to emanate from the same historical source as the image itself (the sound of Churchill's voice or of horses' hooves on a cobblestone street). Situation-specific sound anchors the image in its acoustic reality. Such sound may signal generic aspects of the historical world (gunfire, running water, and so on, such as we hear, in discreet dabs, in the historical films of Ken Burns), recognizable aspects of that world (a familiar tune or a well-known voice such as a music video by Lady Gaga or a speech by Martin Luther King), or something more intimately familiar (the voice of a friend or family member, for example).

Fiction films seized on the viewer's desire to recognize familiar aspects of historical reality to create a pantheon of famous figures. They were not recognizable for their historical significance and not personally known to the viewer, but they became familiar thanks to their featured appearance in film after film. Such figures, or featured actors, became known as stars. With rare exceptions, like *Nanook of the North* (Robert Flaherty, 1922)—which, we should bear in mind, arrived before the term *documentary* was in common use and was, instead, promoted as "a story of life and love in the actual Artic"[8]—early documentary films, especially in the Soviet Union and Great Britain, stressed emotional tone and social issues, common causes and typical people over the charismatic individual. Montage, or collage, to convey concepts and create emotion, more than character, was the order of the day. Documentaries invited recognition of familiar, recognizable social problems and topical issues rather than of charismatic individuals who carried the day.

The use of stars as a powerful form of recognition (and identification by a complex of means such as acting style, plot structure, and editing—

matched movement, eyeline matches, point of view) began to center the fiction film on the singular body and voice of an individual actor, the specific character she or he plays, and the ineffable aura they generated. It simultaneously began a movement in the fiction film away from equally plausible figures of common causes and social issues, coalitions and collectivities, cultures and their transformation. It became increasingly taken for granted that a drama must revolve around actions and dilemmas involving a single individual, or hero, who undergoes a change and is represented by a star.

The representation of real workers, begun perhaps inadvertently by the Lumière brothers, remained central to the tradition of social representation in the Soviet Union and, in an equally hagiographic way, in Great Britain but seldom elsewhere. The worker could appear as hero, the driving force of revolution or the noble cornerstone of social progress, but the economic hardships and political turmoil of the 1930s undercut this image. Most working people were much more hard-pressed than the determined and triumphant builders of roads celebrated in the Soviet film *Turksib* (Victor Turin, 1929) or the good-natured railway postal workers in the British one *Night Mail* (Harry Watt and Basil Wright, 1936). And even when lionized, workers remained generic and unfamiliar, recognizable only as historical types—types whose faith in the economic system they represented most often seemed highly optimistic, if not fabricated, as it might be in a fiction film. They were seen but not heard, their value, and sometimes needs, articulated in voice-over and in powerful musical scores, an image somewhat hard to fathom amid hunger strikes, extreme poverty, and unemployment throughout the 1930s.

Alternative, more charismatic, figures were needed. Such figures could provide the necessary element of social guidance or political perspective. And soon the documentary film found its equivalent to the star: the unseen commentator—a distinctive, disembodied, self-assured if not omniscient, professional voice whose pronouncements guide us through the course of the film and the issues of the day. Through the 1930s men (commentators were always men) like Westbrook van Voorhis and Ed Herlihy conveyed certainty and authority, without the overbearing manner of a pedant. They were to become the models for pioneer television commentators like Edward R. Murrow and Walter Cronkite, who continued to embody the idea of a heroic, knowledgeable figure, now visible but usually sequestered in a studio, away from all the tumult on which they reported. Theirs was the well-modulated voice that could guide us through the mass of images and events that constituted the news of the day.

Throughout the 1930s and beyond, spoken commentary, in its myriad forms, served as the telltale sign of a documentary. The avant-garde generally rejected this device or utilized it ironically, as Luis Buñuel did in *Land without Bread* (1932). Commentary is a decisive element in the splitting off of documentary from the broader, more open-ended exploration of sound and voice in experimental film.[9]

The early use of sound in documentary emphasizes the representation of the familiar historical world, populated with typical representatives and expressed through a powerful collage of sound and images. Creating or gathering such images and assembling them in a compelling manner gave great creative license to the documentary filmmaker, seldom more so than in the Soviet Union and within the avant-garde. Most documentaries, however, edited together images to support the message delivered by the commentary without letting them become a vividly independent source of meaning on their own, what I elsewhere describe as "strange juxtapositions."[10]

Meanwhile, the unique individual occupies a far more marginal position and social issues a far more vital one than in the flourishing feature fiction film. The star, or central point of identification, becomes, for documentary, the spoken word and the commentator who delivers it. It is the literal voice of the film, and it arrives in the form of "He Who Already Knows," a voice that marshals sounds and images in support of a carefully crafted perspective known from the outset. The film conveys this perspective movingly and convincingly. The spoken word stands for the disembodied, omniscient, invulnerable filmmaker who retains full control over the assembly of images and the rhythm of the film. Its persistence is vividly demonstrated in the work of Ken Burns, whose voice-over commentators, from David McCullough in *The Civil War* (1990) to Peter Coyote in *The Roosevelts* (2014), hark back to this classic—if not overused and often tedious—model (the voice-overs tend to drone on in the later Burns films).

Documentary relies on the viewer's recognition of images that refer back to the historical world. To this quality documentary filmmakers add their own voice, or perspective, most crucially in the 1930s by commentary; but editing, composition, depth of field, lighting, music, and reenactments can all contribute to a distinct perspective or "voice" in a more general sense.[11] Documentary therefore occupies a complex zone of representation in which the art of observing, responding, and listening must be combined with the art of shaping, interpreting, or arguing. Viewers come to realize that what they see when they see a documentary is a complex, often semi-visible, mix of the historically real and the discursively constructed. To the pleasure of recognition are added personal journeys, moral imperatives,

political exhortations, spiritual discoveries, cautionary tales, romantic long-
ings, and enchanted idylls.

By the early 1930s the re-presentation of the historical world, combined
with the distinctive voice of the filmmaker, began to give the domain of
documentary a use value that drew the attention of politicians and governments, not to mention poets and adventurers. It was possible not only to
represent reality with great exactitude (something that might have
remained at the level of the early actualités or become primarily of scientific interest) but also to give audiences a perspective on the world that had
never been seen in quite the same way before and to convey this view with
emotional power, thanks, in no small measure, to the use of sound.

These impulses gradually bifurcated into the two main divisions of nonfiction film, the documentary and the avant-garde, but in the beginning
such distinctions were blurred (as the lists of early films discussed as documentary in Ellis, Jacobs, and Barnouw suggest). Those setting out to explore
the world around them and represent it in recognizable form were simultaneously interested in discovering how they might reshape that world, and
our image or understanding of it, through cinematic techniques. The
emerging documentary form allowed viewers to see the world anew, from
a distinct perspective and for a particular purpose.

Another way to think of these two, nonexclusive tendencies toward documentation and voice or, if pushed toward their extremes, documentary
and the avant-garde, is to think of them as cinematic versions of two
twentieth-century tendencies: an anthropological impulse, bent on broad-
ening the scope of the familiar and recognizable beyond our own culture or
worldview, and a corresponding surrealist impulse, bent on shocking or
shaking up existing assumptions about the familiar and recognizable within
our own culture or worldview.[12] Paul Strand and Charles Sheeler's
Mannahatta (1921), Ralph Steiner's *H2O* (1929), Alberto Cavalcanti's *Rien
que les heures*, Joris Ivens's *The Bridge* (1927), and Dimitri Kirsanoff's
Ménilmontant (1926) are among the films discussed in Ellis and Jacobs that
emphasize the surrealist impulse toward strange juxtaposition most vividly, whereas *Nanook of the North* stands as the most celebrated instance
of the strange made familiar.

The question of the filmmaker's voice and the extent to which it
remained unobtrusive or highly noticeable often took precedence over the
fiction/nonfiction distinction. Much of Robert Flaherty's remarkable success in exhibiting *Nanook of the North*, for example, resulted from his
astute combination of a documentary attitude toward a preexisting world
and a narrative strategy with its unobtrusive—because so recognizably

humanist—representation. In Flaherty's romantic voice Nanook becomes the first "star" of the still nascent documentary film (with Flaherty himself not far behind). Nanook's tale of struggles against nature stand as the documentary equivalent of the folkloric and classic Hollywood tale of a hero's quest to overcome obstacles and adversity and reach his goal (in this case survival in a harsh environment).[13]

It is of no small import that Flaherty utilized intertitles in a manner similar to what would, with the coming of sound, become voice-over commentary. Titles, for this silent film, guided the viewer toward the meanings and values intended by the filmmaker, and they provided a narrative backbone for the illustrative scenes of Inuit life.

Flaherty's success in gaining theatrical release for his film is a key factor in his elevation to founding pioneer, and that success is clearly due to his ability to draw on qualities of the fiction film to tell an engaging and carefully conceived story and to convey a specific, appealing (humanist) perspective on man's relation to his world. Flaherty did not want to string together a series of semiconnected scenes of disparate events, as the less commercially successful Edward S. Curtis did before him in his *In the Land of the Head Hunters* (1914), restored and retitled *In the Land of the War Canoes* (1972), a narrative nonfiction set among the Kwakiutl of the Pacific Northwest and told, albeit less gracefully, in a spirit clearly akin to Flaherty's tale of Inuit life in the Arctic.

Flaherty went beyond Curtis's proscenium stage camera style, where a single long shot often constitutes each scene, to adopt many of the editing devices of fiction film (close-ups, continuity editing, matches on action, and so on) while also retaining great respect for the long take when the actual duration of an event had distinct importance. Flaherty also substituted the familiar (and heartwarming) tale of a nuclear family (Nanook's) for Curtis's more lurid story of sexual jealousy, dubious ceremonies, and grim rituals such as head-hunting, all bundled into a tale of melodramatic excess.

Flaherty wanted to tell a story and to document the life of a people. Whether these two aims were at odds with each other, or in what ways they combined to produce specific effects, depending on the voice of the filmmaker, may not have troubled Flaherty himself as much as they have troubled documentary filmmakers and theorists ever since. Narratives are always fictions in the sense that, even if they refer to the historical world, they must still be shaped from the flow of historical events into a tale that has a beginning, middle, and end; corresponds to known facts; and holds together as a plausible account. Narratives are a vital way to make meaning from what happens, without cessation, in the world around us. They form the backbone of all the great myths. Documentaries do so with sounds and images that refer to this historical world and give voice to the filmmaker's vision of it.

Sometimes important events occur when a camera is not present to record them. Reenactment or reconstruction is a logical solution to the paradoxical quandary a documentary filmmaker often confronts: how to film an actual event that occurred before a camera could record it so that it once again appears as it might have appeared at the time it originally occurred. *Nanook of the North* is certainly not the first or only film to rely on reenactments. At least since Curtis's *In the Land of the Head Hunters*, in which he, like Flaherty, "painstakingly reconstructed [settings] for pre-contact authenticity,"[14] the goal of filmmaker, anthropologist, historians, and storytellers—to re-present the historical world in an engaging, essentially authentic manner—seemed entirely compatible.

This goal, however, further blurs any distinction between fiction, which reenactments must, to some degree, be, and documentary, which sets out to represent the preexisting world, not to fabricate another one. Music, sound effects, and speech could all be plausibly added to a reenactment in ways that might seem more intrusive and problematic in the representation of a historical event recorded on the spot. In a reenactment the creative use of sound can heighten what it might feel like to witness a given event for which the camera was not initially present or to increase our awareness of the fictive quality of such a scene.

As long as the filmmaker's intentions were deemed honorable (as long as viewers shared the apparent intentions of the maker), these ways of giving creative shape to reality were readily accepted. They were, in fact, the foundation stone of the creative reediting of existing footage in the work of Esfir Shub's compilation films and many newsreels. Compilation films, like reenactments, attest to the centrality of the filmmaker's expressive voice and distinct perspective. These creative elements, conveyed by sound and image, were also readily accepted by viewers of the British films produced by John Grierson in the 1930s, films like *The Saving of Bill Blewitt* (Harry Watt, 1936) or *The Smoke Menace* (John Taylor, 1937). Similar strategies of reshaping and constructing what would then be presented as reality were also central to Pare Lorentz's U.S. government–sponsored films *The Plow That Broke the Plains* (1936) and *The River* (1937), films that also effectively introduced sound to the American documentary. Music, as well as commentary, became a crucial element in giving an emotional coherence to the argument for soil conservation in the former and flood management in the latter.

For much of the early history of documentary it was the individual shot that retained a special relation to historical reality (and even this left considerable room for fabrication if done in the spirit of an anthropological quest for authenticity that most critics attributed to Flaherty). The combination of shots remained less easily bound by principles of faithfulness or authenticity in any straightforward empirical sense (as Vertov's and Eisenstein's films and the heavily experimental films cited by Ellis and Jacobs remind us vividly). Collage assemblies of images governed by pace, rhythm, and composition often subordinate realist representations of time and space to aesthetic affect and impart a musical quality to the image track. Considerable license reigns when images constitute a form of visual poetry or music. Recent musical scores for early documentaries such as the Alloy Orchestra's lively music (first performed in 1995) for *Man with a Movie Camera* (Dziga Vertov, 1929) crackles with an energy and dynamism commensurate with the film's frenzied assembly of disparate images.

At this larger level of the assembly of shots into scenes or sequences, techniques of joining images together rely heavily on modernist collage even though the dominance of voice-over commentary compelled tamer forms of editing compatible with the principle of reasoned presentation: creative license was not unlimited. Images of illustration, what filmmakers usually refer to as "B-roll" footage, anchor the commentary in the visible world. Such images, such as a collage of people hurriedly eating sandwiches at a lunch counter in *The City* (Ralph Steiner and Willard Van Dyke, 1939), reinforce the verbal message—modern urban life is far too chaotic and rushed—rather than stand as a purely poetic message on their own. Music can support poetic collage assemblies or images of illustration, but if the voice-over dominates, music, like image, needs to subordinate itself to this unseen but controlling voice, as it does to the speech of characters in fiction films.

The tensions and dynamics of early documentaries, as they embraced sound in various combinations of music and voice-over commentary primarily, shifted dramatically in the 1960s. Portable cameras and tape recorders, capable of recording sync sound on actual locations, opened up a new world of possibility. The filmmaker might observe what unfolds before the camera, as if the camera merely recorded what would have happened anyway, or she or he might participate in the lives of others, most notably through interviews. This altered the status of the voice. No longer the disembodied, omniscient, invulnerable voice of He Who Already Knows (often crystallized in a scripted shooting plan and written commentary that could be completed before the start of shooting), the filmmaker adopted an embodied, situated, and often highly vulnerable position as one among many—albeit the one with the movie camera—for whom the future unfolded in the course of making the film rather than having taken shape prior to the start of filming. It was the voice or perspective of He Who Does Not Yet Know and what happens happens outside his full control. Impromptu, spontaneous speech prevailed over the well-polished commentaries of the past.

The filmmaker's new challenge was to find or shape the dramatic quality in life lived before the camera, either in observed moments or through interactions with the filmmaker (where illustrative archival footage often replaced the wild collage assemblies of the past). The image track was no longer a collage of shots that built a mood or attitude; it was instead the visible counterpart to the voice of the speaking subject. The filmmaker now held his or her camera on the one who speaks, in sync. This meant willingly sacrificing full control of the image. Less preconceived, the image as caught served to anchor spoken words to individual bodies. For the filmmaker, listening with a well-tuned ear became as high a priority as speaking, through commentary, with polished eloquence.

Documentary stars akin to Nanook arose at a rapid rate. They were individuals who command our attention with their expressiveness, idiosyncrasy, or emotional intensity. Hubert Humphrey and John F. Kennedy in *Primary* (Drew Associates, 1960), Jason in *Portrait of Jason* (Shirley Clarke, 1967), Paul Brennan in *Salesman* (Albert and David Maysles, 1968), and Edith and Little Edie Bouvier Beale in *Grey Gardens* (Albert and David Maysles, 1975) helped erect a pantheon of documentary figures of memorable proportion through what they said as much as what they typified or did.

The innovations of the 1960s remain with us, but so does the richer stew of experimentation from the 1930s. It is in the 1980s that these two tendencies found common ground in the innovative work of individuals such as Michael Moore, Errol Morris, and Marlon Riggs, who pursued the avenues opened up by Emile de Antonio's *In the Year of the Pig* (1968), which used sound and music expressionistically, and Connie Field's *The Life and Times of Rosie the Riveter* (1980), which introduced archival footage only to undercut and subvert it.

Errol Morris, in particular, with his landmark film, *The Thin Blue Line* (1988), expertly and powerfully coupled the anthropological and surreal impulses of early documentary with the rise of the sync interview in the 1960s to extraordinary effect. (The film helped secure the release of an innocent man sentenced to die for murder.) His 35 mm carefully lit and expertly composed scenes evoked as much as they described. Morris reclaimed the carefully composed image of 1930s documentary, sacrificing nothing to spontaneity, and married his compelling images to the distinct, idiosyncratic speech of his subjects. He reintroduced elements of surreal collage, as well as close-up shots of newspaper reports that tracked across fragments of sentences, making it impossible to treat this standard form of information as source material. It gestured, as Bertolt Brecht might, to this function without fulfilling it. Viewers beheld a familiar visual field rendered strangely unintelligible.

Likewise, his reenactments upheld the intentionality of authentic representation except that what Morris sought to authenticate were the subjective memories, self-serving narratives, and suspect accounts of police investigators and alleged witnesses alike. No single reenactment, of the several included in the film, represents "what really happened," but all attest to the cloud of doubt and self-deception that shrouded what was, in fact, the truth of who did or did not kill the fallen police officer. With no commentary at all the film calls the veracity of individual statements into question and asks whether it is not ourselves whom we often deceive as much as, if not more than, others.

Morris also utilized Philip Glass's musical score to great effect, giving the testimony and reenactments a haunting, ethereal, and yet powerful impact. The subtle, repetitive, hypnotic music functioned less as a supportive backdrop than as a powerful alternative to any voice-over commentary: it conveyed an obsessive perspective and mysterious tone from which any discursive argumentation had been removed.

The film adopted the performative qualities that revolve around social actors, or subjects, who possess distinctive expressive qualities and who populated the observational or participatory documentaries of the 1960s. The two main subjects of his film were both potential heroes in the sense of possessing memorable qualities, even as Morris coupled these qualities with the prevailing tone of the film, carried by surreal images and compelling music, and with a gradual revelation of guilt and innocence. The film spoke engagingly and movingly through sounds and images no longer beholden solely to what happens in front of the camera but liberated to once again speak in an inventive, personal voice that addressed reality and the viewer with equal verve. The qualities that made the nascent documentaries of the 1920s and early 1930s captivating—suspense, narrative, music, a collage of striking images, and a mix of fabrication and observation, staging, and listening—serve to build emotional engagement and intellectual involvement with a world both familiar and, once again, disconcertingly strange.

Sound remains essential throughout this condensed history of the form. From the voice-over commentary that replaced intertitles and gave documentary a nascent form as the locus of one-who-knows to the more stylistically based voice of countless documentaries that avoid commentary but nonetheless convey a distinct perspective and moral attitude toward the world we share, sound provides a major point of identification for the viewer. It guides us through the imagery; it lends coherence, emotional intensity, and sensory rhythm; it draws us into a state of epistephilia as we set out to experience and know the world in a distinct way. The shape of sound's design on us has changed with time, but its centrality to the power of documentary abides.

6 To See the World Anew

Revisiting the Voice of Documentary

Unexpectedly, someone calls out: "Hey, you!" This interpellation served as one of the foundation stones for Louis Althusser's theory of ideology,[1] but we can make a simpler claim: to be addressed by a film—to sense that a film seeks to engage and speak to us about the world we share—functions as a hallmark of documentary film. Seldom as confrontational as the famous Althusserian "hailing of the subject," and tied to more specific forms of ideology than the construction of the subject itself, ranging, in fact, from the soft-spoken "Consider this" of a poetic documentary to the "Listen up" of a didactic one, the documentary's imperative address distinguishes it from the overseen and overheard quality of most fiction and prepares us for a distinct form of engagement.

Technologies change, but the need to have a voice with which to address others, a distinct way of seeing our shared world, remains a constant. It is as elemental as the need to tell a story, present a point of view, or give poetic form to a formless world. Now digitized in myriad ways, the need for a voice persists across the history of the documentary film. More than a style, which imbues an imagined world with its distinct allure, which we then behold, the voice of documentary, as the felt presence of a cohabitant of our shared reality, shapes the historical world from its specific point of view and addresses us directly. Voice calls out to us to acknowledge the presence of an other who strives, by means of sounds and images, to speak to us. (I regard this other mainly as the individual filmmaker, but it may also be institutional, as in the address of network news or reality TV shows.)

Just as the public speaker uses his or her entire body to give voice to a particular perspective, documentaries use all the cinematic means at their disposal to address us. Questions of speech and voice are therefore not sim-ply literal. The spoken word, of course, plays a vital role in most documentary film and video: Alain Resnais's *Night and Fog* (1955) exemplifies the centrality of voice-over commentary, just as Drew Associates' *Primary* (1960) demonstrates the power of the spoken word captured with sync sound as the camera rolls.

Some films, like *Portrait of Jason* (Shirley Clarke, 1967), *Word Is Out* (Nancy Adair and Andrew Brown, 1977), or *Shoah* (Claude Lanzmann, 1985), seem at first glance to be nothing but speech. But when Jason confides to us about his life in *Portrait of Jason*, a key avenue to understanding his words involves what we notice of his inflections, gestures, and behavior, including his interaction with Shirley Clarke, the filmmaker, as she orchestrates their dialogue. And when the various interviewees in *Shoah* speak to us about their past, a key aspect of understanding the force and severity of that past lies in its effect on their way of speaking and acting in the present. Memories, experience, habits, and trauma all get embedded in the body, and it is of them that the body in documentary speaks.[2] Even the most speech-oriented of documentaries—often referred to as "talking head" films—convey meanings, hint at symptoms, and express values on a multitude of levels beyond what is said literally.

Voice has taken on different characteristics over the course of documentary film history, differences we can sketch out in terms of five periods.

(1) With silent films, accompanied only by music, the sense of a voice addressing us came largely through intertitles and nonverbal means such as composition and editing. Scenes of walrus, fish and seal hunting, as well as of igloo building, in *Nanook of the North* (Robert Flaherty, 1922), with their long takes and suspense, say, in effect, "Just watch; see what this man can do against tough odds." The intertitles, like those in many other silent films, tell us what voice-over commentators would soon describe. There is a respectful but suspenseful, anticipatory quality to these titles from Flaherty just as there is an exhortatory, ecstatic tone to the intertitles of Mikhail Kalatozov's delirious tribute to Soviet engineering as it brings a road to a landlocked region in *Salt for Svanetia* (1930), a tribute amplified by the wild but rhythmic editing and music that seem to hew the road from celluloid mountain sides.

(2) With the coming of sound at the end of the 1920s, voice takes firm root in "Voice of God" commentary (unseen but heard narrators who guided us through a situation or issue from the film's perspective), but this was but one component of what conveyed a sense of being addressed by films like *Night Mail* (Harry Watt and Basil Wright, 1936), *Coal Face* (Alberto Cavalcanti, 1935), or *The River* (Pare Lorentz, 1937). Their assembling of images to illustrate their verbal points played just as vital a role.

We witnessed men at work or nature at its most dangerous. As W.H. Auden's poetic voice-over for *Night Mail* attests, commentary need not be didactic or stilted and can engage us affectively as well as factually. And for much of the 1930s and 1940s—and ever since, in fact—commentary has played a decisive role in conveying the perspective of the filmmaker to the audience, be it John Huston's rueful account of difficult, costly struggle to defeat Italian and German forces in his *The Battle of San Pietro* (1945) or Peter Coyote's flat, middle-of-the-road recounting of a presidential dynasty in Ken Burns's *The Roosevelts* (2014).

Time and space as we normally know them unravel to reveal the time and space called up by the film's voice. Images from many different places might be edited together to support a single point. Continuity of time and space matter less than continuity of thought or emotional tone. Classic expository films seldom have a deep investment in any one person, place, or thing. Each shot serves to represent typical qualities needed to support the film's point of view.

These qualities are evident in Walter Ruttmann's *Berlin: Symphony of a Great City* (1927), Dziga Vertov's *Man with a Movie Camera* (1929), Hans Richter's *Inflation* (1929), Harry Watt and Basil Wright's *Night Mail*, and Ralph Steiner and Willard Van Dyke's *The City* (1939). These films share a common theme—life in the modern urban center—but speak with different voices: the formal, abstract power of machinery that seems to function on its own, devoid of human agents, in *Berlin;* the freneticism and excitement of a new human agency in charge of production, its own body, and its environment in *Man with a Movie Camera;* the wreckage brought about by rampant inflation in *Inflation;* the harmony of state and society evident in the work of the British postal service in *Night Mail;* and the overwhelming, oppressive frenzy of an urban pace that reduces individuals to cogs that conform to the rhythm of the machines in *The City.*

Time and space submit to the logic of a point of view; shots support a specific tone rather than build a sense of concrete geographic space. Images come together to create this tone rather than to offer evidence of a fixed location; individuals pass through the films less to attest to their specific circumstances or to reveal aspects of their distinct experience than to represent types and activities the film wishes to speak about. People may lack in individuality or personality, but they contribute to the distinct and powerful voice of the filmmaker.

All these films speak in vivid voices and use a wide variety of cinematic means to do so, the voice-over commentary of a narrator being but one of many devices put into play. These strategies remain commonly adopted ones today. Ali Samadi Ahadi's *The Green Wave* (2010), for example, returns to this tradition even though it adopts new technologies such as computer-generated animation. In this film we don't get to know individuals in any great detail, but their many voices and experiences during the massive protests and political movement leading up to the 2009 elections in Iran give us a vivid sense of what it was like to stand up to an oppressive regime and demand change. Similarly, Tony and Ridley Scott's *Life in a Day* (2010) creates a rich collage of individual experiences on one day that evokes large themes like love, marriage, and birth by taking fragments from thousands of diaries shot on the same day around the world by people using cell phones and digital cameras. We learn almost nothing about any of these people, not even their names, but the footage they provide folds into an impressive sense of what one day, an Everyman's Any Day, was like around the world.

(3) Something happened in the 1960s to change all this. Sound recording became far more manageable, and for the first time the voices of social actors—people—entered into documentary in a major way. Everyday speech, recorded at myriad locations outside a sound studio, could be heard and social actors seen in their immediate environment, doing what they routinely do and saying what they often say. They go about their business, with or without the overt intervention of the filmmaker to interview, challenge, provoke, or otherwise interact with them. Voice now emerges from how the filmmaker encounters others in the moment of filming more than in the process of editing footage and adding commentary and music, footage often recorded without a comparable sense of immediacy and risk.

The very moment of filming becomes the heart of the matter in a way that earlier approaches seldom stressed, be it in the intensity with which Hubert Humphrey and John F. Kennedy campaign for the Democratic nomination as presidential and vice presidential candidates in *Primary*, the pseudo-intensity of David Holzman's effort to capture his quotidian life in the mockumentary *David Holzman's Diary* (Jim McBride, 1967), or Eduardo Coutinho's remarkable ability to draw out personal testimony from near strangers in *O fim e o princípio* (Eduardo Coutinho, 2006) or from not-so-shy teenagers in *Last Conversations* (2015).

O fim demonstrates vividly the new principle of synchronous sound and the change it produced. The film consists largely of interviews with elderly residents of Brazil's less prosperous northeast, and they talk mainly about their views on life, religion, and death. We gain a vivid sense of them as individuals rather than a sense of the filmmaker's controlling sensibility. Indeed, rather than controlling *all* the sound that accompanies the film,

Coutinho controls virtually *none* of the sound. He adds nothing to what he can record in the moment: no music, no sound effects, no voice-over commentary. Coutinho, like other filmmakers working in this new key, respects the spatial and temporal geography of a very specific time and place and captures fundamental qualities of specific encounters with fleshed-out individuals in that geohistorical location. This is also vividly true for *Roundabout in My Head* (Hassen Ferhani, 2015), a respectful observational study of men who work in an Algerian slaughterhouse. We learn little of the larger context save what the men tell us through their casual conversations, but what they say is thoughtful, poetic, and profoundly revealing of a society that seems to lack an underlying cohesiveness.

From complete control over sound to almost no control over sound, but still able to speak about the world in compelling ways, the voice of documentary has changed profoundly. The broad-scale perspective that might have organized films in an earlier period and used individual figures to promote this perspective now becomes the small-scale perceptions of discreet individuals whose views we must measure against our own, knowing that we encounter them through the lens of a filmmaker who nonetheless cedes a large measure of control to his subjects.

After 1960 the individual shot is no longer just a fragment in a montage assembly. The individual who is in the shot is no longer just an example of a larger principle. There is the sense of a direct, personal encounter. Acute questions involving the ethics of encounter arise: how do we acquit ourselves in the presence of others? Do we treat others with respect or disrespect, as full human figures or as symbols or stereotypes that fulfill a larger purpose? The voice of documentary now says to us, in so many words, "This is how I choose to act and film; what do you make of it?" Coutinho confronts these questions with extraordinary eloquence in *O fim e o princípio*. D.A. Pennebaker shows a similarly attentive ear in *Don't Look Back* (1967). He observes and recedes from the frame. People act as if he were not there. He observes how Bob Dylan acts when people seek to interview him, but Pennebaker himself does not interview Dylan; he only observes what happens when others do. Listening attentively becomes as vital as speaking eloquently.

In taking this approach, Pennebaker also demonstrates a new editing style that honors the time and space of a specific encounter. Montage assemblies of shots no longer dominate. Pennebaker, like many other contemporary filmmakers, maintains a continuity of time and space because that is the time and space of encounter itself, the time and space needed for two people to face one another and create a relationship. Pennebaker therefore edits in the camera, panning and zooming to achieve the effect of continuity editing and its shot/reverse shots, its two-shots, establishing shots, and close-ups, except that they all occur within the duration of a single long take. The year 1960 marks not only the rise of a new documentary voice but a new documentary editing style as well.

(4) The 1980s saw a return to the more open-ended, inventive forms of social representation that flourished in the 1930s—from fictional reenactments to formal innovation. This earlier period of experimentation spoke to the commonalties of avant-garde and documentary filmmaking.[3] John Grierson attempted to suppress this comingling in favor of a more promotional form of advocacy, with partial success, but it took the shifts that occurred in the 1960s to propel documentary away from the avant-garde most decisively. It would only be a matter of time before their common root in seeing things anew, in ways that exceed the strictures of capturing the present moment as it unfolds in front of the camera, was rediscovered.

Often this new, more prominent voice includes the personal voice of the filmmaker, which underscores the sense of direct encounter, an embodied perspective, relayed to the viewer. Michael Moore remains almost synonymous with the vivid presence of the filmmaker within his own film, from *Roger & Me* (1989) to *Where to Invade Next* (2015). Something personal is at stake. In a radically different key, Trinh Minh-ha's *Reassemblage* (1982) owes a good measure of its distinction to Trinh's voice-over commentary as she speaks in her own carefully modulated Vietnamese-accented and very forthright style, just as the films of Péter Forgács address us with, among many other things, his own slightly idiosyncratic, Hungarian-accented, minimalist commentary. And although Boris Gerrets chooses written intertitles to speak for him, the sense of something intensely personal surfaces vividly in *People I Could Have Been and Maybe Am* (2010).

Gerrets wants to find out what the lives of strangers are like and what it might be like to enter into those lives. He does this with his cell phone. What we see is how he acts in the presence of people he meets, gets to know, and even in one case has a sexual relationship with. We hear and see someone relating to others on the basis of their mutual participation in the making of a film even as they go on just living their lives. A strong sense of loneliness and need, irrational actions, and turbulent feelings comes across from everyone, including the somewhat detached but deeply invested filmmaker. His life becomes his film, and his film, as the product of a cell phone, becomes an extension of his life. The film has a confessional voice as Gerrets reveals to us how he relates to others and how others relate to him. It is, in its own distinct way, as personal and experimental as the work of Stan Brakhage.

If I were to nominate one film to epitomize the shift that occurred in the 1980s and lay the groundwork for the documentary of today, it would be *The Thin Blue Line* (Errol Morris, 1988), a film about a man sentenced to die for a crime he did not commit. Errol Morris eschews deferential adherence to the observational and participatory modes for something more eclectic. He combines special effects (particularly slow-motion shots), attention-grabbing music (by Philip Glass), an emphasis on emotional affect (with dubbed sounds and suspenseful structuring), and feature-film production values (shooting on 35 mm film with a production designer as part of his crew). These shifts alone proclaim something radically different from the handheld, rough-and-ready style of the 1960s. But Morris also gives us portraits of social actors as far more complex entities than most documentaries allow (people emerge as complex characters with contradictory testimony, hints of deception, self-deception, and as symptoms of the power of institutions, or ideology, to frame how they see and describe the world) and fantasy (reenactments depict claims about what happened at the time of the shooting more than what really happened factually and reintroduce the classic devices of music, sound effects, artful mise-en-scène, and stylistic embellishments such as the slow-motion shot of a flying milk shake). These are the classic forms of speaking through the body of the film that Vertov, Ruttmann, and others pioneered but that were swept aside in the 1960s.

It is, in many ways, the voice of documentary today. In *Regarding Susan Sontag* (Nancy D. Kates, 2014), for example, special effects let us experience the world as Sontag did, serving less to amplify a given historical event than a personal aesthetic. A memorable example involves an image of typed words that decompose into an animated sea of floating letters that slowly cluster back into a Chuck Close–like portrait of Susan Sontag, which then dissolves into a photographic image of her. Nancy Kates uses such effects to speak empathetically about a woman whose life revolved around a love for and profound engagement with words.

This return to its mixed, open-ended origins accounts, in my view, for the explosion of interest in documentary as a theatrically appealing, commercially viable, socially invested, poetically sophisticated enterprise. Documentary has repossessed its affinity not only with the avant-garde but with narrative storytelling as well. It has become less like a narrowly conceived form of social moralizing and short-term advocacy and more like its fictional siblings: a form that explores the depth and complexity of human interaction. Special effects, even animation, as utilized in Ari Folman's *Waltz with Bashir* (2008) and Dennis Tupicoff's *His Mother's Voice* (1997);

the quest, as utilized by Michael Moore in *Roger & Me*, by Morgan Spurlock in *Supersize Me* (2004), and by Banksy in *Exit through the Gift Shop* (2010); complex, deceptive, or self-deceptive characters in Heidi Ewing and Rachel Grady's *Jesus Camp* (2006) and Alex Gibney's *Steve Jobs: The Man in the Machine* (2015); and heightened suspense as deployed in James Marsh's *Man on Wire* (2008), Louie Psihoyos's *The Cove* (2009), and Jeff Prosserman's *Chasing Madoff* (2010) all attest to a willingness to resort to any means necessary to tell a story and involve an audience.

In my original "Voice of Documentary" essay, written before this revived interest in documentary had peaked, my concern was that some films that broke free from the observation mode still relied on archival footage to impart a classic tonal flow; but instead of being coupled to a voice-over commentary offering the filmmaker's point of view, it amplified what social actors said about their experiences through a string of interviews. The filmmaker's voice seemed to succumb to that of the film's subjects. The filmmaker risked sacrificing his or her independent voice by omitting what interview subjects did not want to address. This occurred in *Union Maids* (Jim Klein, 1976) and *The Life and Times of Rosie the Riveter* (Connie Field, 1980). In both of these cases the involvement of interviewees with the Communist Party goes unacknowledged, presumably because it carried a stigma that might discredit their testimony.

My concern then, though real, does not seem central to the direction taken by the late 1980s in which the filmmaker's voice gains increasing clarity and strength. Even in works like *Jesus Camp*, *12th and Delaware* (Heidi Ewing and Rachel Grady, 2010), or *The Act of Killing* (Joshua Oppenheimer, 2012), where many of the social actors espouse views the filmmaker does not endorse, the film's voice makes clear that a distance exists, that these are views to ponder—in terms of how they arise and get sustained—but not necessarily to embrace. There is a mix of "Decide for yourself" and "Can you believe this?" in these films' voices that avoids the dangers of subordination while expanding the range of subjects with whom we are invited to seriously engage, from those with whom we might already agree to those with whom we often do not.

(5) These developments remain with us in the twenty-first century as documentary migrates into the digital universe of recording, editing, and projecting pixels rather than analog traces of what strips of film or video record. Be it the relative ease with which an image can be modified, edited, or combined with sounds and music, or the interactive potential that allows viewers to chart their way through narrative options on interactive websites, the form now exhibits a degree of flexibility, or indeterminacy, that

marks a dramatic departure from its original claims to represent reality with a clear and sober voice. Far more fluidity and participatory potential exist. Documentary film spans a gamut from the IMAX screen to the cell phone for both production and reception, with new opportunities to text, tweet, and blog, to post to YouTube or to send an Instagram. We no longer need to be trained filmmakers to share intimate photographs or to capture events as they happen around us, as participant or bystander, with nothing more than a handheld device. It is despite, or perhaps because of, this bewildering array of forms and functions that documentary finds itself in the midst of a golden age of creative expression.

Do all these possibilities significantly alter the question of voice? Some recent films suggest tentative answers to this question. Many recent films, speak probingly and responsively about the nature of encounter and human relationships, including that between filmmaker and subject. Such a voice typically acknowledges its subject, and audience, as its equal, not its target, victim, or tool. This is a voice that speaks compellingly through the body of the film: through editing; through subtle and strange juxtapositions; through music, lighting, composition, and mise-en-scène; through dialogue overheard and commentary delivered; through silence, as well as speech; and through images, as well as words.

These elements announce a voice that listens with compassion and responds with empathy, be it the plight of immigrants strewn across a European landscape in the poetic and haunting *Those Who Feel the Fire Burning* (Morgan Knibbe, 2014) or the anguish and indignation of the brother of a victim of Indonesian death squads in Joshua Oppenheimer's *The Look of Silence* (2014) as he interacts with the killers and their families, probing, almost always unsuccessfully, for some small sign of contrition or remorse.

We witness an embodied perspective that becomes relayed to the viewer. Something personal is at stake for the filmmaker and the subject. Witnessing the hardships and struggles of others stems from a need to address a sense of social injustice or an inner demon that may never be announced but is felt all the same. The profound anguish suffered by veterans of the war in Iraq in Laurent Bécue-Renard's *Of Men and War* (2014), an excruciatingly honest portrait of men in a life-and-death battle for their souls, arrives as a result of Bécue-Renard's dedication to telling their story over a five-year period of filmmaking. The camera attests to a presence that possesses none of the voyeurism that sometimes mars an observational style. Accepted and integrated with others who expose their darkest deeds and deepest fears, the filmmaker becomes a medium, or channeler, who facilitates our own compassion and understanding. Respect, if not love, marks the camera's presence decisively and imparts a luminous quality to the film's voice.

The end credits of *Of Men and War* attest to this when we see photographs of two of the filmmaker's grandfathers in military uniforms from World War I. In a question-and-answer session Bécue-Renard indicated that these figures haunted him with their perpetual silence at family gatherings. Unlike the veterans he witnesses in intense sessions of group therapy as they struggle to overcome the moral injuries they have suffered, these relatives never spoke of what they experienced at war. Their silence was the great elephant in the room that haunted family relations and that Bécue-Renard sought to exorcise.

Unlike Ed Pincus's groundbreaking personal film *Diaries* (1982), a frank, even intimate, portrait of his personal and family life from 1971 to 1976, shot on 16 mm, films like *The Act of Killing, Of Men and War,* and *People I Could Have Been and Maybe Am* explore how similar intimacy can develop between relative strangers. It quickly seems in all these films as if the participants had long known each other. The camera can exhibit an intrusiveness, for better or worse—vividly felt in Ross McElwee's *Sherman's March* (1985), tragically recounted in Elizabeth Barret's *Stranger with a Camera* (2000), mockingly portrayed in Jim McBride's *David Holzman's Diary*—but in these other works it becomes an embodied prosthetic, a corporeal extension that enables a vibrant, respectful relation to come to the fore and engage us.

Something personal is at stake here, as it always is in an encounter, a fact often masked by concepts and categories that submerge the individual within a preestablished frame, including observation as an end in itself. The filmmaker becomes more than a professional maker of films; she becomes a collaborator and confidant, a partner in life to a remarkable degree. What emerges is a dialogical truth, the type of truth about the self that only arrives in and through encounter, interaction, and relationship. It is radically distinct from factual or logical truth and from personal or subjective truth.[4] It is not what is true for just the filmmaker or just her subjects alone and not what is true about the world in its empirical facticity. It is the manifestation of what is true when two people engage with one another and through their dialogical engagement discover for themselves, and us, aspects of our shared state of being not otherwise evident.

Along with Jonathan Caouette's *Tarnation* (2003), about the filmmaker's tumultuous family relationships; Heddy Honigmann's *Food for Love: A Shtetl That's No Longer There* (2004), in which the filmmaker's seventy-five-year-old mother makes vrennekes as she reminisces with her daughter about family history and longs to return to the Polish shtetl eradicated by the Nazis soon after she left, long ago (in the 1930s), as if this were possible; Alan Berliner's *First Cousin Once Removed* (2012), in which the filmmaker celebrates the life of his cousin, Edwin Honig, as he slowly slides into the obliviousness of Alzheimer's disease; and Laura Poitras's *Citizenfour* (2014), these films speak to the power of the camera to attest to the love and intimacy that can flourish between those aligned across from one another.[5]

The films I am emphasizing sidestep the risk of voyeurism by adopting the position of witness, of one who listens to the words, and testimony, of the other in an act that brings a sense of closure and fulfillment. Like Frederick Wiseman's work, whose early films seem to be the work of a sociologist and sometime voyeur, his more recent films—especially *La Danse* (2009), *Boxing Gym* (2010), *National Gallery* (2014), and *In Jackson Heights* (2015)—radiate a profound respect, appreciation, and even love for their subjects. This affection flows from the rhythm of the films and their patient absorption into the everyday rehearsals of ballet dancers; the routine practices of aspiring boxers; the encounters among staff, visitors, and art at England's National Gallery; and the vast array of interactions and political tensions swirling through a highly diverse section of New York City. Clearly, it could be otherwise, but these films reverberate with the voices of those who encounter others who fascinate and inspire them.

What common qualities emerge from how filmmakers engage with this twenty-first-century digital world and adopt the technologies now available? I want to suggest four ways this contemporary voice emerges:

1. Time and space collapse into a vivid sense of simultaneous event and overlapping space.

2. History from below gains a striking prominence over the classic model of history from above. The reliance on archival material of humble origin, such as home movies, is a vivid demonstration of this tendency.

3. Affect and emotional engagement, similar to what we experience in face-to-face conversation, come to the fore.

4. Performance, or the presentation of self, gains complexity as fantasy and reality, deception and self-deception, social reality and psychic reality blur in increasingly sophisticated ways.[6]

1. The collapse of time and space.   People can be in more than one place at once. This defies what we know from physics and yet becomes increasingly vivid as the devices that "transport" us become more and more sophisti-

cated. *Life in a Day* strives to locate us in a transnational, indeed global, present where cultures, languages, social status, and nations fade into the background. Our identity moves into alignment with others elsewhere at a highly quotidian, even moment-by-moment, level. In *The Green Wave* we enter a world inhabited by those who stood up to the Iranian regime and demanded reform at the time of national elections in 2009. We shift not only from location to location, and from one participant to another, but also from what was live, on-the-spot cell phone recordings to animation and interviews conducted after the fact, as if these were all part of a single continuum.

Time and space take on a mutability that no longer speaks to a world of fixed geographic coordinates so much as a field of experience and memory that continues to evolve. This quality links up with affect and immediacy as these immersive, subjective dimensions imbue time and space with an indeterminate fluidity quite strikingly in *Leviathan* (Lucien Castaing-Taylor and Verena Paravel, 2012), where multiple fishing voyages couple with numerous acts of hauling nets and sorting fish to generate a vivid sense of what it is like to fish the open sea rather than to locate a particular boat and crew on a specific trip. And, as I have noted, the body acts as a palimpsest for past memories, experiences, and trauma so that how the body moves, gesticulates, or self-protects, and how the voice evidences emotion in the density of its grain—in films from *Shoah* and *Chile, Obstinate Memory* (Patrizio Guzmán, 1997) to *Waltz with Bashir* and *Of Men and War*— speaks to a past still affectively present in the how and why of what subjects say and do.

2. History from below and the archive effect. As *People I Could Have Been and Maybe Am, The Green Wave, Tehran without Permission* (Sepideh Farsi, 2009), which Farsi made as she explored the streets of Tehran with her cell phone, and *A Sinner in Mecca* (Parvez Sharma, 2015), where Sharma takes us into the forbidden city of Mecca (forbidden to non-Muslims) via his cell phone as he tries to reconcile being gay and being Muslim, suggest, those who wield the cell phone or digital camera and share the results with others are typically not those who hold power and expect others to carry out their commands. They are typical citizens or individuals. We see events unfold from the bottom up. The revolution Louis Marcorelles proclaimed in his book *Living Cinema* (1973), about the rise of direct cinema in the 1960s, reaches a new level as filmmakers no longer have to find ways to represent those who cannot speak for themselves.[7] Instead, they reassemble the sounds and images made by those who, with

these new technologies, do, in fact, speak for themselves and do so compellingly, offering a history of our times but from below.

This is nowhere more vividly demonstrated with archival footage than in the work of Péter Forgács. His films, made almost entirely from the home movies of others, function as a "private history," as he calls it, of bygone times and cultures. Many, such as *The Maelstrom* (1997), *Free Fall* (1998), and *Miss Universe 1929* (2006), revolve around footage of European Jews in the 1930s and 1940s, before they fell beneath the murderous boot of Nazism. Their lives, families, and entire culture were almost entirely erased. And yet they return to us, in moving images, as a precious gift made possible by the creative interventions of Forgács, who reworks the footage considerably, tracing out a narrative line that runs parallel to the larger social history, until these lines intersect in disaster. No fiction film could have so vivid an effect as these simple home movies do when they are spun into mesmerizing tales of exuberance, perseverance, love, life, and loss.[8]

3. Affect and emotional engagement. This quality emphasizes what it feels like to see the world a certain way, to be immersed in a given situation, or to live in a distinct part of the world in a specific way. It includes the relational intimacy of filmmaker and subject that I discussed above as well. Films from *Sweetgrass* (Ilisa Barbash and Lucien Castaing-Taylor, 2009), with its intense sights and sounds of sheep amid the high plains of the Rocky Mountains; *Être et avoir* (*To Be and to Have*, Nicolas Philibert, 2002), with its patient immersion in the day-to-day life of a rural schoolteacher and his pupils; and one of the most inspiring works of this kind, *Koyaanisqatsi* (Godfrey Reggio, 1982), itself a radical revision of the city symphony films of the 1930s, all attest to the ability of the documentary to speak about the world poetically and movingly, as well as politically and motivationally. This remains a powerful tendency in documentary in the early twenty-first century, even as the idea of documentary as a tool for addressing social issues and promoting political advocacy continues to play a dominant role.

4. Performance, the presentation of self, and the thin line between fantasy and reality. Clearly foreshadowed by *The Thin Blue Line* and its conflicting, sometimes self-serving, and often self-deceiving accounts of a murder, how filmmakers tackle the presentation of self has become a central concern for many. A certain hall-of-mirrors effect occurs in films like *David Holzman's Diary*, with its mock diary and realist style mimicking perfectly the realism of the new documentaries of the 1960s, an effect taken to a different level in

a film like Werner Herzog's *Grizzly Man* (2005). Here the surviving footage of Timothy Treadwell, who sought to protect wild grizzly bears by living among them, commingles with footage shot by Herzog himself. The self-promotional quality of Treadwell's footage, designed to cast him as a noble hero, erodes in the face of more self-deprecating outtakes and Herzog's own sharply divergent values. What did Treadwell accomplish, and was he wise to attempt to do so at all? Who was he that he would seek to live among bears? Herzog gives us a layered view of a man who appeared to be one thing, may well have been another, and was all the more fascinating for the complexity that results.

Something similar but with higher social stakes occurs in *Enron: The Smartest Guys in the Room*, where the public personas of its chief executives, so carefully calculated with an eye on the market value of their corporation, unravels under the relentless scrutiny of Alex Gibney. We see their self-presentation in interviews and press conferences but then learn about what they knew and what they hid about the house of cards they built. It is one thing to present a somewhat different side of oneself in different social settings, but Gibney shows how this quality can go hand in glove with manipulation and deception, and possible self-deception, as these men seem to believe the very things they fabricate to try to keep ahead of looming disaster. (Gibney pursues this search for contradiction in many of his films, including *Steve Jobs: The Man in the Machine* [2015], discussed herein in a separate essay.)

On a more individual level films like *Catfish* (Henry Joost and Ariel Schulman, 2010), about a woman who takes on a full-blown but false online persona and the filmmakers who appear to believe her fabrication but with hints that they may not, or *I'm Still Here* (Casey Affleck, 2010), about Joaquin Phoenix's "retirement" from acting only to star in this mockumentary about his life after he decides to stop acting—except when he's in this film—performance no longer revolves around social actors being themselves, as if this were a singular thing, but around individuals whose self-awareness and self-presentation involves layers, roles, and calculation, some of it consciously conveyed and some of it less so. This becomes a central motif in Sarah Polley's *Stories We Tell* (2012), about the layers of storytelling that wind around her own family's tangled history.

But few films confront this complexity more powerfully than Joshua Oppenheimer's *The Act of Killing*.[9] Here we meet former death squad leaders in the massacre of more than a million citizens in Indonesia in the 1960s for alleged communist ties and antigovernment politics. These men reenact their killing methods with great flair and complete impunity. Treated as heroes by the government even at the time of filming, they go through the motions of their former crimes with a clear pride in their inventive adaptation of murder techniques that they first saw in Hollywood genre films. Not only that, but they construct a modern-day fantasy for themselves: a gigantic fish constructed in a verdant landscape serves as home to a chorus line of beautiful women who emerge to praise them as the gods and saviors they themselves think they are.

The film mutes its own voice to allow these killers the chance to have their say, perplexing, if not flummoxing, us with their matter-of-fact tales of torture and murder. Oppenheimer's withholding of moral judgment compels us all the more to assess these acts for what they are. Oppenheimer's silence—a crucial element of classic rhetoric—speaks volumes, nowhere more so than in the pan of his camera to a volunteer victim who breaks down in deep distress after being depicted as having been tortured and killed in one of the reenactments. Now "dead," he can be ignored as the killers discuss the potential impact of this very scene on audiences: it may be too graphic and may show that it was they who were cruel rather than the communists. Oppenheimer's camera says, "So very true," without his uttering a word.

Throughout the film fantasy becomes reality and reality fantasy, and it is up to us to uphold the distinction. The subdued voice of the film serves as a vivid reminder that history is not just the dead and gone, the resolved and settled, to be recounted in instructive morsels, as "Voice of God" commentary so often assumed, but a force that haunts the present and must be accounted for by us, as well as the filmmaker.

These qualities suggest that the voice of the filmmaker remains central and strong but with new distinctiveness. New technologies make possible new ways of seeing and responding to the world around us but do not in and of themselves create new ways of speaking, of seeing the world anew. They do not relieve us of the need to speak in our own voice about our own experience, perceptions, and perspectives and those of others.

It is not new technologies that hold our attention, although they may very well attract it. It is the old, even ancient, drive to tell a story, convey a point of view, and render reality with a sensitive eye, to, in short, give aesthetic form to lived experience in a way that engages and moves us, that makes documentaries worth our attention. Without a voice that addresses us in a compelling and convincing way, these films would collapse into heaps of mere footage, into documents of fact and information rather than documentaries of affect and engagement. Filmmakers have constantly had to respond to new technologies, from the advent of color film and synchronous sound to videotape and digital cameras to the evolving world of the Internet and ubiquitous cell phone. They do so as masters not of technology alone but of the well-told story, the carefully shaped point of view, and the movingly evocative impression. Documentary filmmakers are masters of an art, not a science, and it is this mastery that we find on display in the works that resound in our hearts or trouble our sleep.

7   The Sound of Music

I know firsthand how important music is to documentary. For several years
my university had a 16 mm print of Dziga Vertov's *Man with a Movie
Camera* (1929). The print had no sound track at all. It was truly a silent
film, even though most silent films of its time were accompanied by live
music. When I projected it in class, students fell asleep. The onslaught of
rapidly edited images felt arbitrary and inconsequential. This wasn't true
for every single student, but the impression of a less than rapt reception
remains vivid in my mind.

Then in 2003 the Alloy Orchestra, which has created sound tracks for a
number of films, released a new version of the film with their remarkable
music, performed on a striking mix of nontraditional and traditional instru-
ments, as accompaniment. Reception changed overnight. The film took on a
vitality and coherence it had had all along that the completely silent version
eviscerated. The Alloy Orchestra's music gives tempo to the day that structures the film; it gives vitality to the machinery that awakens and begins to
produce the goods that will benefit the people; it organizes an affective
response to the film that makes the editing cohere in a way it did not do
when the film was simply a visual cascade without any sound track at all.

Examples proliferate. Consider Werner Herzog's extraordinary film
Grizzly Man (2005), an examination of the life of Timothy Treadwell, a
solitary defender of Alaska's grizzly bears whose own stunning footage of
his life among the bears forms a significant part of Herzog's film about him.
Grizzly Man possesses a haunting quality in its view of a majestic but
deadly nature and a disturbed but impassioned man. It would not do so as
powerfully as it does were it not for the unforgettable music, composed by
Richard Thompson, formally of Fairport Convention. The guitar solos that
punctuate the film add a deeply felt resonance to the sense of tragedy and

loss on which Herzog meditates (Treadwell and his girlfriend are both killed by a bear).

A kindred documentary spirit to Herzog is Errol Morris. (They served as coproducers of Joshua Oppenheimer's *The Act of Killing* [2013].) Morris's third film, *The Thin Blue Line* (1988), utilizes a score by the well-known avant-garde composer Philip Glass to convey something of the eerie, almost somnambulant world of painful ironies and nightmarish experiences along with the crucial but illusive issue of guilt and innocence that surround the murder of a Texas policeman. Glass had previously created the music for Godfrey Reggio's poetic film *Koyaanisqatsi* (1982), a film composed solely of stunning images and memorable music that together stress the need for balance and harmony in our relation to the earth. For *The Thin Blue Line* Glass gives the sometimes surreal images that Morris mixes together with more straightforward interviews even more potent impact. Nothing is what it seems—or almost nothing. Morris contradicts the criminal justice system to show that the real killer escaped prosecution and that the wrong man sits on death row. The tendency of Glass's music to establish a tonality that is both hypnotic and repetitive gives effective embodiment to the sense that the police and prosecution had circled around and around the events, repeating their own mantra of assumptions and beliefs, only to let the truth slip through their fingers like the elusive spirit that hovers near but not quite in Glass's music.

So far, this parade of examples of music that makes a difference in documentary may seem to only prove that it is a valuable support to the underlying and more fundamental aim of the film as words and images convey it. I want to take the argument further. Music may be considered a supplement, valuable, or even invaluable, to a film's point, perspective, or thematic impression if we take documentary to be a form of film that conveys facts and makes arguments. Some documentaries do, though many might be better labeled instructional, informational, or educational (in the limited sense of servicing an educational market that may not always seek out the best of documentary filmmaking to meet very specific curricular needs). Much journalism also leans toward facts and arguments, or at least reports, and in these cases music can be a valuable complement to bring the argument alive, to give it greater intensity, to engage the viewer to the point of heightened attention.

But what if this is not the fundamental goal of those documentaries that stand as the most exemplary documentaries through the decades? What if there are other goals at work? What if documentaries aren't simply informational but rhetorical? What if they aren't only rhetorical but also poetic and story driven? We then begin to drift toward familiar territory: fiction. Elsewhere, I've described documentaries as "a fiction (un)like any other" as a way to suggest that many of the same techniques and structures occur in documentary as in fiction.[1] But beyond techniques, the two forms also share another common goal: to give sensory embodiment to a representation conveyed by a voice that will engage us, a representation that is more imaginary than not for fiction, and a representation that is more historical than imaginary for documentary. (By *historical* I mean that documentaries address the socially constructed world we occupy in common, whether it is a previous incarnation of this world, the historical past, or some aspect of its present condition.)

What does giving sensory embodiment to the historical world mean? In part it means finding a way to represent reality so that we will entertain, if not adopt, a particular perspective, a way of understanding or explaining some aspect of this world, which is the perspective embedded in the voice of the film. A recitation of facts does not a documentary make. Documentaries engage us as ways of seeing the world, much as fictions do, by means of their imagined representations of some aspects of human experience. The best documentaries give us a vivid sense of what it feels like to occupy or consider the world from a particular perspective. And few things help us understand what it feels like to be in a particular time or place, in the midst of a specific challenge or situation, better than music. In this sense music is not a supplement, a filling in of an outline already sketched, but part and parcel of what we come to understand it feels like to be in this world, seen this way—to live and perceive and act and dream in a particular manner.

The examples I've cited do more than supplement a complete message. They serve as testimony to the vital role of music in giving sensory embodiment to what it feels like to spend a day in 1929 Moscow *(Man with a Movie Camera)*—an act, it seems, if my students' responses are to be believed, that proves essential to engaging and comprehending the film; to be only a few paces from huge, carnivorous grizzly bears and hundreds of miles from any other person *(Grizzly Man)*; to be snared in a legal maze of contradictory but prevailing judgments that may kill you *(The Thin Blue Line)*; and to experience viscerally, affectively, as sentient human beings, what it is like to enter into the thousands of other situations and dilemmas documentaries attend to.

What does it feel like to experience a specific aspect of the world in a particular way, and what does it feel like to be addressed by a voice that displays the timbre or grain of another human soul, a filmmaker who speaks to us with enchantment or irony, anger or love, curiosity and detachment, passion and intensity? Music gives an answer: it feels like this. Music gives embodiment to emotion. It draws us in, engages us, attests to qualities of voice that are complex, affective, even ineffable. And as Luis Buñuel reminds us in his *Land without Bread* (1932), it can disorient, baffle, and befuddle as readily as it can charm, enchant, or immerse. Its uses vary, but when used effectively (a crucial qualification), music becomes a vital part of what the documentary experience means as a way of engaging the world.

Music belongs to the heart and soul of a film form that strives to represent what it feels like to experience the historical world from a particular angle, with specific people, in specific places and at specific times. It takes the concreteness of such images and imbues them with an emotional glow. It brings them alive in a way similar to how our own bodies and sense organs receive the world around us as far more than a conglomeration of facts and much more as a force field of intensities and lures, focal points and empty spaces. Music may make the world go round, but it also makes documentaries ascend and swirl and engulf us in this world in richly compelling and uniquely memorable ways.

PART III

Beyond "Just the Facts"

Evidence, Interpretation, and Social Context

PART 3 TACKLES THE QUESTION OF EVIDENCE. Documents are factual; documentaries are evidential. What constitutes evidence, and how do documentary filmmakers utilize it? Facts provide information but do not necessarily serve as evidence. These essays examine how verifiable, and sometimes unverifiable, information becomes transformed into real, or apparent, evidence in documentary film.

Beginning with the differentiation of evidence from facts, the first essay, "The Question of Evidence," provides a general overview of the issues and argues that evidence comes into being to support an argument or perspective and often possesses a rhetorical dimension as much or more than a scientific or rational one. Facts, in other words, must be recruited into a narrative or argument, whose validity may well remain in doubt, before they can serve as evidence.

A look at evidence as it arises in the thick of the moment forms the backdrop for the second essay, "The Terrorist Event." This article revisits the events of 9/11 and explores what it felt like to experience television news coverage of the two planes that hit the World Trade Center towers in the morning hours of that very day, before it became blatant evidence of a terrorist attack. This was information without a context or explanation. The question of how to interpret it before it became a definable event loomed large in those morning hours. What psychic state does something that resists our usual framing, or sense-making, procedures induce? What changes when a flow of actions condense into an event? How does a prevailing or dominant narrative about an event come to shape our understanding and response to that event, with what implications and consequences? The essay tries to come to grips with these questions. It does not address very many specific films so much as lay some groundwork for thinking about trauma, narrative, and documentary.

The Further Reflections in this section consist of a book review—
"Remaking History: Jay Leyda and the Compilation Film"—and two commentaries that began as posts on my blog. The raw footage of what happened
during the attacks on 9/11 is a classic example of factual documentation that
will later become a building block of documentaries. It becomes an archival
resource as footage has done since the beginning of cinema. This is painfully
true of the amateur records of violent, sometimes deadly, confrontations
between police and civilians—shot on a small video camera by George
Holliday during the beating of Rodney King in 1991 and, in many other cases
since, on cell phones. The idea of taking preexisting footage and using it for
new purposes, in a new conceptual or explanatory frame, stems from what Jay
Leyda called the "compilation film" in his groundbreaking book *Films Beget
Films* (1963). Leyda adroitly raises numerous issues that he traces back to
silent cinema in the Soviet Union and related theories of montage but that
extend into contemporary practice (in the postwar period). It is one of the rare
books on documentary with a keen theoretical edge prior to the introduction
of contemporary film theory to documentary study in the early 1990s.

The second reflection, "*Restrepo:* A Case of Inadvertent Evidence," somewhat expanded for this volume, discusses *Restrepo,* an observational chronicle of the daily lives of a small group of U.S. soldiers in Afghanistan, to pose
a larger question than the film itself addresses: how does this "nonpolitical"
film stand as evidence of failed political policies? How do these soldiers'
actions serve as evidence, even if they are not recruited into an argument by
the film itself? The essay affirms the idea that evidence is a construct based
on but distinct from information. In this case it requires the viewer to posit
a frame the film itself resists: can the actions and conduct of the American
soldiers we follow serve as evidence of what went wrong in Afghanistan?

The third reflection, also revised for inclusion here, "The Symptomatic
Biopic: *Steve Jobs: The Man in the Machine,*" argues that Alex Gibney's
film, with its judicious mix of Jobs's great achievements and underhanded
deeds, only makes complete sense when we understand Jobs as symptomatic of the type of personality that often stands as evidence of corporate
success. This adulation amounts to a process of fetishization, not unlike
commodity fetishism itself. It necessarily suppresses more disturbing personal qualities and economic relationships to celebrate such a person's
achievements or a commodity's magical aura. Gibney places these contradictory dimensions of Apple's founder in juxtaposition to each other, allow-
ing us to see his status as symptomatic evidence of larger issues and processes than the usual hagiographic (or demonizing) depiction of corporate
heroes allows.

8 The Question of Evidence

The Power of Rhetoric and the Documentary

All discourses, including documentary film, seek to externalize evidence—to place it referentially outside the domain of the discourse itself, which then gestures to its location there, beyond and before interpretation. It's like fly-fishing, where an artificial fly is cast into the water, where it will then appear as a natural part of the environment, luring a fish, which mistakes the fabricated for the authentic—to its eternal regret—to bite.

Granting evidence an external authenticity beyond that bestowed by the discourse itself makes its visibility appear a fact rather than an invention. Evidence does indeed refer to a fact, object, or situation—something two or more people agree on, something verifiable and concrete—but facts and events only acquire the distinctive status of evidence within a discursive or interpretive frame. Evidence, then, is that part of discourse, be it rational-philosophic, poetic-narrative, or rhetorical, that is charged with a double existence: it is part of the discursive chain but also gives the vivid impression of residing external to it. In other words facts become evidence when they are taken up in a discourse, and that discourse gains the force to compel belief through its capacity to refer evidence to a domain outside itself. This is what makes the creation of credible evidence like fly-fishing, or ventriloquism, performed, in the case of documentary films, by the filmmaker.

The compelling documentary *An Injury to One* (Travis Wilkerson, 2002), about the history of Butte, Montana, as a mining town and the murder there of a Wobbly (Industrial Workers of the World) organizer, Frank Little, in 1917, demonstrates vividly how facts convert to evidence and how their evidential status is contingent on the discourse to which they attach. At one point Wilkerson recounts the story of a large flock of geese that land on the enormous lake that fills the open-pit mine that still dominates the town. The lake is extremely toxic, loaded with copper, cadmium, zinc, nickel, lead, arsenic, and sulfates; it has a pH of 2.5, "roughly comparable to battery acid," Wilkerson tells us in his intense but flatly spoken commentary. A storm takes the geese by surprise and they land on the lake. In the morning 342 geese are dead. They are blistered with lesions, their esophagi and tracheae corroded, and their livers bloated with toxic quantities of heavy metals. Wilkerson recounts that representatives for ARCO, the company that owns the mine, assured the townspeople that the water was actually safe; the geese died "because of something they ate," not from exposure to the lake water. Wilkerson concludes this section of his stunning film with an observation: "As the geese help to demonstrate, history, in this case, cannot be so easily expurgated [as the company's original name: Anaconda]. In an act reminiscent of a mass suicide, the geese hurled themselves into the open wound in the heart of the town. Perhaps using the only manner they knew, these creatures were trying to tell us something because it seemed to have escaped our notice. They were directing us to the scene of a crime."

The facts do not, as Wilkerson's sardonic tone suggests, speak for themselves: they must be seen, and heard, and thence interpreted, an act that fissures in multiple directions depending on the purposes and goals of the interpreter. ARCO interprets the death of 342 geese as evidence of a bad diet. Wilkerson sharply disagrees: he interprets it as evidence of a "mass suicide," a costly symbolic gesture pointing to a past crime. The event, however, can only be seen as accidental death, testimony, or anything else within the interpretive frame provided for it. Cast back by discourse into the external world, facts take up a place outside discourse and are made to do so in a way that allows their reincarnation as evidence to overlay perfectly the fact to which they correspond.

The indexical quality of the photographic image is ideally suited to this purpose. A perfect tautology appears to come into being between fact, object, or event, on the one hand, and evidence and interpretation, on the other, so that reference to a piece of evidence marries signified and referent in a single stroke. As the story of the geese suggests, the fact or event does not come into being as evidence; this status accrues later, when it is recruited to a discourse: "bad food," "mass suicide"—these labels become affixed to that which simply was. And they seem to stick because of an indexical bond between image and referent, that which exists outside the discursive chain.

Sometimes facts speak in ways not intended by the speaker or filmmaker. The viewer, too, may convert fact to evidence, sometimes in ways that run against the grain of their initial recruitment. In Marlon Riggs's powerful documentary about being black and gay in America, *Tongues Untied* (1990), Riggs crosscuts between a protest march in Selma, Alabama, in the 1960s and a gay pride parade in New York City in the 1980s. For Riggs the parallel is evidence of a continuous lineage of protest and struggle for civil liberties and individual rights among African Americans. But there is a tremendous difference in the two pieces of footage if we examine them not as part of Riggs's stunning visual testament but as visible evidence of two distinct historical moments.

In the Selma march what is most striking is the rich diversity of the marchers themselves: young and old African Americans, young and old whites, male and female, primarily but not entirely well-dressed, religious leaders and laypeople, all marching to confront a racist society with their visible, demonstrable protest. The two most prominent banners read, "We March with Selma" and "We Shall Overcome." The gay pride march footage features a contingent of young black men, with two bare-chested black males carrying a banner that reads, "Black Men Loving Black Men Is *The Revolutionary Act.*" The goal of mobilizing a broad, inclusive range of people to confront racism and champion civil rights has yielded to the proclamation of difference, the affirmation of an identity and a politics that seeks to embrace the like-minded and gain the public recognition of others. The spectrum of ages, classes, and races incorporated into and patently visible in the Selma march has disappeared. Belonging and activism are now predicated on a specific combination of race, gender, and sexual orientation. The male and female onlookers, mostly younger but occasionally older, along with a number of primarily white police officers lining the route of the gay pride parade, are a far more diverse group than the marchers themselves. The unity of purpose of an earlier time has yielded to the identity politics of a later one, or so an interpreter could argue just as forcefully as Riggs can argue for a line of continuity.

Similarly, Edward R. Murrow's powerful broadcast *Harvest of Shame* (1960), now inadvertently serves as evidence of massive historical shifts in the composition of the migrant-labor workforce: the migrant workers depicted in the film are almost entirely white or black, but now, several decades later, migrant workers are almost entirely Hispanic. The racial composition of the workforce was taken for granted at the time of broadcast—a fact rather than evidence—but now the film provides evidence of a remarkably thorough transformation that may once again seem natural, or taken for granted.

Careful consideration of this act of converting fact to evidence occurs in R. G. Collingwood's book *The Idea of History*, written in 1946 and dedicated to the idea of history as a scientific undertaking. During an extended discussion of "historical evidence," Collingwood debunks the view that history amounts to citing the testimony of credible authorities whose remarks can be cut and pasted together to provide the requisite history. This out-dated method relies on facts drawn from earlier, authoritative accounts—and whose status as evidence can go unquestioned for that reason—that now form the backbone of a new narrative. By contrast, Collingwood argues that good history writing requires making inferences that are always based on questions directed toward a careful examination of the facts themselves. They can only come to serve as valid evidence when freshly taken up in the author's own interpretive discourse. The historian must pose questions based on his or her inferences about what really happened rather than adopt the views of others. Wilkerson's comment about the geese, "Perhaps using the only manner they knew, these creatures were trying to tell us something because it seemed to have escaped our notice," becomes a stand-ing assumption of critical inquiry: facts and occurrences exist, but their conversion into evidence and events depends on the analytic powers of the interpreter, be she or he historian or filmmaker.

But in the middle of this call for a methodologically rigorous history, Collingwood suddenly takes a surprising turn. A subheading entitled "Who Killed John Doe?" announces the detour. Contrary to the strictly expository style of all the previous sections, Collingwood now adopts a semifictional voice. The section begins, "When John Doe was found, early one Sunday morning, lying across his desk with a dagger through his back, no one expected that the question of who did it would be settled by means of testi-mony."[1] Here is a case where Collingwood can demonstrate the necessity of inferential analysis that, when done properly, will lead to a clear-cut solution.

Using Collingwood's own dicta that "everything in the world is potential evidence for any subject whatever"[2] and that we should focus not on the content of statements but on the fact that they are made—in other words, that our analysis must not accept what others represent the case to be but must ask, "What light is thrown on the subject in which I am interested by the fact that this person made this statement?"—we can ask, Why does Collingwood tell this whodunit in the middle of his disquisition on history?

Clearly, it serves as an example, if not allegory, for good historical inves-tigation. It serves Collingwood's goal of giving the impression that history writing can become a science, capable of determining what really happened in an unambiguous manner through an independent examination of facts and testimony. Inferences lead to knowledge and knowledge leads to the one and only logical solution: the rector did it, in this case. Ambiguity is dispelled thanks to the hard work of the historian laboring in the vineyards of the local, empirically verifiable, event. Not all rectors should now be suspected of murder, nor should all murders be attributed to rectors, but in this concrete case, with these facts and statements and with this set of questions to transform facts and statements into evidence, the rector's guilt can be cleanly determined.

By presenting a Sherlock Holmes–like murder mystery, Collingwood can arrive at a specific solution to a concrete question. The solution, though, lacks generalizing power: it tells us nothing about the behavior of rectors or the causes of murder in general. The example offers a definite conclusion, based on asking questions whose answers generate evidence: a footprint in the wet soil of the lawn becomes admitted as evidence as soon as we ask a question such as, "Who might have crossed the lawn that fateful night but only after the rain fell?"

Though instructive, Collingwood's choice of a murder mystery as metaphor reduces his method to factual determinations that cannot account for historical complexity. He neglects to add to his assertion that "everything in the world is potential evidence for any subject whatever" *and can therefore support a wide range of interpretations.* Or, as Wittgenstein put it, "Everything we can describe at all could also be otherwise."[3] The murder mystery involves facts, questions, evidence, and interpretation of a different order from those involved when we ask what brought about the transformation of communism into totalitarianism, why capitalism undergoes cycles of growth and recession, whether observational documentaries convey a higher degree of authenticity than expository ones, or how funding sources have shaped the form and content of documentaries over the last decade or two. Questions such as these propel us into a realm rather remote from the indisputable evidence, clear-cut verification procedures, and singular conclusions that Collingwood naturalizes as the common stuff of history through his exemplary fiction.

Collingwood, in fact, builds his conception of proper historiography on the Aristotelian notion of "inartistic proofs"—evidence, that is, that exists outside, or can readily be made to appear to reside outside, the discursive chain. Examples include laws, witnesses, contracts, oaths, documents, and confessions obtained by torture (a practice reserved, in Aristotle's time, for slaves since citizens would give their own testimony artistically, that is, with benefit of the rhetorical arts). This is the evidence that can most easily be "thrown out" of the discourse as fact in order to be reeled back in as evidence. Science, like murder mysteries, works with objective facts; the form a precise account of them takes is of minor consequence. Form, for Collingwood, is little more than a question of elaborating a style; the proof is in facts that serve as evidence. Careful interpretation leads us down a straight and narrow path to the truth, not into a labyrinth of competing interests and multiple interpretations whose merits may be decided more by power, or at least rhetoric, than by logic.

Although seemingly the most irrefutable of evidence, inartistic proofs were of minor concern to Aristotle. The "artistic proofs" that were the heart and soul of rhetorical discourse concerned him much more. Though necessary, inartistic proofs still have to be incorporated into a discourse where they become convincing. Alone, the inartistic proofs might be necessary but hardly sufficient. Only when such proofs took on their second life as evidence inside a body of signification—discourse—did it become possible for a convincing argument to emerge. *How* inartistic proofs become incorporated into the discourse thus matters more than *what* these proofs reveal in and of themselves. It is here that the voice of the filmmaker, like that of the orator, enters the scene.

What concerned Aristotle, Cicero, and Quintilian, among others, were the artistic proofs that strove to guarantee the ethical credibility of a speaker, the emotional response of an audience, and the convincingness of an argument (including the convincingness of inferences or interpretations drawn from inartistic proofs). These are questions regarding rhetorical, not philosophic or logical, discourse. The protocols of science eschew such discourse. Rhetoric or persuasive speech, it is said, mires us in deception; it lacks a moral compass; it leads to ideology rather than knowledge. Or so it seemed to Plato and to Roland Barthes, when, in 1964, he wrote his seminal essay, "The Rhetoric of the Image," and so it seems to those who attack filmmakers like Michael Moore for "distorting" or "inventing" facts that serve as tendentious evidence, as if there could be any other kind once we enter the arena of human affairs, where science no longer reigns supreme.

Barthes's essay, which, for me, marks the beginning of the end for an understanding of the crucial role of rhetoric in contemporary culture (except as handmaiden to ideology), asks questions about the meaning of an image, in this case, an advertisement for Panzani pasta sauce in the form of a photograph of a shopping net filled with fresh vegetables and Panzani products, their labels clearly legible. Like Collingwood, Barthes is moved to question authority, to refuse to accept the advertisement at its word. Barthes asks of the image, as Collingwood did of his suspects, How does it disguise what it says as something natural and obvious?

Like Collingwood's whodunit, Barthes's analysis of the ad reduces the mystery of meaning to one and only one conclusion. The image represents ideology. It does so because it sets out to naturalize Panzani. The advertisement equates a can of pasta sauce with the fresh, wholesome bounty of the farm by making a collage of the two images. A perfect tautology exists:

fresh vegetables are Panzani; Panzani is fresh vegetables, nothing more or less. We harvest the product, Panzani, from the same rich bounty of the earth as the ingredients it contains. Like the fly cast by the fisherman, it is at one with its natural surroundings. Or as Barthes puts it himself, "To the general ideology, that is, correspond signifiers of connotation which are specified according to the chosen substance [sound, image, gesture and so on]. These signifiers will be called *connotators* and the set of connotators a rhetoric, rhetoric thus appearing as the signifying aspect of ideology."[4] It is no longer the rector who did it but ideology. The power of rhetoric to move an audience by establishing a credible, compelling, and convincing case of any kind, on any subject, for any purpose becomes reduced to the power of rhetoric to put ideology into practice.

This line of thought returns us to Plato's attack on rhetoric as a corrupting form of flattery or deception. Plato terms the proper cultivation of the body "gymnastics," which strengthen the body's innate capabilities, and its corrupt form cosmetics, or *kosmètikè*, an ornamentality that renders appearances false and leaves the body's innate capacities untouched.[5] In an attempt to preserve the centrality of rhetoric as discourse measured by its effects without dismissing it as sheer deception, Quintilian differentiates between the use of cosmetics such as color, ornament, gesture, and emotion for venal and noble purposes.[6] His negative example involves slave dealers who use cosmetics to increase the value of those whom they sell by giving them a flattering appearance. Such an appearance renders the slave overvalued, a form, that is, of fetishization, and any subsequent transaction dishonest. This would seem to be the category in which advertisements, and certainly the Panzani ad, fall.

Venal purposes contrast, for Quintilian, with the art of the noble orator who sees speech as an instrument for the expression of views strongly believed and compellingly conveyed.[7] "In place of the cosmetic body Quintilian puts a political body.... As the place of political relations, the body escapes from the moral disdain of metaphysics.... The body—image, passion, pleasure, effect, and affect—gains legitimacy in politics and in rhetoric too.... By all these shifts Quintilian succeeds in justifying the definition of rhetoric as wisdom.... To ensure the victory of justice, eloquence is thus within its rights to apply itself not only to instructing the soul but also to moving the body."[8] This "eloquence" is what I term "voice" by another name.

Rhetoric, in other words, may deceive, but it is the only means we have as social actors, or filmmakers, for conveying our beliefs, perspectives, and convictions persuasively. A rhetoric of persuasion strives to move others; it shocks, disturbs, provokes, inspires, galvanizes, or defamiliarizes, displaying the old in a new, revelatory manner. In this case the rhetoric of the image belongs to a struggle for power in which the meaning and effect of an image or film cannot be determined in advance as simply and always ideological in the sense of serving the interests of the status quo by the use of deception. Instead, the rhetoric of the image, or film, speaks, as narrative or logic might speak, with multiple purposes and to different ends but in ways that strive to compel belief as much as they might please or prove. Rhetoric gives a distinct voice to those who wish their perspective and their interpretation to enter into dialogue with that of others.

Voice refers to the ways in which a documentary film speaks to its audience. *An Injury to One, Tongues Untied, The Revolution Will Not Be Televised* (Kim Bartley and Donnacha O'Briain, 2003), *The Agronomist* (Johnathan Demme, 2003), *Fahrenheit 9/11* (Michael Moore, 2004), *Chile, Obstinate Memory* (Patricio Guzmán, 2004), and *The Maelstrom* (Péter Forgács, 1997), among others, evidence a voice that speaks probingly and responsively to others as well as angrily to injustice, abuse, exploitation, racism, antisemitism, cruelty, and other barbarisms. It acknowledges its subject, and audience, as its equal, not its object, target, victim, or tool. If style turns attention to the one who addresses us, voice turns attention to the audience addressed.

Often, this voice includes the personal but untrained voice of the filmmaker him- or herself rather than the impersonal, professional delivery of a voice-over commentator. The filmmaker's voice stresses the sense of direct encounter, an embodied perspective, relayed to the viewer. Something personal is at stake, as it clearly is in Marlon Riggs's film: his own experience as a black, gay man gave him a distinct perspective on racism that now inflects the voice that speaks to us.

This is no less true of Yervant Gianikian and Angela Ricci Lucchi's *Oh! Uomo* (2004), which, without spoken commentary of any kind, speaks nonetheless compellingly through its compilation of archival footage of abandoned orphans, scavenging youths, and disfigured veterans from the First World War. The eyes of the starving, traumatized, and lost engage the camera that encountered them so many decades ago with a vivid openness and acute intensity that cries out for response. The filmmakers, through the duration of shots that accumulate into a requiem to catastrophe, offer a delayed response that engages us in a near hypnotic séance with survivors and victims who are fleetingly reanimated before us.

Such films face the challenge of how to speak of that which escapes our notice, like the "mass suicide" of the geese in *An Injury to One*. Hubert

Sauper confronts this question forcefully in *Darwin's Nightmare* (2004), when all he can find are the horrific consequences of a highly lucrative fishing industry that flies frozen Nile perch from Lake Victoria, in Africa, to Russia and Eastern Europe. Meanwhile, the massive and accidentally introduced perch devour every other species of fish in the lake, indigenous residents of the lake's surrounding land live off the thousands of filleted fish carcasses left to rot in the sun, and some tribal women have little choice but to enter into prostitution. Like Wilkerson's geese, these carcasses of fish heads and bones direct us to the scene of a crime.

Monstration, the act of asking viewers to look at what the filmmaker hopes they will convert from fact to evidence, increases in difficulty when the subject lies buried in the past and when the visible signs of a mass political movement flicker uncertainly. Like *Lone Star* (John Sayles, 1996), with its discovery of a buried badge that launches a quest to learn the consequences of what happened many years before, films like *An Injury to One, Chile, Obstinate Memory, Life and Debt* (Stephanie Black, 2001), and *Maelstrom* all address the political landscape of past and present but with no expectation that interpretive frames are readily available for application. Voice now functions to guide viewers toward an interpretive frame that they must help build.

The documentary voice that has taken form in recent times is clearly an oratorical voice but not a dogmatic one. It is the multidimensioned, embodied voice of films that speak to viewers in the hopes of moving them, predisposing them, inducing a sense of political and historical consciousness that represents a step toward going beyond established boundaries by means of a truth that had escaped awareness. As Werner Herzog put it, in speaking of the quality he seeks in his documentary work (the particular reference was *Grizzly Man* [2005] and what we learn of the horizon at which the animal and human conjoin), "In great moments of cinema you are hit and struck by some sort of enlightenment, by something that illuminates you. That's a deep form of truth, and I call it ecstatic truth, the ecstasy of truth, and that's what I'm after in documentaries and feature films."[9] Hit and struck. This is a form of knowledge or a way of seeing that is closer to a paradigm shift than the accretion of information in the service of conventional learning, mystery solving, or the marshalling of evidence to serve a preexisting form of political activism. Herzog's ecstatic documentary is the work of orators who set out not to show but to move, to establish movement that may come in a flash and extend forward in an altered temporality.

This form of knowing presupposes finding the means to bring to a condition of visibility what has remained less visible, or not visible at all. It sets out to identify what may attain visibility and yet still not be seen (understood) since what is seen is a trace, sign, symptom, or consequence of that which remains beyond the net of words and the reductive aspect of naming. The geese, perch, wounded soldiers, and even grizzly bears speak with their actions. The mining pit turned toxic; the African lake, source of the Nile, turned killing field; the shattered jaws and missing noses of the veterans of World War I in *Oh! Uomo;* the grizzlies that lurk, waiting and following instincts beyond the reckoning of Timothy Treadwell—all speak of consequences that "hit and strike" us. This is a form of speech that can predispose us to see anew and, in seeing anew, to make a radical shift in what is both true and yet still a mystery. No words can contain such mystery, but some forms of speech can render it visible.

A powerful example of such speech, one that requires a retroactive reading, occurs in *The Revolution Will Not Be Televised,* about the attempted coup that ousted Hugo Chávez from power in Venezuela for a brief period. At one point President Chávez arrives at the Presidential Palace, where the Palace Guard stands at attention and salutes him. Chávez casually starts a conversation with one officer and then, as he enters the palace, playfully rubs his hand on the belly of the soldier standing at attention, guarding the entrance. Chávez was an officer himself, and he clearly retains substantial rapport with these officers. Later, after the coup has taken place and Chávez is held captive, the insurgents, remarkably, are routed from this very palace. And who was responsible? The Palace Guard. At this point the viewer may well realize that prior events—a casual conversation, a pat on the belly—can function as evidence in an interpretive argument about how Hugo Chávez returned to power. The film need not say anything directly; the evidence is in the image, if we can see and interpret it. The film speaks through its imagery as readily as through its verbal commentary.

The voice considered here is often a poetic voice that seeks to convey what it feels like to enter into the past, what it feels like to enter into other lives, what it feels like to experience oppressive, violent conditions and to emerge with an altered sense of self by being placed in relation to others who pass before us. In *An Injury to One* Wilkerson scans across a long procession of mug shots of the hundreds of miners arrested as Wobblies in Butte. This "night train" of shots moves past in the center of the frame, with large black borders at top and bottom. The photographs serve as a reminder of the repressive uses of what was a relatively new technology at the time, photography, but it now restores these men to visibility and celebrates them as heroes who, once silenced, stare defiantly, not at arresting police officers but us.

The oratorical voice of documentary uses previous times and disparate places to establish the multiple points necessary to form a trajectory that moves forward with a utopian desire to uphold a set of principles and expose a series of consequences. It brings these consequences—exploitation, oppression, poverty, destruction, military coups, neocolonial occupations, economic deprivations, global immiseration, social degradation, torture and murder, injustices to one and all—to a condition of visibility, if we can see and understand what this voice brings forth as fact without necessarily explaining verbally. This is a voice that can no longer assume we all see things the same way, as Barthes and Collingwood did. The political base in shared experience seen the same way, with shared principles and common goals, is too fragile, too precarious for that, and even if it were not, affirming what is already known is different from seeing anew what stands before us.

The voice with which an image or film speaks is capable, of course, of innumerable effects—many of which may well be ideological but not necessarily ideological in the sense of reinforcing the status quo. Speech and images may embody counterideologies designed to subvert or reject the status quo.[10] To reexamine the tradition of "downcast eyes" and suspicion about the rhetoric of the image as ideology invites an investigation of, among other things, representational film practice, where speaking on behalf of counterideologies is frequently the raison d'être of the work in the first place.[11] Documentary filmmaking, with its strong ties to a tradition of liberal amelioration and radical transformation is one such practice. The body of the film, and filmmaker, with its expressive mix of passion and knowledge sets out to move us. Such movement can contest the status quo as readily as it can confirm it; such movement is the constitutive domain in which power and pleasure combine to achieve political effect.

Collingwood rightfully advocated an approach in which evidence is seen as what is made to appear in response to a question. From this perspective a fact can become evidence despite itself, despite reticence or a lack of any intention of serving as evidence. (Symptoms consistently possess such a quality.) A fact or object can suddenly turn into evidence once we put a question to it. Questions do not stem from the image, or from the fact, object, or event to which it refers, but from what we ask of it. Barthes own questions had this quality about images, but Barthes seemed content to locate a meaning and effect *in* the image as if his interrogation exposed what the image itself sought to conceal through its cosmetic application of a "lustral bath of innocence" to a consumer product.[12] When we recognize that evidence emerges as a response to the questions we pose, we are in a position to recognize the ambiguity of that evidence: with a different question, different evidence, and different arguments, different conclusions would have emerged.

The radically different interpretations, resulting from sharply distinct questions, of the Rodney King footage are a vivid example. Rhetorically, these questions retroactively fabricated quite different "lustral baths of innocence," as it were, for Mr. King or for his assailants, members of the Los Angeles Police Department who pursued, beat, and arrested him for speeding, fleeing, and then resisting them. That is to say, opposing perspectives and different questions led to radically disparate interpretations by the prosecution and the defense at the two trials of the police officers accused of beating Mr. King.[13] The voice of documentary is largely given over, as a rhetorical utterance designed to move us, to shaping and focusing the polysemous quality of sound and image. Innocence and other qualities emerge after the fact, as that which a rhetorical voice desires to confer on what will be identified as evidence.

Despite the certainty that rhetorical utterances wish to confer, images retain a fundamental ambiguity that whodunits, advertising, and other forms of reductionism minimize. Barthes's later writing embraces such ambiguity, although he never went back to revise his earlier writing about the image and its ideological effect. For every social issue divergent positions emerge, with overlapping forms of evidence used as answers to different rhetorical questions. No denotative plane of certainty underpins these differences. The voice and gestures of the orator or the film's body seek to move us in relation to those social issues and conflicts that do not lend themselves to scientific determination and unanimous agreement.

Style, form, and voice are the heart and soul of persuasive engagement, and persuasive engagement is at the core of political discourses and social practices, whatever their ideological underpinnings. We inhabit an arena that remains fully within the shadow of ideology. There is no exit, only the constant effort to pose questions, present evidence, and make arguments that move us beyond what has come before. Leaving certitude behind moves us into an arena of radical doubt that cannot be dispelled so much as deferred, suspended, and, ultimately, embraced as part and parcel of a movement whose direction and intensity remain open to all the vicissitudes of history.

9 The Terrorist Event

White House officials see a pattern of terrorism which they believe
may be an attempt to test the will of . . . the American people.

—Leslie Stahl, *CBS News (regarding hostages on TWA Flight 847 held in
Beirut, June 1985)*

More and more American servicemen are going peacefully about their
peaceful rounds and being murdered for it.

—Bruce Morton, *CBS News (regarding six Americans killed in El
Salvador, June 20, 1985)*

BRUTUS. Let's to the Capitol,
And carry with us ears and eyes for th' time,
But hearts for the event.

—*Coriolanus,* 2.1

VIEWING DISASTER

September 11, 2001, introduced the United States to the experience of
domestic terrorism as no other event has ever done. For most people, word
of this event first arrived as live television bulletins: we are at home, or
work. We see images of disaster of an extraordinary magnitude. A plane
slices into the World Trade Center. Flames and smoke billow from the
wound. Lives are surely lost.

As the morning unfolds, television news anchors interrupt regular programming to speak to us from their studio chambers as they report what
eludes comprehension but portends tragedy. Their reports and images
offer evidence of a catastrophic event but provide no context or perspective.
If it be evidence, of what might it be so? It is as if live television coverage
rips the flesh from the face of the world and hurls it into our living
rooms. Shocking, grotesque, obscene—this should not be imaginable let
alone real. And yet it occurs—as rippled relays of incomprehensible destruction, catastrophic ruin. What has happened? What may happen as a consequence?

Live television coverage tumbles forward as interminable flow. The usual interruptions for advertisements and changes of program disappear. "Breaking news" gives an irregular rhythm to the syncopated, postmodern mix of images and comments, graphics and live broadcasts, recaps and conjecture, descriptions, repetitions, and interviews that tumble forward. News anchors in the studio, reporters in the field, witnesses and survivors, news footage taken and transmitted, still images and maps, later that morning, amateur footage found and recycled—this work of our media bricoleurs confounds, compels, and terrifies.

In the case of a live, simultaneous unfolding, "news" occurs outside any context. Facts are scarce. Background information does not exist. No one can narrate the trajectory of a story line when the actual existence of a story remains uncertain. Mayhem refutes narrative. Chronology is all we have. When did it happen? What happened next? What does it mean? In what sense can it be called an event? What is its origin, and when will it end? Can we stop watching before we know the answer?

What happened on September 11 began unburdened by such considerations, which began to take shape, retrospectively, in medias res, as the search for answers gained momentum. A plane has crashed into the World Trade Center. Almost certainly a terrible example of the new order of magnitude that modern technology provides to the accident. How many are injured and what can be done? Is the building in any danger? Or others on the streets?

Such questions abruptly shift with the sight of a second plane plunging into the second World Trade Center Tower, news of a third plane slamming into the Pentagon, bulletins of a fourth plane crashing in western Pennsylvania, and reports that the president of the United States is aboard Air Force One, his response and location unknown.

What grows to near certainty is that no accident could present so vivid but unfathomable a pattern. Hours after the first occurrence, the conviction of these occurrences as part of an attack by an unknown, almost inconceivable enemy looms large. Who would do such a thing? How could they do it, with commercial airline planes? For what purpose? As part of what larger plan? Invasion? Diversion? Warning? No one knows. Telecasts paper over this fundamental ignorance with hypotheses and speculation. Viewers—as well as survivors, witnesses, political leaders, and military commanders—grope for a frame within which to place this affront. Comprehension lacks a foothold. Understanding falters. Meaning proves elusive. The news catapults the nation into the grip of trauma, of shock without meaning. By midday it grows clear that an attack has taken place, but by whom and for what end remains a mystery. . . .

MAKING MEANING

Although the sudden disruption of media programming makes confusion itself into an event, viewers experience profound uncertainty about what this succession of occurrences might signify or within what chain of signification—within what story or account—it might be explained.[1] Such uncertainty multiplies enormously for those directly caught up within the maelstrom of disaster whose nature, contours, and extent remain utterly unknown. Viewers respond to the imperative, "Stay tuned," but those on the scene must respond to life-altering imperatives of a different order: stay or flee, ascend or descend, assist others or save oneself. Decisions must be made, swiftly, without knowledge of what it is, exactly, to which one is responding.

Maurice Blanchot comments that "since the disaster always takes place after having taken place, there cannot possibly be any experience of it."[2] Blanchot's remark pinpoints a paradox: occurrences coalesce into an event after the fact. Henceforth what seemed utterly confounding will bear a name and at least partial meaning. But our encounter with what will become an event precedes the act of identifying it as an event—disaster, attack, or otherwise. Such an encounter cannot, therefore, stand as an experience of what has yet to be named or understood. Experience is retroactive; encounter is traumatic.

No one experienced what took place on the morning of September 11 as an event (except the perpetrators). Instead, the ghastly succession of appalling images and dumbfounding information confronts us as the kind of occurrence that defies all categories of experience. Calamity, catastrophe, disaster, holocaust, and terrorist attack—such names mark, and bind, what has occurred but cannot contain what is still in the process of taking form as an event. No words are adequate, not simply in the sense of being of an incommensurate order of magnitude with what takes place but in the more basic sense that this encounter exists outside the domain of language, discourse, and comprehension altogether. Naming it is an act of dragging it back into the realm of reason and language. Once named as an event, it possesses a form that allows experience and response to take shape around it. It becomes evidence rather than raw fact.

But in the initial moments of unfolding, grasping for words offers minimal consolation and no coherence. Speech merely gestures toward the loss of meaning, a gash in the social fabric. The effort to name unfathomable, inexplicable, terrifying experiences signifies a certain desperation. We stand at the abyss, tottering, with little more than language and its power to spin webs of signification to prevent our fall.

If a disastrous occurrence can be identified as an event, as 9/11 was to be, it becomes a candidate for topical address and historical placement. That which arose at the boundaries of the social order passes the border checkpoint that permits entry into the realm of comprehension. This, however, does not settle the matter. "Is it an event?" yields to a more politically fraught question: "What kind of event is it?" Every answer carries moral, political, and ideological implications. Agreement about the *fact* of the event converts a series of incidents into a conceptual whole. Debate about the *kind* of event recruits this incident to a larger discursive chain. As evidence, the "event unit" enters into discourse that embeds the event within an unfolding social debate where different interpretations and proposed responses contend. I will return to the question of what kind of event 9/11 was shortly.

Unlike documentary representations, including television news, which set out to tell a story about a familiar, historical world, live media coverage of a disaster finds itself shorn of both a historical perspective and a narrative frame. Commentators and witnesses may revert to mythic evocations of a primordial chaos prior to the "in the beginning . . ." of a discernible order. Images arrive as remains, the remains of the referent, fragments bereft of meaning. Live media coverage finds itself taken hostage by an unfolding drama it cannot comprehend. (*One Day in September* [Kevin Macdonald, 1999], about the capture of the 1972 Israeli Olympic team by pro-Palestinian terrorists, makes the utter confusion of the media during this event abundantly clear.) Television news, in fact, disseminates the mise-en-scène of terrorist desire itself: confusion, loss, shock, silence.[3] Terrorism holds the media hostage to the emergent event much as the media does its audience.[4]

Live television coverage differs in this regard from "real-time" but mediated interactions. Real-time interactions link a set of occurrences with an agent who can control or manipulate these occurrences from a distance, at a remove. The event is the sum of the occurrences plus the interventions of the interactive agent. The agent may occupy a position in the same cybernetic system or may simply have a means of access to it: a drone pilot may activate weapons that attack a target at a distance but within the same real, historical world as the operator, whereas a video game player may interact with elements of a spatiotemporal world conjured by and existing solely within a computer simulation. Real-time interactions represent a technological prosthetic for the extension of power. Live television coverage of a disaster represents a technological prosthetic for the extension of powerlessness.[5]

Live media coverage of any disaster puts us on the scene, live but vicariously; the reporting dramatizes the disaster's magnitude and simultaneously reassures us of our remove from it. The 1989 Loma Prieta earthquake in California exemplifies the simultaneity of a virtual presence and a corporeal absence. Within minutes of its occurrence, images of chaos and devastation arrive. The nature of the event as earthquake was almost immediately known, and this made a considerable difference in the nature of the coverage. Motives and plans, the full extensiveness of the action and the options available for response, crucial to deciphering what happened on 9/11, were either not relevant or not immediately known. Live coverage could afford to be smug in the face of a natural disaster. It functioned on the occasion of this massive earthquake with the calm of a puppet master who, largely unseen, orchestrates, controls, and establishes the frame that mediates response. The reporter or news anchor belongs to a spatiotemporal margin between those directly affected and the audience. The structure of a known event excuses the reporter, and audience, from full, participatory engagement; it prepares a space for observation and spectacle.

"Professional" in one sense, this detachment or marginality also renders the news of catastrophe irrelevant to those caught up within it. The needs of those who experienced the effects of the Loma Prieta earthquake greatly exceeded the pathos of spectacle. Practical, tangible information was paramount: What roads were open? Which homes or buildings remained safe, and which did not? Where were shelters available? How could groundwater be made drinkable? But news coverage circumvented victims and their needs to address an audience always presumed to be elsewhere. Marginality converts itself into centrality, adding to the trauma of victims who now find themselves serving as an index of the magnitude of a catastrophe for an audience barred from intervention.[6]

The attacks on the World Trade Center and Pentagon were different in degree if not kind. The lack of a framework of comprehension for the incidents heightened the sense of participatory identification. Everyone seemed caught up in the same inexplicable chaos. Empathy grew, globally in fact, and trauma spread as no one proved able to give punctuation to the event and mark it closed or to give a name to the event and render it available for interpretation.

As a telemediated crisis, September 11 was exceptional. The stupendous monumentality of it, the horrific trauma, the sheer uncertainty about its nature, extent, or purpose—all of this put to the test the process of making sense of what first appeared as senseless annihilation. Did passing this test mean making a string of occurrences coalesce into a familiar shape that confers the status of event on that which operates at the boundaries of all those events that constitute a culture, a civilization, and a history? And how was this act followed by the act of locating this event within a narrative account that assigned agency, inferred intentionality, and planned a response?

Both these operations—identification and narration—serve vital functions, but at what price do our media commentators and politicians deploy them when the occurrence itself tests the limits of these processes, exposing the phantasmagoric underbelly of a response that, on its surface, is forthright and measured?

IN SEARCH OF A PATTERN

Identification with and narratives about the attack of September 11 invite consideration of "the modernist event." The modernist event involves those technologically assisted events of such scale and horror—genocide, nuclear warfare, mass starvation, "ethnic cleansing," and so forth—that the very notion of an adequate historical narrative falls into question.[7] The term *modernist event* is Hayden White's, and he explains it this way:

> [Modernist events] function in the consciousness of certain social groups exactly as infantile traumas are conceived to function in the psyche of neurotic individuals. This means that they cannot be simply forgotten and put out of mind, but neither can they be adequately remembered; which is to say, clearly and unambiguously identified as to their meaning and contextualized in the group memory in such a way as to reduce the shadow they cast over the group's capacity to go into its present and envision a future free of their debilitating effects.
> . . . It is the anomalous nature of modernist events—their resistance to inherited categories and conventions for assigning them meanings— that undermines not only the status of facts in relation to events but also the status of "the event" in general.
> . . .[One result is the difficulty] felt by present generations of arriving at some agreement as to their *meaning*—by which I mean, what the facts established about such events could possibly tell us about the nature of our own current social and cultural endowment and what attitude we ought to take with respect to them as we make plans for our own future. In other words, what is at issue here is not the facts of the matter regarding such events but the different possible meanings that such facts can be construed as bearing.[8]

The media and American government have concurred, for the most part, on what the events of September 11 mean, but they have done so, I would argue, by treating the event as a traditional rather than a modernist one. The difficulty leaders have experienced in acknowledging the traumatic nature of the event and the work of mourning relative to the prosecution of "war" against an ill-defined, extraterritorial and extragovernmental enemy (terrorists) is one indication. The uncertain application of categories of agency, responsibility, policy, or purpose to such an enemy is another.

How have we conferred meaning on these images of disaster? Not, I would suggest, via the "indexical whammy" of images of giant jetliners slicing through concrete and steel nor of entire buildings plummeting to earth. Such images disseminate the shock of such experience and induce a desire for therapeutic knowledge. Indexicality attests to the *fact* of the occurrence but offers nothing by way of an interpretive account or explanation. Evidence of what remains an unanswered question.

Nor, I would also argue, is meaning conferred via the more sociological or Marxist claim that the truth of the image flows not from its own interior but from its controlling surround. In this view the meaning of these images becomes assigned to them by (1) an institutional framework that promises to distinguish images of evidence from images of fantasy, (2) a nonfictional "discourse of sobriety" that assumes an instrumental power capable of interacting directly with the social reality of which it is a part,[9] (3) the political agendas embedded in these discursive conventions—from maintaining market share by performing a public service at any cost for media outlets to maintaining a sense of social order for political and civic leaders, and (4) the ideological assumptions that underpin these operations, from the sanctity and innocence of the American nation-state to the stress on individual responsibility that makes possible the identification of crimes and the distribution of punishment.

Instead, I would like to suggest a third framework that stresses a zone of ambiguity within indexical or institutional arguments: is it possible that the "ultimate referent" that points toward "what really happened" exists neither in the image per se nor in the material conditions of its production and circulation but *in* the relation entertained among the image flow, its social or semiotic context, *and the viewer?* Our gut-response, our interpretive gestures, our willingness to suspend disbelief all suggest that we remain prepared to discover meaning in the image itself. Our reliance on knowledge of genres and conventions, institutions and their discourses suggests that we temper what we see with an awareness of how it is produced. But is there anything about the image, or how it is produced, that *guarantees* its status independent of our own activity? Is any guarantee anything other than a necessary fiction? This question underscores the fundamental ambiguity of the image, an ambiguity that is only exacerbated in modernist events that take place at the margins of traditional ideas about the event and its representation. Neither the indexical nature of the image nor the discursive character of the surrounding social frame, particularly traditional realist ones, guarantees comprehension. Neither makes meaning alone; the act of constructing a story—the making of meaning—demands a viewer.

In the case of 9/11 the interpretation of live media coverage involves the *assignment* of meaning to an information flow that stupefies more than it illuminates. Recognition of this continuous sensory flow as signifiers requires its conversion into meaningful units, not the emanation or application of meaning to already existing units, which we acknowledge and understand. It is we who actively distinguish the figure from its ground, who see a gestalt take shape phantasmagorically. (It is not there to be seen; it takes shape within the subject.) Sensory impressions arrive as an ebb and flow of shock and sensation, spectacle and information, without division into clear and distinct signifying units. Signifiers dissolve in a reflux of sensory impressions. Narrative structure proves elusive. We respond to an initial disturbance, a violent launching of narrative energy, but with what heroes and villains, with what sense of agency and responsibility, suspense and resolution? The *desire* to answer such questions is intense, but the modernist event thwarts them at every turn.

The assignment of a signified literally hands over to the image forms of meaning that are of the viewer's own devising. In one sense of the word this assignment is *fantastic*; it mimics the work of fantasy. It posits meaning where there would otherwise be none. A psychic investment of considerable magnitude comes into play. Its fundamental goal is to overcome the experience of meaninglessness, of unbounded confusion, and the singular shock of trauma. One key step in this process is the designation of certain occurrences as evidence of an "event" so that it can be recruited to a larger narrative or to contending narratives.

WHAT'S THE STORY HERE?

"What's happening?" is a question that invites a story. The story of an event, however, remains unavailable during its duration. The act of assigning a set of occurrences to the category "event" itself signals the event's completion, or at least an anticipation that it will be brought to completion. Identifying an event prepares it to join yet other events, functions, or actions in the construction of a narrative. In the heat of the moment, before recognition of the boundaries of an event takes place, such as those moments that seemed to commence at 8:46 a.m., September 11, 2001—when the first plane struck the south tower of the World Trade Center—the meaning and magnitude of the catastrophe eludes comprehension. The sequence of occurrences defies the traditional signs of an event such as the presence of clear causes, natural or human, and, if human, plausible intentions. "What's happening?" remains a confounding question of staggering proportions.

As a word, *event* harbors the difficulty of assigning meaning in its very definition. Definitions such as "occurrences of some importance," "something that happens," or "that which follows from a course of proceedings" make it clear that events lack a coherent, internal structure; their identification follows from the retrospective impression that an "occurrence of some importance" has taken place. (That historians regard accidents as prototypical events stresses the way in which the event appears to stand out and define itself against a more uniform ground.) The etymology—from L. *evenutus,* fr. past part. of *evenire,* fr *ē + venīre* [out + to come, hence, to come out]—also points toward an origin that defines it. And yet this origin in a prior moment proves elusive since it is only *after* its occurrence that the event proves identifiable. The sense of an origin is, perhaps, the fiction necessary to disavow the impression that events occur sui generis even if this is how they may be initially experienced, especially traumatic ones. Ritual or predictable events such as a parade or birth might appear to have specific causes or origins, but these points of origin themselves dissolve into larger and longer chains of preconditions that do more to establish the possibility of the event than to guarantee its occurrence. Our understanding of history as contingent, and perhaps intrinsically meaningless, is at stake here.

At the time of its unfolding, the beginning of an unanticipated event does not stand in a metonymic relation to the entirety of the event. The whole of which it is a part has yet to be determined. Rather than *stand for* a whole, the part awaits *assignment* to a whole, something that can only occur in a retroactive act of recognition. The familiar processes of fantasy, dream-work, or narrative construction, be it fictional or nonfictional, comes into play to carry out the necessary assignments and generate the effect of recognition. This is why the viewer or social actor is a necessary supplement to the indexicality of the image or the institutional framework of its circulation.

On September 11 no one knew what hit them. Everyone underwent an experience of intense magnitude, possibly of physical travail and loss, certainly of confusion and anxiety. Each person had a perspective on the occurrences as they happened but not in the form of a linear model, in which all aspects of the occurrence cohere by arising from a known origin and receding toward a common destination. The occurrences of September 11, which retroactively constituted an event, the event that live television coverage strove mightily to discover, had not yet arranged themselves in an orderly grid of specifiable spatiotemporal coordinates, a precondition to causal explanation.[10] Efforts to establish a spatiotemporal field centered on a singular vantage point necessarily entail misrecognition as well as recognition.

The process of recognition/misrecognition occurs in a heightened way in relation to trauma. As White points out, the experience can be neither forgotten nor understood. It casts a shadow across our lives and continues to do so as long as its meaning remains elusive. We rework the event to assign meaning that will free us from its "debilitating effects." The assignment of meaning establishes a horizon to chaos, panic, and trauma, and it identifies or misidentifies an agent responsible for it.

FRAMING THINGS

There is no satisfactory meaning to a traumatic event; this is what makes it traumatic. As a set of sensory impressions, or as signifiers with incomplete signifieds, the experience, image, or event stands vacant. Bestowing form enacts a misrecognition of the fundamental nature of the experience itself, what Blanchot termed our inability to experience a disaster that is always defined as a disaster after the fact. The emergence of a gestalt betrays the very thing to which it retroactively refers. This infidelity to staggeringly hurtful experience is what, I take it, those who stress the unrepresentability of catastrophes and traumas such as the Holocaust wish to emphasize above all.[11]

As an ex post facto label, "9/11" signifies the temporal contours or boundedness of this event: it began and, in retrospect, sufficiently concluded on that specific day to allow the date to name it. Such punctuation is of a different logical type from the occurrences themselves.[12] It is not a "context" that extends the series in spatial or temporal directions, potentially without limits, but a *category* that encapsulates the series. Such punctuation is a metamessage that tells us what kind of occurrence a set of sensory impressions is or, at a yet higher level, what kind of event an event is. We group sense impressions into an overall pattern such as "This is a memory," "This is a fantasy," or "This is an event."

The identification of a figure/ground relationship, a gestalt image ("accident," "evil," or "terrorism," for example)—may be fundamental to all communication and behavior. It generates the discrete units necessary for discourse. Once accomplished, the dynamics of recognition/misrecognition lead to a historical narrative that will explain its importance and locate it in relation to that from which it comes out. "This is an act of God," "This is an accident," or "This is terrorism," tell different stories of origin and meaning. In the case of 9/11 the dominant story so far tends to reassert the primacy of the individual victim and the generic quality of the perpetrators, the centrality of terrorist strategy, the need for homeland security, the combination of innocence and righteousness that characterizes Americans, and the necessity of retaliation. Once named, the mourning of a traumatic event can commence. But once named in this particular way, within this particular narrative frame, the work of mourning may find itself minimized or subordinated to goals other than the arduous working through of loss.

Roland Barthes notes that "the sequence exists when and because it can be given a name, it unfolds as this process of naming takes place, as a title is sought or confirmed."[13] Titles or names signify a bounded condition. As Gregory Bateson remarks: "We assume that the psychological frame has some degree of real existence. In many instances, the frame is consciously recognized, and even represented in vocabulary ('play,' 'movie,' 'interview,' 'job,' 'language,' ['terrorism'], etc.). In other cases, there may be no explicit verbal reference to the frame, and the subject may have no consciousness of it. The analyst, however, finds that his own thinking is simplified if he uses the notion of an unconscious frame as an explanatory principle; usually he goes further than this and infers its existence in the subject's unconscious."[14]

The psychological frame that identifies a figure against a ground, or a pattern to a constant flux of sensory impressions, often snaps into place all at once. This "click of recognition" is what Lacan refers to with Köhler's term, "*Aha Erlebnis*" (Aha experience), in his discussion of the infant's discovery of a more perfect whole in the image of an Other or the reflected image of itself during the mirror stage.[15] The "click" or "Aha" yields a conceptual frame that provides a category and a boundary. The "Aha" moment establishes a signifying unit—the event, in this case—of a conceptual order different from any of its constituent signifiers. This unit then stands ready, like the functions of Vladimir Propp or the actions of Barthes, to take on its full measure of meaning through syntagmatic linkage with other units, other events, which brings its own "click of recognition" as we recognize the transformation from chronological to story time.[16]

FRAMES AND FETISHES

This process of recognizing a frame or gestalt assigns wholeness and boundaries to elements that do not intrinsically possess such qualities, even though the sense of coherence seems inextricable from them.[17] When Lacan discusses the gestalt image of a coherent, powerful Other that characterizes the mirror stage, for example, he makes clear that the Other does not, in fact, possess such qualities. The search for coherence and wholeness signifies the work of desire, where we construct a "*mise-en-scène* of desire"[18] on which individual or collective dramas play out.

The impression of a coherent gestalt amounts to an overvaluation or misrecognition. The "click of recognition," the "*Aha Erlebnis,*" snaps a sense of meaning or identity into place, be it to events or the self. This, as Lacan noted, simultaneously effects a destabilization. The subject constituted by this process imagines a coherence and autonomy for itself that is, in fact, dependent on an image of others that is, in a profound sense, imaginary. The overvaluation of wholeness and coherence goes hand in hand with a disavowal of partiality and fragmentation. When we overvalue, we fetishize.

Eric Santer proposes a distinction between the work of mourning and narrative fetishism:

> By narrative fetishism I mean the construction and deployment of a narrative consciously or unconsciously designed to expunge the traces of the trauma or loss that called that narrative into being in the first place. . . . [It contrasts with the work of mourning in that] narrative fetishism . . . is the way an inability or refusal to mourn emplots traumatic events; it is a strategy of undoing, in fantasy, the need for mourning by simulating a condition of intactness, typically by situating the site and origin of loss elsewhere. Narrative fetishism releases one from the burden of having to reconstitute one's self-identity under "posttraumatic" conditions; in narrative fetishism, the "post" is indefinitely postponed.[19]

Mourning begins with the acknowledgment of trauma and proceeds to work through its destabilizing effect on the psyche. Narrative fetishism, by contrast, begins with the disavowal of trauma and any destabilizing effect it might have. For historical events, narrative fetishism provides meaningfulness to events just as the mirror stage provides identity to the self. Coherence persists because loss comes from somewhere beyond the domain of imaginary intactness. This is a story of loss that identifies traumatic events as coming from *outside* the boundaries of culture and society, the field of social relations in which we constitute our own identity. This fetishism cannot be recognized for what it is, a fantastic story of disavowed trauma, and still achieve the desired effect. Its own origin outside the field of trauma, in the realm of myth or ideology, must be disavowed. This is a *political* strategy, a choice of one among numerous choices but one that has played itself out to a considerable degree both in news coverage by domestic media and in foreign policy by the federal government.

Mourning has certainly occurred for the trauma of September 11, but the bulk of the subsequent political response and media coverage displays more of the characteristics of narrative fetishism than of mourning, especially through its focus on presidential action and a fantasy of an invincible, implacable America that will remain intact to the extent that the villainous enemies (the site and origin of loss) are located in the radical "elsewhere" of a presumably alien religious fanaticism and nihilistic political philosophy beyond the bounds of culture, society, and even civilization.

Terrorism instills fear. It signals sudden, abrupt, catastrophic, barbaric, and traumatic acts that lie beyond the pale of law, reason, or judgment.[20] To the mind of the terrorist who is so constructed, the social order he opposes appears as obdurate, unyielding, impenetrable, and overwhelming—beyond the pale. No dialogue is possible, no warnings necessary, and no larger strategy than terror itself required. Terrorism confronts a "barbaric" enemy, an alien foe, an evil empire beyond the law of those beyond the Law. The only response conceivable is eradication; the only action possible is terrorism. Civilization condemns the terrorist to those very acts that exile him to beyond the pale, beyond the civilization that has itself constructed this barbaric figure and in which it can effect a negative identification with its own values and beliefs.

Naming the 9/11 event a terrorist act by Osama bin Laden and his Al Qaeda network clearly affirms the intactness of a sovereign, benign identity for the United States and locates the origin of terror decisively elsewhere, in a realm of antidemocratic, anticapitalist, fundamentalist fanaticism. It simultaneously disavows the complicity that might be understood to follow from the history of U.S. foreign intervention—often military or paramilitary assistance in Latin America, Africa, and Asia—and, in this case, support of the ultraconservative Saudi Arabian royal family and the perceived degradation of honorable Saudi values by figures such as Bin Laden himself.

Disavowed, and subject to narrative fetishization, terrorism facilitates the misrecognition of its quasi-legitimate counterpart, state terrorism. State terrorism as a covert implementation of power favors (1) invisibility (as embodied in the Nazi policy of *Nacht und Nebel* [night and fog] or the Argentine government's policy of "disappearing" suspected dissidents), (2) masking of overt signs of torture, (3) absence of an identifiable subject to whom accountability can be assigned, and (4) cultivation of a state of diffuse anxiety by dissolving any sense of specific events back into a general condition or situation through denial or disinformation. Nonstate-defined terrorism such as the attacks of 9/11 contests state power by turning this sense of powerlessness back on the state itself. It relies on (1) visibility (violence is less strategic, as it would be in a revolutionary movement, than dramaturgical), (2) overt violence—from 9/11 to beheadings—staged as spectacle, using the mainstream media to propagate its disregard for any "rules of engagement" or "human rights," (3) identifiable perpetrators of the immediate event who assume accountability for the deed (to the point of becoming, as in the case of suicide bombers or the 9/11 hijackers, indecipherable apart from the event), and (4) the cultivation of a widespread state of immediate shock and persistent fear brought to a focus by media coverage.

In *The Believer* (Henry Bean, 2001) the anti-Semitic Jew Daniel confides to several people that he wants to kill a Jew. The self-proclaimed fascist Curtis asks him how, and Daniel answers: "on a New York City street, midday, with a small-caliber automatic, without a silencer." A young woman, Carla, asks, "Why no silencer?" And Daniel responds: "You want it to be an event."

And in the documentary film *One Day in September*, one of the surviving terrorists from the capture of the Israeli Olympic team as hostages at the Munich Olympics, Jamal Al Gashey, proclaims, at a news conference, "I'm proud of what I did at Munich because it helped the Palestinian cause enormously. Before Munich the world had no idea about our struggle, but on that day the name 'Palestine' was repeated all over the world." Al Gashey fantasizes that this incomprehensible distortion of the usual process of nation-building achieves terrorist goals in a way that no state-sponsored act of terror would ever dream of doing.

FETISHISM AND FANTASY

Fetishes are fantastic, but, even more, their construction follows the path established by fantasy itself. As a framing device, the "terrorist event" has served to assert mastery over trauma by situating the origin, if not the site, of loss elsewhere and vowing to bring the site of loss home to the enemy. The dominant narrative of fiendish terrorists beyond the law and any human values has pushed attention beyond the traumatic event and the work of mourning. The mise-en-scène of desire constructs an enemy wholly alien and utterly inhuman. The task taken up by such narrative fetishism is well described by Freud: "[Following a trauma] there is no longer any possibility of preventing the mental apparatus from being flooded with large amounts of stimulus, and another problem [rather than self-defense] arises instead—the problem of mastering the amounts of stimulus which have broken in and of binding them, in a psychical sense, so that they can then be disposed of."[21] Disposition, for Freud, meant mourning, in a successful case, and melancholic neuroses in unsuccessful ones. In relation to 9/11 the flood of stimuli that overwhelmed us became framed and narrativized as a fantasmatic fetishization of something utterly alien and absolutely reprehensible rather than mourned as trauma. This disposition becomes, for the subject who believes it and on the level of the *unconscious* mechanism of fantasy propelling it, real, regardless of whether the occurrences narrativized belong to the imagination or history.[22]

What betrays the fantasmatic dimension to the "terrorist event," as the dominant narrative of our government and media have termed it, lies in the narrative of its wholly foreign origin. Trauma registers as all the more shocking and inexplicable. Innocence has gone unprotected. Something sacred has been defiled. Mourning seeks to find a way to conciliate profound trauma with its absence of moral, political, or social meaning. Narrative fetishism, however, launches a story that converts catastrophe to evil, trauma to crime. It moralizes in the name of the Law and the beleaguered nation-state that embodies it. The crime bears resemblance to the miscegenation at the root of Freud's analogy about fetishism; the penetration of an alien race into our midst has betrayed itself by the disaster it has wreaked.[23]

FANTASY CONTINUED: THE DOER OF THE DEED

Given that experience often arrives in a way that defies our desire for bounded coherence and recognizable form such as that which a story provides, what would we see if we confronted the gaps and contradictions, the incoherencies and fragmentations that elude meaning—a ground without figure, strewn with the remains of the referent? Do these gaps and contradictions attest to a genuine incoherence to occurrences themselves? What process of disavowal or fetishization do different processes of bestowing meaning entail?[24]

When we see more in what we overvalue or fetishize than is there to be seen, we enter into a realm of fantasy, which is tightly tied to the real, not isolated in a private world of reverie. To speak of fantasy is not to speak of pure acts of imagination or visual fallacy alone but of a process integral to our relation to reality itself. To protect private fantasy from the clutches of the Law may belong to a liberal tradition, but, as the authors of *Formations of Fantasy* argue, "the imperative to maintain this particular limit to the jurisdiction of the state has no doubt contributed to that climate of hostility which today prevails, on the democratic left, against *any* consideration of psychology in connection with the political. One consequence (perhaps most conspicuously displayed in the consistent failure of the left to understand nationalism) has been that the mobilizing force of *fantasy* has been effectively ceded to the right."[25] In fact, if videotapes broadcast by the news media are to be believed, Osama bin Laden and his followers sought to realize a plot partially based on a fantasy in which the devastation of the World Trade Center would prove paramount to the destruction of Western capitalism and culture as a whole. The terrorist fantasy utilized this particular site to stage the mise-en-scène of a murderous desire.

Large psychic investments are at work here. The stories encouraging individuals to "dispose of" a traumatic event prompt subjects to one course of action rather than another. The social rituals of mourning facilitate emotional confrontation and the resolution of trauma, but the government's narrative gives priority to the destruction of the distant cause of this grievous attack and to seek out those "striking features" (fanaticism, secretiveness, isolation, mysterious sources of funds, and so on, even, for some "Arabness" of any kind) that "betray" a terrorist intent. The mainstream media and the Bush administration created an unfinished story—so far, fifteen years later—of terrorism. This tale offers a vantage point from which the event's origin can be identified and a vanishing point toward which the event recedes ("elsewhere").

Such a picture locates an agent or subject "behind" the event, as he from whom it issues. If it did not come out of nothing, it must have arisen from something or someone. That something in this case is the subject, an imaginary coherence but one necessary to the assignment of responsibility. To recognize such a subject—Osama bin Laden, the Al Qaeda network, or, more recently, other similar groups—as the one responsible nullifies the sense of traumatic meaninglessness by assigning, paradoxically, an *agent* to meaninglessness.

Recognizing the identifiable figure of the terrorist, and naming him, provides a doer for the deed. As such it reinstates the rule of law in the midst of an event that would seem to originate from a locus beyond the law. "A being is hurt, and the vocabulary that emerges to moralize that pain is one which isolates a subject as the intentional originator of an injurious deed. . . . The subject is not only fabricated as the prior and causal origin of a painful effect that is recast as an injury, but the action whose effects are injurious is no longer an action, the continuous present of 'a doing,' [what

I have termed occurrences] but is reduced to a 'singular act.'" Furthermore, "the subject appears only as a consequence of a demand for accountability; a set of painful effects is taken up by a moral framework that seeks to isolate the 'cause' of those effects in a singular and intentional agent, a moral framework that operates through a certain economy of paranoid fabrication and efficiency"[26]

Trauma converts to injury, and injury requires redress; redress demands we produce the subject responsible. The mise-en-scène of desire conjures up the terrorist as the evildoer of the deed. The continuous present of "a doing" that would diffuse responsibility and acknowledge trauma collapses into a singular enemy, one whose status challenges the very law that calls it into being. The Bush administration's term for captives at the Guantanamo military base in Cuba, "unlawful combatants," identifies a subject accountable for injurious deeds, but it also locates this subject beyond the very law that calls such a subject into being. Accused criminals, like prisoners of war, remain subjects of the law, protected by those guarantees accorded to all citizens or soldiers. "Unlawful combatants," like undocumented guest workers, illegal immigrants, and the inhabitants of refugee camps, exist beyond the law. Special rules apply. They occupy a liminal space that justifies extraordinary measures, beyond the customary rule of law in order to preserve the rule of law, protect the peace, and maintain order.

The fantastic process embodied in the mirror stage returns as a political process of "othering." Slavoj Žižek puts it this way: "In short, 'enemy recognition' is always a performative procedure which brings to light / constructs the enemy's 'true face.' [Carl] Schmitt refers to the Kantian category of *Einbildungskraft*, the transcendental power of imagination: in order to recognize the enemy, one has to 'schematize' the logical figure of the Enemy, providing it with the concrete features which will make it into an appropriate target of hatred and struggle."[27]

The name *terrorism* gives a face and a figure to the excess that typically escapes the categories of history, narrative, and meaning. We can address our future intentions toward that figure to which we assign responsibility for the unconscionable in the very moment when we misrecognize this figure ("elsewhere") as an agent of history. And we can justify forms of recourse that exceed the rule of law or the conventions of war since that which we oppose occupies a liminal space between the human and inhuman. In other words, the law requires fantasy as a vital fiction. It requires a mise-en-scène of desire populated by those subjects on whom it can exercise its power and whom it can hold responsible, even in their capacity as excess.[28]

What is at stake is not whether specific terrorists mounted the attacks of September 11 but whether the form of narrativization given to the event by the Bush administration misrecognizes the fantasy involved by individuating the doer and singularizing the act, by segregating the doer and the deed out from a continuous stream of historical "doings" and consequences, and by constructing a special entity, the terrorist, from whom stems the rejection of law, the nullification of being, and the rule of terror.

THE TERRORIST FANTASY

The "remains of the day," 9/11, lie strewn with the latent fragments of a narrative, if only they can be assembled into one. "Attack on America," "Terrorism," and "America Strikes Back" give name to the three-part story that unfolds. Like other events of catastrophic proportion that result from the conjunction of technology, determination, and evil, this event raises the question of whether any narrative frame can prove adequate. Modernist events—of which the Holocaust is the most paradigmatic for many commentators but which can also include other campaigns of genocide or ethnic cleansing; nuclear, biological. and chemical warfare; mass starvation; and terrorism—poses a distinct challenge to narrative representation.[29] To stay with our specific example, *terrorism* names the unfathomable. Terrorism assigns human agency to that which exceeds the bounds of civilized (human) conduct. It converts to history that which defies the premise of historical meaningfulness. It freezes a traumatic moment into a mythic binary of Manichean struggle: them/us, love/hate, good/evil; civilization/barbarism. ("You are either with us or against us," as President Bush put it.) The melodramatics of terrorism enable a narrative production in which a purely benign state strikes out against a totally malevolent enemy.

This particular story of a profoundly uncivilized and un-American terrorism alleviates the event of its sting, and mystery, by disavowing its full traumatic impact. This story also disavows the painful effects of injustice and exploitation, of economic dependence and cultural hegemony on the peoples of other nations and other values. It favors a fantasmatic scenario that reduces terrorism to a unilateral act of cold-blooded violence that comes out of an unfathomable void, a heart of total darkness.

Like *unlawful combatant,* the term *barbaric agent* bears an oxymoronic ring. Historical narratives require human agents—be they individual or collective. Human agents are those that possess a conscience and stand morally responsible for their actions. Yet terrorism stands for unconscious emanations of hate and violence beyond the pale of law or reason. How can the terrorist be assigned responsibility when, by definition, he or she exemplifies the one who acts unconscionably? How can we think we recognize a familiar historical agent of any kind in the terrorist? Modernist events in all their guises, including terrorism, continue to call for narratives of cause/effect, agent/action, yet their technologically amplified magnitude compels such narratives to betray their own "special features" as alien impositions on that which defies the categories and representations of traditional narratives or a moral human order.

It is little wonder that the first extended reexamination of the events of September 11 on network television was a two-hour special, *9/11*, broadcast on CBS on the six-month anniversary of the event and organized around the footage of a pair of independent documentary filmmakers from France, the Gaudet brothers.[30] The filmmakers began their film, on the everyday life of a New York City fireman, in the months before September 11, but they found their fireman, and themselves, swept up in the maelstrom of the event itself. Their efforts took them inside the World Trade Center buildings and captured the collapse of the towers. It observed the extraordinary conduct of their hero and his comrades as they risked their own lives to save others, not knowing at the time what had happened in any detail or how acute the risks actually were.

Heroic firemen made an understandable choice for a focus. Such figures come closest to the human agents of old. They, both during and in the aftermath of the event, afforded a way of "indexing the irruption of fate, destiny, grace, fortune, providence and even of 'history' itself into a life" to yield meaning. The fantasmatics of melodrama recur. As their hero fireman says regarding his choice of profession, "I just wanted to do good with my life." It is no wonder Americans have seized on these men and women as heroes in a classic and profound sense (and rightly so). They offer linkage to a past tradition of courage and sacrifice, and they restore some shards of meaning to a landscape denuded of the significance it had once been made to bear.

Evil, however, is entirely elsewhere. It comes out of nothingness, out of that which lies beyond the pale of democratic institutions and civil society. It occupies no place in the documentary tribute to sacrifice and heroism, as if it cannot be accounted for within the same narrative frame. The film *9/11* is the story of heroism on the scene of disaster rather than of crime and punishment in its aftermath.

The story of "terrorism" eradicates the mythic story of heroic endeavor in favor of a fantastic story of moral triumph over absolute evil. What Leslie Stahl reported in 1985, as "a pattern of terrorism which [the government] believe[s] may be an attempt to test the will of . . . the American people" requires no concrete referent. A permanent state of Manichean struggle prevails: the national continues to be tested; evil terrorists and good Americans continue to confront each other across the chasm between history and society, on the one hand, and eternal evil, on the other. Attention turns to the crusade ahead and away from the iterative pattern of occurrences in which the complicity of state power would replace the innocence of human goodness, the continuous process of doing that understands the specification of an event as a work of fantasy. Civilization disavows association with the ground of barbarism from which it must consistently stand out. It directs attention to a future time populated by revenge, triumph, retribution, and memorialization. "Terrorism" allows "civilization" to reassert itself as its diametric opposite. Once so named, the event carries forward the paradoxical logic of a fantasy in which the nation strives to eradicate that which simultaneously belongs to the ground of its own being.

10 **Remaking History**

Jay Leyda and the Compilation Film

A slim volume of 176 pages, with an original paperback price of $1.95, Jay Leyda's *Films Beget Films* remains one of the most insightful, stimulating books on the compilation film yet written.[1] The initial champions of documentary—Dziga Vertov, John Grierson, Paul Rotha, and others—stressed the creative treatment of reality, or as Rotha put it in his *Documentary Film*, documentary film involved a "dramatic statement of facts."[2] Editing was a pivotal part of this treatment, as was reenactment, but reusing found footage was not. Found footage, already understood as a rapidly accumulating resource, simply did not have the immediacy of freshly recorded material, be it staged, reenacted, or captured on the fly. And with the technological innovations of the early 1960s that made capturing the encounter of filmmaker and subject in the moment of filming a defining act for documentary—be it in an observational or participatory mode—the idea of compiling new films from old, despite Esther Schub's remarkable example,[3] remained a largely neglected, secondary consideration.

In that sense Louis Marcorelles's *Living Cinema: New Directions in Contemporary Filmmaking* captures the spirit of the 1960s far more accurately than Leyda's book does, but it fails entirely to consider the value of this well-established and vital tributary of documentary filmmaking.[4] Similarly, A. William Bluem's *Documentary in American Television*, published just a year after Leyda's book, devotes one chapter (almost entirely on NBC's Project XX acclaimed series of compilation films), and Eric Barnouw's classic text, *Documentary: A History of the Non-fiction Film*, published a decade later, makes no more than passing mention of this form.[5]

None of these books scrutinize the aesthetic, ethical, and political complexities of the compilation film. In fact, we have had to wait for the recent publication of Jamie Baron's *The Archive Effect: Found Footage and the*

Audiovisual Experience of History to find a significant elaboration on the insights Leyda offered in this seminal book.[6] There is a reason for this. In *Representing Reality* I argued that the collage-like principle championed by Leyda as a foundation for the compilation film never gained a solid foothold in the United States, not even among leftist filmmakers: "The formalist concept of *ostranenie,* the 'making strange' of things familiar through the manner of representation and juxtaposition, the Brechtian concept of *Verfremdungseffekt,* using alienation devices that break the empathetic bond to promote a broader level of insight . . . all seemed too distracting when priorities favored the direct, immediate, and obvious."[7] Strange juxtapositions seemed too contrary to the sense of immediacy and transparency that formed the basis for documentary realism. It is not surprising, therefore, that the compilation film became little more than a side current to the mainstream documentary and that its analytic treatment should be neglected apart from this one outstanding book. (*Representing Reality* is as guilty of this neglect as any of the other books I have mentioned.)

Leyda spent considerable time in the U.S.S.R. during the birth of the Soviet cinema of the 1920s and 1930s. He returned to the United States in 1936 as purges and show trials abounded but retained his faith in a communist ideal. His *Kino: A History of the Russian and Soviet Film* remains a unique, firsthand account of the rise of Soviet cinema.[8] Leyda understood well the importance of montage as a cinematic principle and, more broadly, the centrality of strange juxtapositions as both an artistic and political tool.

Although Eisenstein's theories of montage, and John Heartfield, Hannah Höch, and Alexander Rodchenko's practice of photomontage do not receive extended discussion in *Films Beget Films,* they clearly form the bedrock for the book's treatment of the compilation film. All of them understood the shot or image as part of a greater whole whose sum could be constituted by parts chosen for their *dissimilarity* of type, origin, or affect rather than as a contribution to continuity and transparency. This was a very different principle from capturing reality as it unfolded before the camera, however creatively this reality might be shaped then or after. Juxtaposing images in fresh, unexpected ways could become, in Walter Benjamin's words, "dynamite" to shatter customary perception and habitual behavior so that "in the midst of [the cinema's] far-flung ruins and debris, we calmly and adventurously go traveling."[9]

Likewise, the *archive,* a term far more frequently invoked today, also makes a significant appearance. Bluem and Barnouw acknowledge that more than half a century of newsreels provide an extraordinary resource, but the unique problems this resource generates and the distinct qualities it possesses go unexamined. (The main problem discussed by Barnouw is how the technique of "stretching"—inserting duplicate frames—allowed older footage originally shot at sixteen frames per second to be converted to twenty-four frames per second.) Leyda, however, astutely points to the crucial role played by a catalogue or "index": the system by which elements within an archive can be identified, retrieved, and used for new purposes. By what means will archival footage be inventoried? How can specific effects be found amid a vast sea of old footage, initially created for reasons that almost certainly no longer govern its new use? Using images in new ways means seeing them from fresh perspectives, and this makes any classification based solely on their previous usage, without regard for their as yet unfulfilled potential use, problematic. Leyda, in fact, envisions "punched cards, run through sorting machines" as a possible solution that would allow for an imaginative and highly expansive categorization, an idea that is quite prescient in its basic conception.[10]

The core idea of the compilation film revolves around not only montage and photomontage but also *ostranenie*, the basic tenet of Russian formalism as put forward by Victor Shklovsky: "the purpose of art is to impart the sensation of things as they are perceived and not as they are known."[11] An "aha" occurs when something familiar and known is seen in an unfamiliar, new way. Old documentary footage, already associated with reality in one way, becomes associated with reality in a new way. New meanings and insights become possible. New tonalities and emotional states arise. Czar Nicholas II's celebratory home movies of life in Russia as seen by a monarch become transformed, through Schub's editing, into a condemnation of poverty, exploitation, and arrogance in *The Fall of the Romanov Dynasty* (1927).

As Leyda claims, a "new art" is brought into being in Schub's work. Much later but following in these vivid footsteps, Emile de Antonio revived the practice of scathing political critique by turning television coverage of the Army-McCarthy hearings conducted by the rabid anticommunist senator from Wisconsin, Joe McCarthy, into a condemnation of his irresponsible, bullying tactics in *Point of Order* (1964). He later refined the use of archival footage in his rebuttal to official justifications for the war in Vietnam in *In the Year of the Pig* (Emile de Antonio, 1968). His films demonstrated the enormous potential of the compilation film during the heyday of the observational film. Following his example, government propaganda films, designed to draw women into the workplace during World War II, become the butt of a biting critique when juxtaposed with real-life stories told by actual women workers in Connie Field's *The Life and Times of Rosie the Riveter* (1980), and instructional films on how to survive nuclear attack become subverted in a trenchant send-up of Cold War madness in *Atomic Café* (Jayne Loader, Kevin Rafferty, and Pierce Rafferty, 1982).

Leyda is quick to point out a crucial quality of the compilation film with regard to its capacity to help us see anew: we first need to have some familiarity with the original source of the footage so that we can then see it in a new light. To watch a compilation film as if it were made entirely from new footage, just as to mistake a reenactment for the actual (reenacted) event, would negate a significant part of its impact. Leyda pushes this point repeatedly, although a quote he offers from Siegfried Kracauer conveys the idea with particular lucidity: "The most familiar, that which continues to condition our involuntary reactions and spontaneous impulses, is thus made to appear as the most alien. If we find these obsolete sights funny, we respond to them also with emotions which range from fright at the sudden emergence of our intimate being to nostalgic melancholy over the inexorable passing of time."[12]

Like irony, where what is said is not what is meant, the full effect depends on recognizing that what is being signified is not what the presented footage originally signified but is, instead, a transformation of that initially intended meaning.[13] Emotional impact in terms of identification with specific characters and their psychological complexity was quite secondary for Leyda, as it was for the Soviet filmmakers and for Brecht. Favored was intellectual impact. Leyda saw the compilation film as an ideal vehicle for a cinema of ideas (and propaganda), but it is the humanist tendencies of Flaherty that have governed a great deal of compilation film production. Leyda, for example, makes factual note that NBC's *Victory at Sea* (broadcast in 1952–53) was the first compilation film made for television after World War II, but he neglects to comment on its nostalgic, memory-laden evocation of the war even though this tone is strikingly different from the galvanizing, patriotic documentaries made during the course of the war.

This powerful series, directed by Harold Solomon and with memorable music by Richard Rodgers, demonstrates the capacity of compilation films, like other forms of documentary, to convey what it feels like to perceive and engage the world in a particular way. The evocative, emotional power of this series carried more pertinence than Leyda allows, but it also skews the compilation film in a different direction.[14] This is the quality that struck many as the mark of a fresh historical voice that could render human scale to epic events. It was the quality that A. William Bluem seizes on as the unique contribution of *Victory at Sea*. A similarly respectful, insightful but non-defamiliarizing, use of found footage marks the entire career of Ken Burns, a filmmaker now regarded as a major historian of American life in the nineteenth and twentieth centuries. The "aha" moment becomes a more gentle "Ah, so that's the way it was."

Bluem approvingly cites at length a review of *Victory at Sea* that appeared in *Harper's* magazine by Bernard de Voto. He concludes his review by noting, "The exhaustion, anguish, agony, sullenness, apathy, despair, or exaltation which the screen shows are not histrionic; they are actual. *But the faces blend and generalize and build up and create a realization of men in war, and this is not a function of fact but of art.*"[15] This is precisely what Leyda did not value: blending and generalizing to create an abstraction: "men in war." Leyda did not value mythic abstraction so much as historical revision. The vague, milky, "we're all in this together," and "all men love, suffer, and die" type of sentimentality was what Roland Barthes excoriated so incisively in his short essay on Edward Steichen's photo exhibition *The Family of Man*, where Barthes writes about one of the exhibit's themes, work in different cultures, as a universal and unifying act: "It is . . . historified work which we should be told about, instead of an eternal aesthetics of laborious gestures."[16] For Leyda the compilation film was a way to understand history in a new way, not a technique for the perpetuation of more of the same. The latter, however, has proven enormously lucrative, as *That's Entertainment* (Jack Haley Jr., 1974), on the MGM musical, and the TV series *That's Hollywood* (1976–82), let alone the work of Ken Burns, make clear. Defamiliarizing work remains far less so. Burns's work is a far cry from de Antonio's, but it also amply demonstrates the vast potential of the form.

Ideas were not only generated by what viewers made of new assemblies of previously shot material but also by the addition of spoken commentary, usually voice-over. Here, too, Leyda perceptively identifies a major problem vis-à-vis the role of the archival image: if the commentary carries the bulk of the argument, or idea, to what extent is the image evidentiary, and to what extent is it merely a "stopgap" filler to accompany the sound track?[17] As Leyda notes, elaborating on another point made by Kracauer, not only may the image seem extraneous, but the argument itself may prove uncinematic: it could just as readily be a lecture or essay. Specific images seldom correlate well with highly conceptual abstractions such as rights, values, needs, criteria, goals, or principles, yet such terms may form the basis for the commentary. A dialectic of voice and image was far more preferable to Leyda than a clear, seamless commentary that merely strung together a series of images of (dubious) illustration. Specific images and concrete examples seldom soar to the desired level of generality, and they may well signify something else entirely or draw the viewer into the emotional complexities of a situation that the commentary treats more abstractly. This is both their virtue, for Leyda, and their danger when used carelessly.

Since voice-over commentary has dominated the expository mode of documentary ever since the 1930s, these considerations retain great currency.[18] Leyda himself slips into the second person to warn budding filmmakers of the dangers of choosing any image whatever to represent a general principle or idea:

> The pieces of actuality on your cutting-table are not protection enough for you [from the risk of being remote from the original event]—it is still too easy to display your ignorance or to succumb to superficiality or wishful thinking in putting them together. Won't any skyscraper do to represent Wall Street? Won't one plough do as well as another? (Who will appreciate your search for the *right* plough shot?) Who will know the nationality of that crowd? The pitfalls of easy abstraction are on every side and grow ever wider and deeper—even before you begin work on the commentary! . . . It will do your morale no harm to tell yourself that there will be an astonishing number of viewers who will know at least as much as you do, if not more, about your subject.[19]

His final sentence is particularly apt. It is not with binding principles or ethical imperatives that the filmmaker using archival material must concern him- or herself but with the effect on viewers. What is the impact of selected images in a given context?

Not all issues involving compilation films belong purely to compilation films; many travel along with archival material to any film employing this vast and fertile resource. In *Honest Truths,* an online guide to ethics in documentary, there is the following selection of comments by filmmakers:

> Louis Messiah reiterated this: "A good film often has many lives, and one of the lives is in educational institutions, within schools and libraries. The film becomes a historical document. So to use archival footage . . . inaccurately, for mood or tone, . . . not looking at archival footage as a document of a particular time and place, becomes problematic." Peter Miller noted that the more fundamental questions are related to matters of life and death. "With the Holocaust, you really don't want to show anything other than the exact day or place. [You have to be] obsessively careful. In a world where people deny the Holocaust, you don't want to give wind to that fire. And you want to be honorable."[20]

These considerations can be extended to reenactments, as Leyda does. He points out that the risks of "a body too many"—the body of a performer or social actor who reenacts something that has already occurred—does not arise with archival footage.[21] What we see is what there was, with the original actors intact. This degree of authenticity is then jeopardized when it succumbs to ignorance, superficiality, or wishful thinking in reenactments as in editing, to rephrase Leyda. (Reenactments, of course, have many uses and values; Leyda's point is not to dismiss them wholesale but to stress the importance of the scrupulous use of archival material when that route is chosen instead.)

Leyda pushes the issue still further. He notes that some filmmakers compile shots from other documentaries that staged or composed their shots to a high degree such as *The Plow That Broke the Plains* (Pare Lorentz, 1936). The practice of composing shots carefully helped documentary earn status as an art, but if such images are imported to a new work, they may appear to have the same evidentiary value as shots that involve minimal interaction with the situation or events represented. This can readily be seen as a distortion or deception, if discovered. Here Leyda expands a debate that had revolved around the use of fiction-film footage, as occurred sometimes in the *Why We Fight* series of seven films (Frank Capra, 1942–45), for example, as a stand-in for archival footage. Leyda astutely cites uses, or abuses, of *The River* (Pare Lorentz, 1937) and *Triumph of the Will* (Leni Riefenstahl, 1935) in subsequent work. He convincingly argues that such footage cannot be treated as the equivalent of stock footage since much more craft, and even collaboration between filmmaker and subject, went into the making of images whose status hovers between fiction and documentation.

This distinction between fiction and nonfiction has blurred considerably now that staged footage, particularly of the collaborative sort found in *Triumph of the Will*, has become a trademark of press conferences, political conventions, so-called reality TV shows, and most sports coverage, but Leyda treats the distinction quite seriously, especially if the source is not identified and thereby gets passed off as more authentic than it might otherwise be: "this seems as good a time as any to define what is and is not proper material for the 'normal' compilation. Such quotations [using footage from 'controlled' films where the shots are carefully staged or made with the subject's collaboration] are as unnecessary and can be as intrusive as shots from a fictional film."[22] However we decide the immediate issue, Leyda's deep engagement with the ethical foundation for and rhetorical impact of the selection and identification of archival material remains a basic consideration for documentary filmmaking in general. It is here that he extends the more routine acknowledgment of this form by other authors into a rigorous examination of its uses, principles, and values.

Jay Leyda's book is clearly a product of its time and its author in ways that complicate its continuing pertinence today. Leyda held strongly progressive beliefs and was heavily involved in leftist causes, hardly grounds for dismissal, but the terms and conditions of progressive, leftist thought have shifted considerably since the end of the Cold War, when *Films Beget Films* first appeared. The vast majority of the films Leyda discusses focus on issues pertaining to the nation-state—not only the United States but just about any country where compilation documentaries appeared, most notably East Germany, China, and the Soviet Union. There are almost no examples of films that address individual lives or social issues that did not yield pride of place to the need for government guidance or intervention. There is also no mention of home movies as a valuable resource, something Leyda would no doubt correct if he were writing his book today.

Ironically, some twenty-five years after the fall of the Berlin Wall, the vast majority of the films Leyda cites as examples that originated on the other side of the Iron Curtain, works that constitute a sizable part of his overall sample, are unavailable for viewing. His discussion of these films is difficult to evaluate when they can now be numbered among the casualties of the Cold War and its aftermath. In this regard the book is an indispensable record and guide to what has been, like so much potential archival footage, lost, suppressed, or "disappeared." From Alberto Cavalcanti's *Yellow Caesar* (1940), made in Britain, to the films of Annelie and Andrew Thorndike in East Germany such as *Du und mancher Kamerad* (1956), *The German Story* (1956), and *Operation Teutonic Sword* (1958), and from Ilya Kopalin's history of the Soviet Union *Unforgettable Years* (1957) or Joris Ivens's and Vladmir Pozner's *The Song of the Rivers* (1954) to Chris Marker's *Description d'un combat* (1960), a great many of the films Leyda singles out have become difficult if not impossible to locate.[23]

Jay Leyda clearly stands as one of the most important pioneers of film studies, and this slim volume remains an indispensable introduction to the use of found footage—the now vast expanse of not only an audiovisual archive but a digital one as well. Published before film studies became an entrenched discipline within the academy and in the shadow of the Cold War, which made books like this politically suspect for many who did not share Leyda's emphatically progressive views, *Films Beget Films*, like the novels of blacklisted screenwriters, failed to receive extensive review or a positive critical reception.[24] Leyda's exploration of this form was, itself, something of a "strange juxtaposition" to the tenor of a time when documentary stood as a beacon for a democratic way of life. Most other writers on documentary prized this medium for the representation of history and culture, which, even if critical of one or another component of the overall social system, had little use for defamiliarization, alienation effects, or intellectual montage. As times change, examining standard doxa about the past to revise its relation to an altered present proves indispensable. Not simply neglected but marginalized by the tenor of its barely post–Cold War times on initial publication, *Films Beget Films* is a powerful case in point.

11 *Restrepo*

A Case of Inadvertent Evidence

The war against terrorism, with its gospel of counterinsurgency as a military strategy and its contorted interpretation of war crimes and torture, makes a perfect stew of unrealistic goals, inadequate means, and misguided thinking. After the horrific attack of 9/11/2001 anything less than a rousing call to arms carried the air of compromise, weakness, and self-doubt, even if it truncated the importance of mourning as a necessary first step. Not to mention reflection. War—a knee-jerk response by leaders with a black-and-white, "either you're with us or against us" mentality—was politically efficacious and strategically disastrous. Well over a decade later, and near the conclusion of a second president's subscription to magical thinking, its folly—in massive cost, death and destruction, maimed and traumatized soldiers and civilians, diminished moral authority, forgotten domestic needs, and an invisible, amorphous enemy stronger and more diffusely spread around the globe than ever—demands address.

Sometimes evidence of misguided efforts, inappropriate means, and failure arrives directly before us as it does with the enormous cache of documents released by Edward Snowden or with almost any objective assessment of the state of affairs in Afghanistan and Iraq after more than a decade of U.S. intervention. And sometimes evidence arrives inadvertently, as a by-product of a different endeavor, a virtual slip of the tongue, which, as Freud made clear, is not always a simple slip at all.

A case in point is the documentary film *Restrepo* (Tim Hetherington and Sebastian Junger, 2010), identified as "nonpolitical" because, unlike *Why We Fight* (Eugene Jarecki, 2005), *Iraq for Sale* (Robert Greenwald, 2006), or *Taxi to the Dark Side* (Alex Gibney, 2007), it claims no political position, casts no moral judgment, and advocates no specific course of action. Depending on what we make of what we see, however, it provides compelling evidence of the sheer folly of it all. The facts of everyday life for a platoon of American soldiers as they battle the Taliban and try to win the hearts and minds of the local inhabitants become transformed into evidence of the most damaging kind.

The soldiers are part of a larger effort to secure Afghanistan's Korangal Valley, a Taliban stronghold, over a period of fifteen months. The soldiers demonstrate valor and courage; they express fear and ignorance; they are no match for the challenge they face, and at the end of the film the mission is abandoned. We follow these men in a largely observational mode, with no voice-over commentary and a smattering of interviews done after they have concluded their "tour." They go about their mission day by day, demonstrating, as they go, the impossibility of victory. In later 2010, when the military abandons the mission to occupy the Korangal Valley and defeat the Taliban, it provides no clear explanation and no visible recognition of the cost of this mission in American lives or disillusioned Afghani hearts and minds. This is what, to some degree, *Restrepo* provides instead.

Tactical reasons for the failure may apply, but deeper ones emerge as well. The group's leader, Captain Dan Kearney, clearly has a mind of his own; the problem is its vacuous grasp of where he is. He tells us, "When they told me I was going to the Korangal Valley I didn't read up anything on it. I wanted to go in there with an open mind." And a closed book. Even tourists know better. How can the American military engage individuals who have a culture and tradition going back centuries without attempting to gain even the slightest bit of local knowledge? Why was he not trained in confronting an enemy and in working with civilians who belong to a radically different culture? Is not reading up on a society with whom successful communication is crucial standard operating procedure for the military? Like the State Department, the Peace Corps devotes considerable resources to training its members in local customs, mores, history, and language, but such training, it seems, holds minimal value to the military. Translators and informants will do the job. Capt. Kearney's idea is to kill the bad guys, save the civilians, and protect his men, just like in the vintage Hollywood westerns, except these bad guys don't circle around covered wagons as obliging targets for the good guys to shoot down.

We never see a single enemy combatant, although they make their presence known with random attacks, sometimes intense, that arise and fade away inconclusively. We do see American soldiers, looking like invaders from Mars with their massive, intimidating combat gear stalking through the countryside and villages. It would be one thing to chat with a policeman on his beat, but to talk with a cop in full riot gear would only begin to suggest how alienating and intimidating soldiers, prepared more for combat than outreach, appear. The thunderous roar of helicopters ferrying men and supplies to and fro hardly inspires awe from a local population more concerned with herding their cattle and tending their crops. Drones are not apparent, but one can readily imagine how greatly they would add to a looming sense of fear among the local civilians. Meetings with townspeople take place in the course of danger-laden patrols from a relatively secure, and totally isolated, operating base, named Restrepo in honor of the first American soldier to be killed. The patrols venture to nearby villages, with the risk of ambush and the detonation of improvised explosive devices always present. Of course, the filmmakers, Tim Hetherington and Sebastian Junger, share the risks, and much of the power of the film comes from their immediate presence in the face of mortal danger. There is no overt editorial commentary, and the sense of what it feels like to fight to stay alive in enemy territory—and, for the villagers, to attempt to communicate with strangers who understand next to nothing of their culture—takes on a dense, palpable quality throughout the film.

To his credit Capt. Kearney conducts weekly shuras (meetings) with village elders, but he doesn't inspire much confidence. He talks of roads and security and yet can do nothing until he can defeat or drive away the insurgents. He and his men retreat to their outpost at night, leaving the villagers at the mercy of the omnipresent but invisible Taliban. The villagers are understandably hesitant to sign up to help when, apart from their fortifications, the Americans only control the countryside when they patrol it, and not always then since ambushes are frequent. Nor is there much reason to buy into one captain's plan when he will be gone in a year or, at most, two. As Capt. Kearney himself says in one meeting, "Everything that happened in the past, when Captain McKnight was here, we're kinda like wiping the slate clean." And soon another captain will wipe this slate clean, just as the overall American presence will eventually vanish, leaving little tangible change in its wake.

Restrepo doesn't make it clear, but the film may well be a depiction of tactics advocated by General Petraeus in his Field Manual on how to combat insurgencies.[1] Military minds prefer identifiable enemies, and powerful weapons to defeat them, the sort of thinking behind the Powell Doctrine of overwhelming force used in the first Gulf War, as an antidote to the gradual, and usually inadequate, escalation of force used in Vietnam. When the enemy is an invisible fraction of the local population, though, overwhelming force has nowhere to apply itself and simply provokes fear, resentment, and resistance. Petraeus, to his credit, realized this. Force becomes second-

ary to "the controlled application of national power in political, information, economic, social, military, and diplomatic fields and disciplines."[2]
Military force is clearly but one facet of what is, in essence, a political struggle for legitimacy in the eyes of the general population. Without a legitimate government characterized, for Petraeus, by fair elections, popular participation, low levels of corruption, and an effective social infrastructure,
success is unlikely. For this reason alone success against insurgencies in
both Iraq and Afghanistan is highly unlikely, and Petraeus himself, along
with anyone who read his manual, should have said so.

We see no evidence of any of the qualities that define legitimacy for
Petraeus, only the brute application of military power. These beleaguered
soldiers, who barely control the valley they are sent to occupy, spend much
of their time trying to befriend the local population. But misunderstand-
ings and conflicts constantly arise. A cow, for example, dies after being
caught in a razor-wire barricade the soldiers put up. Negotiations ensue, but
Capt. Kearny does not seem able to understand why the village elder won't
take food staples as compensation for the lost cow instead of cash (even
though briefcases full of cash to win over warlords, politicians, and religious
leaders seem to have been a common sight in Afghanistan). Kearny insists
he cannot replace the cow. The film captures the elders' looks of frustration,
disbelief, and powerlessness. They clearly have no recourse. No democratic
infrastructure within which to file a complaint or begin a lawsuit exists, and
no one seems interested in building one. The village elders are at the mercy
of a twenty-something army captain whose word is final. From this, rapport, respect, and democracy cannot grow.

But other problems run still deeper. The invaders from Mars syndrome
so obvious in all the footage of American soldiers on duty makes it clear
that the first priority is protecting members of the military from harm, not
the local population from insurgents. Civilians, therefore, often suffer considerable, apparently indiscriminate, harm. Yet General Petraeus had
stressed that protecting the local population deserves the higher priority.
Again, the vast discrepancy between what he calls for and what was done
looms. To protect the population and build the prerequisite infrastructure
of democratic institutions would require a massive occupying army and a
vast number of civilian advisers and experts. It would call for an effective,
indigenous police force instead of a military occupation as well, but the war
on terror never seems to get past the shoot-'em-up phase of military intervention.[3]

None of Petraeus's vision matches the reality, dictated, it seems, more by
short-term domestic politics than long-term foreign policy. Petraeus calls

for soldiers able to collect reliable information from local sources, empathetic to the needs of the civilian population, familiar with local customs, and able to use the local language and to liaise effectively with the numerous other nonmilitary agencies that have a stake in a successful outcome. None of these criteria are even remotely evident in *Restrepo*. It is hard to imagine them being fulfilled by young, not always well-educated, soldiers who are mainly eager to survive and get back home. Officers may be somewhat better trained, but as Captain Kearney makes clear, their training seems hugely disparate from the counterinsurgency tactics Petraeus hoped to implement.

In fact, General Petraeus's ideal soldier is more diplomat than combatant. Such a concept runs directly counter to the basic precepts of military training and deployment. Under the administration that chose to wage war on terror, diplomacy was anathema. Far better to journey to the "dark side," as former vice president Dick Cheney once said, than to mourn loss or help others go through the slow, difficult process of building a democracy from what amounts to feudalism. Negotiation and compromise with zealots, tyrants, and dictators, which was, until the recent rise of terrorism as a basic tactic, a common occurrence in Washington, became unthinkable in the war on terror. In this worldview, diplomacy, and the State Department that practices it, become subordinated to an increasingly powerful and unchallenged Department of Defense.

Petraeus definitely thought outside the box, and he devised a brilliant plan for counterinsurgency but stopped short of the most logical conclusion of his own work: that control of such a plan belonged in civilian, not military, hands. It was a plan no traditional military force could hope to implement.

What *Restrepo* inadvertently offers as evidence—it isn't the thematic or emotional point of the film but is there to be seen in any case—is that wars on poverty, drugs, crime, and terror all fail for the same reason. It's the wrong metaphor, and vividly so when it comes to terrorism. Programs and policies that give people real alternatives and genuine hope trump wars whose ruthless efforts to eliminate bad guys breeds the very conditions that bring forth more bad guys. It can be argued that the best recruiter for Al Qaeda is the U.S. military: Al Qaeda had no presence in Iraq before the second invasion to eliminate nonexistent weapons of mass destruction. Al Qaeda and other similar entities have lost many top leaders but have also spread globally, constantly drawing new, zealous recruits from those enraged at American acts of liberation that bring more destruction than democracy. And the Islamic State of Iraq and Syria, ISIS, has arisen from the ashes of American ineptitude, beginning with Ambassador Paul

Bremer's disastrous policies and continuing with President Obama's escalation of drone and special forces attacks in multiple countries that are not at war with us and that may have killed key insurgents but have also painted America as a terrorist nation with little regard for due process or civilian deaths. We no longer model how democracy works but how terrorism, conducted by a world power, operates.

As General Petraeus rightly notes, police actions tolerate zero collateral damage, whereas military operations almost always exact a serious toll on innocent civilians. In a war on terror anything goes. From these men in the Korangal Valley to their leaders in Washington there appears to be but dim awareness of the folly of dangerous, heroic efforts that become a deadly, indiscriminate force unto themselves, moving the vision of a flourishing democratic society closer and closer to a delusion than a reality.

12 The Symptomatic Biopic

Steve Jobs: The Man in the Machine

Alex Gibney's on a tear. He's one of the few documentary filmmakers who is releasing more films than most folks can keep up with, including *Client 9: The Rise and Fall of Eliot Spitzer* (2010); *We Steal Secrets: The Story of WikiLeaks* (2013), on Julian Assange; *The Armstrong Lie* (2013); *Mr. Dynamite: The Rise of James Brown* (2014); *Sinatra: All or Nothing at All* (2015); *Going Clear: Scientology and the Prison of Belief* (2015); and *Steve Jobs: The Man in the Machine* (2015). Gibney himself narrates *Steve Jobs* and seeks to answer a simple question: why was a man who was as much a terror as a genius, as much a heartless cad as a savior, as much a ruthless businessman as a tech guru mourned by millions who never met him?

The film follows what is a familiar Gibney tack, dating back to *Enron: The Smartest Guys in the Room* (2005): give successful men their due, but expose their feet of clay as well. Hubris radiates from their very being, or as Job's first long-term partner and mother of his first child, Lisa, notes, he was one of those rare individuals who achieves enlightenment through his ego rather than despite or beyond it. He never exhibited empathy toward others and even tried, in slanderous fashion, to deny the paternity of his first child, until DNA evidence made his lies impossible to sustain. (There is an echo here of Lance Armstrong's vehement denials of drug use until the test evidence became too overwhelming to deny, but it is just one of many lies Jobs spins in the course of the film.)

But all is forgiven, we want to say. After all, Steve Jobs single-handedly gave us the iPod, iPad, and, most radiantly of all, the iPhone! His product announcements were major media events, and he was, without doubt, The Man in the machine, expressing the wonder and awe we all feel at the magic that digital technology can work.

So, does this explain the vast wave of mourning?

Gibney doesn't answer the question so much as use it as a pretext to explore Jobs's contradictions, the thing he also does with Eliot Spitzer, Lance Armstrong, the Enron guys, scientology, and Julian Assange, among others. He is our best documentarian when it comes to setting black-and-white contradictions side by side so that icons and heroes remain so, but with a newfound sense of their flawed, sometimes fatally flawed, human nature. (I hope he considers making a film on Walt Disney, a man who was, like Jobs, driven, obsessive, vindictive, petty, and greedy but also a technological savant, genius storyteller, and charismatic to an extraordinary degree.)

And Jobs? Wasn't he the charismatic face of an entire industry? Other names, from Melissa Mayer to Bill Gates, make the news, but none have the charisma of Jobs, who was not only a highly savvy geek (and what he didn't know, Steve Wozniak, cofounder of Apple and early casualty of Jobs's callous ways, did); he was also a born salesman. He gave gadgets a human face. He made us not just want but need them.

This moves into terrain Gibney fails to explore: fetishism—commodity fetishism, to be exact. We overvalue an object because, as Marx explained, and as advertisers have exploited ever since, we fail to see the real human labor that went into it and behold it, instead, as a magical talisman of great power or beauty that arrives magically before us or in the hands of a god as a wondrous offering. The fetish stands apart and possesses an aura we come to worship and experience with awe. And when we want to associate this with a human face, there it is: not the buxom model standing next to the latest sports car but Steve Jobs, the man in the machine.

In that sense the mourning for Jobs was mourning for a dead god, a figure who did not so much produce the magic as stand as its iconic representative. That this face was Janus-like is not surprising. How can a commodity be both a thing of beauty and the result of mass pollution, grossly underpaid and overworked employees in foreign lands, suicides, and despair?—all of which the film details. How can a thing earn our deep admiration and also be the source of egregious profit ($300 per iPhone, e.g.!) that, following the logic of the market place, is not even taxed because it's tucked into overseas accounts? How can Jobs be a guru and a genius but also a man who lied, deceived, and intimidated to get his way?

Is he not an emblem for the contradictions of capitalism itself, a system that uses the fetish object as a distraction from the wreckage that lies behind the marketplace? And as the only such emblem in the entire IT sector, it is little wonder that his passing was profoundly mourned. We are left with the image of a dark, secretive industry of anonymous but revered drones that Jobs himself helped create in the famous Super Bowl ad—

a dark, totalitarian *1984* world. The totalitarian world that characterizes the ad stems from the gray-flannel ethos of IBM—unnamed but clearly implied. Our liberation arrives in the form of one cute little Apple product after another. But Jobs's Apple became, in fact, the IBM of today, and in doing so, it demonstrated, when we pull back the veil his company has done so much to maintain, the contradictions of a system he never attempted to alter (even closing down Apple's philanthropic ventures).

Jobs clearly expanded the reach and aura of a company on the verge of collapse; he seemed to have the power of a god to resurrect the close to moribund, even if his powers were little more than the bluster and charisma of the brilliant but diabolical egotist. In that sense Jobs was more machine than man, but that is the very thing fetishism urges us not to see.

PART IV

Ethics and Irony in Documentary

PART 4 ASKS WHAT COUNTS AS ethical forms of representation, how ironic or mock documentaries subvert these assumptions, and what is at stake in representing torture and murder from the point of view of perpetrators. Participants in fiction films normally enjoy the safeguards provided by contractual agreements, but in documentary films the ethical or unethical representation of social actors (real people) remains essentially in the hands of the filmmaker. Documentary filmmakers typically secure a "release" from all participants in their films. Such a document normally states that subjects relinquish any and all rights to how what is recorded of their lives gets used despite their being unpaid for their participation. Such a release resembles less a contract than a capitulation, with minimal compensation or no control left for the subject. Hence the question of ethics is both sidestepped—"They gave away all their rights; I'm free to do what feels right to me," says the filmmaker—and intensified—"It's my actual life you're representing, and I don't want to see it stereotyped, mocked or distorted," says the subject.

Such an arrangement may seem unfair, but it is the norm. It arises from the reasonable idea that, like historians and social scientists, filmmakers need to be free to make the work they envision, with due regard for ethical considerations, and not the one their subjects expect from them. Journalism and most documentaries would suffer significantly if it were otherwise, though some films, like *Two Laws* (Alessandro Cavadini and Carolyn Strachan, 1982) and most of the Challenge for Change series from the National Film Board of Canada, insist on a high degree of collaboration and consensus between filmmaker and subjects.[1] Unlike journalism, sociology, anthropology, and other disciplines, however, there is no code of conduct, no set of ethical standards that governs all documentary filmmaking, although such codes may exist within particular institutional frameworks such as broadcast outlets or funding agencies. Documentary filmmakers bear considerable responsibility for the ethical decisions that inform their final film.

The first essay in this section, "Documentary Ethics: Doing the Right Thing," proposes some basic principles about how filmmakers might interact with their subjects and audiences. The principles are not surprising ones. The true test is in the particulars, and every filmmaking effort and every viewing experience will bring a distinct set of circumstances to bear. Should a filmmaker help a subject who cannot pay his or her electric bill, or will this compromise the underlying professional relationship? Is it acceptable to add sound effects to intensify a dramatic scene, knowing that many viewers may mistakenly assume that the sounds were part and parcel of the actual event? Can archival footage from similar but different events be mixed and matched to represent one particular event? Questions such as these abound. This essay sets out a framework within which to consider them.

The second essay, "Irony, Paradox, and the Documentary: Double Meanings and Double Binds," takes the opposite tack. It examines what happens when filmmakers reject the principle of showing respect for their subjects and earning trust from their audience to subvert, or mock, these very principles. The term *mockumentary,* exemplified by films such as *This Is Spinal Tap* (Rob Reiner, 1984), *Forgotten Silver* (Costa Botes and Peter Jackson, 1995), or *David Holzman's Diary* (Jim McBride, 1967), attempts to identify this type of film. These films may at first appear to be typical documentaries, but eventually they confound or overturn our assumptions and expectations. Ironic and paradoxical documentaries turn their back on the usual principles of the form and its ethics. They explore what happens when these principles are violated, deliberately, and may well prompt us to examine our own assumptions and responses more closely when we realize that what we see isn't quite what it appears to be.

The short pieces that follow include a letter and a book review. The letter is to Errol Morris and is about his film *Standard Operating Procedure* (2008). Morris's film invites the guards found guilty of torture at Abu Ghraib to tell their side of the story. Not members of the CIA or other groups who conducted the actual interrogations, or torture sessions, these men and women were prison guards with no responsibility to extract information, but they wound up torturing prisoners anyway.

Unlike the vast majority of Morris's films, which clearly rank among the most important works of the last three decades, I found the film unbearable. Standard academic essay writing felt as if it would legitimize this film as a subject for investigation like any other, when my gut response was that the film went beyond the pale of the usual topics a studied, reasoned response would address. My letter tries to explain how these feelings arose and why I found the film fundamentally misguided. A postscript, added for this volume, explains why I praise Joshua Oppenheimer's film *The Act of Killing* (2012), which also deals with perpetrators, but condemn Morris's film here.

The basic question raised by *Standard Operating Procedure* is How can the actions of perpetrators be addressed in documentary? The vast majority of documentaries that deal with abuse, injustice, torture, exploitation, or genocide present the perspective of victims. They give voice to those rendered voiceless. Are there ethical ways to examine such situations from the point of view of perpetrators? Not all perpetrators are equal; some realize the grave injustice of what they've done and seek to make amends, sometimes by testifying to what they did in a film. Some perpetrators, as we see in *The Act of Killing,* have no remorse whatsoever, and their representation, and self-representation, jars us in unexpected, paradoxical, and revelatory ways. These issues have special significance in Israel and in its relations with its neighbors. This is the context for Raya Morag's *Waltzing with Bashir: Perpetrator Trauma and Cinema* (London: I.B. Tauris, 2013), a major work on documentaries that examine the subjectivity of perpetrators. A number of recent films explore this topic, from the work of Rithy Panh (*S21* [2003]; *The Missing Picture* [2013]; *Duch, Master of the Forgers of Hell* [2011]) to that of Joshua Oppenheimer (*The Act of Killing; The Look of Silence* [2014]), and in my review of Morag's book I explore how she lays out the key issues such work raises.

13 **Documentary Ethics**

Doing the Right Thing

Can we establish standards for an ethical documentary film practice? This is not a purely rhetorical question, as was indicated by the debate within the Academy of Motion Picture Arts and Sciences on whether *Mighty Times: The Children's March* (Robert Hudson and Bobby Houston, 2004) deserved its Oscar. The film merged reenactments and historical footage indistinguishably and used archival shots of violence in one time and place to represent violence in another. Some charge that these practices mislead the viewer and create a false impression of what actually occurred in a given time and place[1]. Did this film breach an ethical standard? What might such a standard be?

All ethical codes function within an institutional context, be it anthropology, law, medicine, or journalism. These professions, like television networks, have definite ethical codes—something documentary filmmakers as a whole have seldom explored, let alone adopted.[2] Anthropologists, doctors, and journalists are expected to comply with the standards of their own profession or face consequences for failing to do so. Their ethical codes serve at least two purposes: (1) to protect the vested interests of the professional group from outside intervention by providing a self-policing mechanism, and (2) to safeguard the well-being of those who come into contact with this professional group.

The Motion Picture Association of America's rating system (G to NC-17) used for feature films also serves these two functions, even though they do not amount to an ethical code. They fend off government and pressure group intervention. They assist moviegoers in gauging the content of given films. The even more informal and universal rating of XXX for adult movies that are not submitted for rating to the MPAA has a similar, sometimes tongue-in-cheek, role for works that contain sexually explicit material, more commonly called pornography, a category to which the rating calls immediate attention. This rating is less warning than promise: it may, indeed, warn some away, but its primary purpose is to promise others that a film so rated will most assuredly provide graphic adult content rather than spell out any form of ethical accountability or moral standard for this content.

Furthermore, films receive MPAA ratings after they are completed and submitted for review. In contrast, an ethics would guide the act of filmmaking itself in terms of the relationship of the filmmaker to his or her immediate subject and eventual audience. A rating system for documentaries seems implausible. What categories might be established? Who would administer them, with what authority, and with the threat of what consequences? Perhaps answers will emerge, but the question of what ethical standard should be applied to documentary possesses no immediate solution.

What obligation do filmmakers have not to actors—with whom they can establish a well-defined, contractual relationship—but to actual people whose lives spill beyond the frame and whose conduct before the camera may itself pose acute ethical, if not legal, issues? What obligation do filmmakers have to avoid distortion, misrepresentation, or coercion, be it overt or extremely subtle, even if such acts appear to serve a higher goal, such as "getting the story" or "exposing injustice"? What further obligation do they have to an audience that will come away with a fresh understanding of some aspect of the historical world based on the representations made by a film? The film may join important and timely issues. The filmmaker's moral or political perspective on those issues will be conveyed by expressive techniques that strive to move and perhaps persuade the viewer: what responsibility does the filmmaker have for ensuring that persuasive techniques do not mislead or distort established facts, manipulate chronology or causality, or disregard basic rules of evidence?

Documentary filmmaking is an art that involves other people directly. It is fashioned from the lives of others, sometimes in very raw, unmediated forms. Ethical guidelines would seem to be a necessary precondition to responsible forms of interaction and representation when the lives of others are the signifying substance of a film. Most film schools do not offer courses in ethics as such, although few documentary filmmakers can practice their craft for long without experiencing ethical quandaries in need of solution.

Documentary film is a rhetorical art. Like the orator of old, the documentarian's concern is to win an audience's assent, not serve as an "information transfer" device. The persuasive goal may be to see the world poetically, afresh, as films from *Rain* (Joris Ivens, 1931) to *Koyaanisqatsi* (Godfrey

Reggio, 1982) have done, or politically, as films from *In the Year of the Pig* (Emile de Antonio, 1969), on the left, to *2016: Obama's America* (Dinesh D'Souza, 2012), on the right, have done. But, as rhetoric, the stress is always on what's fitting or what works (what used to be called "decorum"—a tone, examples, and level of appeal that fit the occasion). One might think "anything goes," as long as it achieves the desired result, but as the word *decorum* suggests, not all tactics are aesthetically suitable or ethically acceptable.

Yet rhetoric is not an immoral art. Its reliance on expressive technique points to its primary reliance on commonly held assumptions and expectations, values and beliefs. Crucial though such things are, they are not established by logic or science alone, or else they would not be shared *beliefs*. Values and beliefs form the bedrock of a society, and in a complex, diverse society more than one set of assumptions and expectations, values and beliefs will exist. They will contend for dominance. Outside a theocracy, monarchy, or dictatorship, it cannot be otherwise. Rhetoric provides the means of contending effectively.

Documentary film is one form in which different values and beliefs contend. For some, an issue may loom as so vital that a "by any means necessary" ethic may appear justified, as when D'Souza dismisses the slaughter of Native Americans in the "winning of the west" by noting that many died of or would have died of disease anyway. A less extreme ethic might say, "a little bit of sleight of hand is worth risking for the potential impact it will have," a notion perhaps behind the editing decisions in *Mighty Times: The Children's March*. For others a standard of "fair play" and "historical accuracy" may be more fundamental than persuasion at the cost of factual accuracy or historical truth. Hence the difficulty of imposing a singular ethical standard. Such a standard or, better, guidelines, since a prescriptive set of rules is unrealistic, would need to apply equally well to a socialist, fundamentalist, or feminist perspective. The basic question is if any general ethical guidelines seem applicable. The rhetorical tradition and its understanding of ethics may begin to suggest an answer.

What guides an ethical rhetoric is that it provides the expressive tools for speaking from the heart as well as the mind. It serves its own purpose poorly if it lies, distorts established fact, misuses evidence, or trades in little more than half-truths. Deliberate deception does not come from the heart. (Self-deception is a different, more complex matter.) A rhetoric, for example, that flies in the face of proper reason or that uses false syllogisms— propaganda for various political positions or electoral candidates may come to mind—can be effective to a degree, but it also leaves itself open to refutation, rejection, and a loss of trust. It is too easily exposed as the deception that it is and loses its power to persuade. The combination of reenactments and archival footage, in which the one could not be distinguished from the other, in *Mighty Times: The Children's March* is an example: for some it seemed in keeping with the spirit of civil rights protest and violent confrontations with police to stretch historical accuracy to present a visceral embodiment of what this moment felt like; for others it discredited the film.

Reason is often insufficient to move us to adopt new values or alter our beliefs, but any effort to have us do so that flies in the face of reason returns us to a pre-Enlightenment, antiscientific worldview based on mystification or, in more modern terms, spectacle. Such a view may have appeal for some, and it can be persuasively championed—as fundamentalist religious groups and other zealots demonstrate. It can be championed with sincerity, with heartfelt belief. The presence of mystification can also serve as a litmus test to search for an ethics that insists on respect for established fact, accepted evidence, and the basics of reason—even as we recognize that facts, evidence, and reason prove an insufficient basis for our most fundamental values and belief.

What does this mean in practice? A code of documentary ethics needs to focus on protecting the well-being of two groups: (1) film subjects (whom I have also termed social actors since they act out social aspects of their lives before the camera but are usually not trained as actors) and (2) actual viewers or audience members. No legal contract beyond granting consent for the use of one's images pertains in the first case (via "release" forms), and no formal contract at all spells out rights and responsibilities in the second. In each case an ethical code needs to give primacy to respecting the subject or viewer as an autonomous human being whose relationship to the filmmaker is not governed by expedience, deception, or abuse.

But when we focus on the film subject, the link between ethics and power becomes an important point of entry. The successful careers of many documentary filmmakers have been built on the misfortune of others. Brian Winston has written indignantly and with some persuasiveness that there is a "tradition of the victim" in documentary, especially in journalistic reporting.[3] The relationship between filmmaker and subject can be similar to that between a benevolent, or perhaps not so benevolent, dictator and his subjects. What limits should be voluntarily adopted to safeguard the dignity and rights of the subject as a human and as more than a victim?

When we focus on the viewer, the link between ethics and representation takes on comparable importance. To what extent are filmmakers responsible for the truthfulness of what they say? As Jon Else, coproducer of the series *Eyes on the Prize* from 1987 to 1990, indicated to me in an email, viewers will believe certain things to be true of documentaries, and the filmmaker needs to shoulder responsibility for upholding those beliefs or for subverting them in a productive way. To what extent and in what contexts is misrepresentation or deception justifiable?

These questions boil down to issues of trust, a quality that cannot be legislated, proposed, or promised in the abstract so much as demonstrated, earned, and granted in negotiated, contingent, concrete relationships in the here and how. Any ethical code would attempt to support and maintain trust. It reaches beyond what a contractual agreement might stipulate, a Production Code require, or a ratings system evaluate. Basically, how will filmmakers acquit themselves in face-to-face encounters with subjects and in mediated form with viewers to earn their trust?

In sum, an ethical code of documentary filmmaking practice allows us to address the imbalance of power that often arises between filmmakers and both their subjects and audiences. It affirms, among other things, the principle of informed consent for subjects that respects their dignity and earns trust from the viewer, inflected to acknowledge that documentary filmmaking is more of an artistic practice than a scientific experiment.

In a nutshell, a guiding statement might propose, "Do nothing that would violate the humanity of your subject and nothing that would compromise the trust of your audience."

Such a statement is blatantly vague, or fuzzy. What compromises trust? What violates another person's humanity? The vagueness is not accidental. It is of a similar order to any definition of documentary itself. It speaks to the situated, that is, not absolute or timeless, historical context in which ethics are put to the test. Grierson's famous definition of documentary as "the creative treatment of actuality" certainly leaves lots of room for ambiguity, and another, 1948 definition does no better: "All methods of recording on celluloid any aspect of reality interpreted either by factual shooting or by sincere and justifiable reconstruction, so as to appeal either to reason or emotion, for the purpose of stimulating the desire for, and the widening of, human knowledge and understanding, and of truthfully posing problems and their solution."[4]

These definitions are not flawed because of ambiguous terms like *creative, sincere, justifiable,* or *truthfully.* What is forgotten, sometimes by Grierson himself and others since him, is that there is indeed more than one form for creativity to adopt, more than one justification available for a given choice, and more than one truth to argue. Documentary conventions, and the standards to which they refer, change. With these changes judgments about what compromises trust or violates another's humanity will change as well. What is fitting (decorous) in one context may not be fitting in another. We will not see a Ten Commandments or Dogme 95–like set of Vows of Chastity for documentary film, except, perhaps, from political pressure groups (or as another Lars von Trier joke). That said, it is still possible to sketch out some of the ethical issues that arise with contemporary documentary practice in further detail.

FILMMAKERS AND THEIR SUBJECTS

The difference in the power of filmmakers and their subjects can often be best measured by their relative access to the means of representation. Do subjects have the means to represent themselves; do they have alternative access to the media apart from that provided by a given filmmaker? To the extent the answer is "No," the filmmaker's ethical obligation to avoid misrepresentation, exploitation, and abuse rises correspondingly. Subjects who are dependent on the filmmaker to have their story told—subjects, that is, who generally occupy the lower social strata and who can most readily be cast into the position of victim—are most vulnerable to abuse.

As an article in *International Documentary* demonstrated, many filmmakers are highly sensitive to the ethical dilemmas of representing others who may not be able to represent themselves.[5] They have lent material assistance to subjects when failing to do so could have had dire consequences. Renee Tajima-Peña, for example, filmed a family's immigration efforts for the PBS series *The New Americans*. She, however, chose not simply to observe the Flores family's desperate race to get to a government office in time to claim the visa papers that would reunite the family after some thirteen years. She knew that the public transit they planned to take could not possibly get them there in time. Instead of watching a tragedy unfold, she chose to intervene and drive the family to the office herself so that they could claim the papers. Her act altered the story's outcome, but her sense of ethical duty overrode the desire to tell a story as if she were not actually there as a responsive and responsible social actor, or person, herself.

Another positive example of ethical encounter occurs in *Born into Brothels: Calcutta's Red Light Kids* (Zana Briski, Ross Kaufman, Geralyn White Dreyfous, and Pamela Boll, 2004). The film is a brilliant demonstration of how the ethical responsibility of the filmmaker can become the subject of the film itself. Fittingly, by helping the children of sex workers learn photography, which is subsequently used as a means of self-representation, Zana Briski addresses the balance of power between filmmaker and subject. The refusal to maintain a detached perspective regarding children

whose future will be severely limited without her intervention clearly conflicts with a journalistic ethic of objective reporting, but this is why documentary filmmaking is more an art than a news report. A crucial part of the
story, in this case, is how the filmmaker acquits herself in the presence of
others, something we can see and judge ourselves. A similar and even more
controversial form of intervention occurs in Joshua Oppenheimer's *The Act
of Killing* (2012). Oppenheimer grants carte blanche to thugs, who killed
alleged communists and others at the behest of the Indonesian government,
to reenact their crimes and to visualize their own fantasies of themselves as
deities and saviors. Was this giving a voice to the incarnation of evil, or was
it letting murderers hang themselves, figuratively, with their own distorted
worldview?[6] Was it justifiable in either case? I discuss the film in greater
detail in the next chapter.

When power flows the other way, when subjects are *not* dependent on
the filmmaker to have their story told, the ethic of responsible encounter
gives "getting the story" a higher priority. Public figures often have an
"image" to maintain that the filmmaker may not feel obligated to respect
or perpetuate. Deception may be necessary with those who feel little sense
of dependency and may have values and beliefs (often involving their own
use of power) they prefer to minimize or whose representation they wish
to carefully mold. News coverage of government press releases and "official
statements" would be one example where American journalism has consistently failed to challenge the power of subjects who wish others to
believe that all they say is the whole truth and nothing but the truth.

Enron: The Smartest Guys in the Room (Alex Gibney, 2005) is a virtual
catalogue of the ways in which the powerful, represented by the chief executives at Enron, set out to use the media to practice systematic fraud and
enrich themselves at the expense of others. Even after Enron's fall and the
arrest of its chief executives, these individuals continue to tell a story about
Enron's success that denies any wrongdoing on their part. Like the killers
in *The Act of Killing* they see themselves as saviors, financial geniuses in
this case, whom the media have turned into culprits and scapegoats. Gibney
engages in a struggle for control of the means of representation with a
once-powerful corporation and its former leaders by juxtaposing their public statements with highly incriminating behind-the-scenes interviews,
recordings made in unguarded moments, and interviews with journalists
skeptical of Enron's apparent success.

Distortions and misrepresentations remain a potential issue when the
film's subjects object to their media representation and apply pressure to get
their way, but the resolve to tell a story other than the one preferred by the

film's subjects calls for intervention less on behalf of the unrepresented than on behalf of a deliberately disguised truth. *Enron: The Smartest Guys in the Room* does not present the prosecution's case against Enron so much as it provides the perspective and background necessary to understand this case in light of the vehement denials by Enron executives of criminal wrongdoing.

FILMMAKERS AND THEIR AUDIENCE

An ethical documentary practice honors reason as fully as possible by using accurate claims, proper syllogisms, and historical facts while knowing its goals exceed the bounds of logic. Documentary film seeks to evoke feelings, alter or strengthen commitments, and propose actions that are propelled by shared beliefs. These beliefs derive from what is sometimes called the heart and sometimes ideology, but they exert a guiding power that reason alone can seldom replace.

How then might filmmakers address the vexing issue of deceptive practices, practices that run from rhetorical suasion to misrepresentation and lies—the systematic effort to mislead, cover up, or deceive? Misrepresentation may involve appearing to present authentic historical footage that is actually reenacted or taken from a time and place other than the one ostensibly depicted. The responsible use of archival footage is a clearly fraught area of debate, and no single standard prevails in current practice. Like reenactments it is an area where consensus about what works, what audiences will accept or trust, remains open to debate and the influence of new approaches. Errol Morris's famous flying milk shake did just this when he staged reenactments of different people's accounts of what really happened in relation to the murder conviction of an innocent man in *The Thin Blue Line* (1987). No one refers to this milk shake's flight through the air at the crime scene as a significant or even real event; hence, no one gave such an occurrence any evidential weight. Morris never determines "the truth" regarding the milk shake nor, for the bulk of the film, the truth of who really killed the police officer, but he does make clear that each witness or participant has a different story and that not all of these stories can be true. The flying milk shake becomes a signifier of subjectivity in the domain of memory.

Misrepresentation may also involve appearing to "get the story" of a historical event that took place independent of the filmmaker when that event was actually orchestrated for the purpose of being filmed. This was the case with *Triumph of the Will* (Leni Riefenstahl, 1935). Reshooting various scenes and combining shots from different times and places to give the illusion of one continuous arrival scene for Hitler complied with what were contemporary standards for documentary representation, whereas the orchestration of the entire Nuremberg rally itself for the purpose of presenting it as a cinematic spectacle did not. The viewer is led to believe the documentary representation of a historical event is authentic by means that are themselves deceptive.

Misrepresentation can also take the form of deceiving subjects into thinking they are participating in one type of activity when, in fact, they are participating in another. In this case the audience is let in on the secret but may also be left in a highly uncomfortable position. The long-running TV show *Candid Camera* avoided discomfort by trading in practical jokes played on unwitting but good-sport subjects, whereas *Obedience* (Stanley Milgram, 1965) recruited unwitting volunteers for a "scientific" experiment in which they think they are testing another person's learning skills by administering increasingly severe electrical shocks. In fact, they are themselves being tested for their willingness to obey commands to continue administering these shocks even when the "learner" appears to suffer pain and perhaps even death. Even when the tester hears howls of pain, the actor playing the researcher tells him, "The experiment requires that you continue." The faux researcher concludes the test when the tester refuses to go on or the shocks reach their maximum (apparently lethal) level.

The tester is then debriefed and learns the truth about what happened (no shocks actually reached the supposed learners). This setup, which yielded compelling evidence of the willingness of ordinary citizens to obey authority regardless of the consequences, is clearly unethical by contemporary standards. Subjects who were asked to administer the shocks had no opportunity to grant informed consent. They must now live with a potentially traumatic, patently manipulative experience and with a public record—the film—of their actions, for better or worse. Viewers may appreciate the new knowledge about conformity and a willingness to obey authority that they gain but may also feel deeply distressed at the plight of subjects who display clear signs of stress and anxiety, even when they do not comply with the dangerous commands. Both the film's subjects and its viewers may question whether an imbalance in power has been exploited in unethical ways. (Milgram himself hadn't expected the degree of compliance with commands that subjects demonstrated and had his own regrets about the experiment, despite its revelatory nature.)

CONCLUSION

A documentary ethics would seem to approach a foundational level when it addresses the need to respect the dignity and earn the trust of subjects and viewers alike, as well as acknowledge that a struggle for power and the right to represent a distinct perspective are at issue. This foundation does not produce "Do this, Do that" dogma but instead acknowledges that questions of ethics remain situated in an evolving historical context. What is to be done is a question to answer in the particular moment, using basic guidelines rather than rules. These guidelines will vary in relation to individual motives, institutional goals, and historical contexts.

An open-ended or situated ethical standard, one rooted in the concrete contingencies of time and place, like an open-ended documentary definition, places the onus for determining the ethics of a given film onto the community that constitutes the actual domain of documentary film practice. This community includes filmmakers, subjects, distributors, exhibitors, critics, scholars, and audiences, all of whom share a vested interest in the form and future of documentary. It is this community that bears responsibility for what is shown and how it is received. It is within this context more than within a specific institutional frame such as the studio system, network television, or the Motion Picture Academy of Arts and Sciences, which have more institutionally specific interests, that documentary film has nurtured its deepest awareness of ethical standards. It will be to a constantly evolving sense of "community standards" that filmmakers, subjects, and audiences alike will turn to give more pointed inflection to the ethical guidelines suggested here.

14 Irony, Paradox, and the Documentary

Double Meanings and Double Binds

> Don't our looks perpetually bounce off the others, as in the hasty encounter of the night, and leave us behind with nothing but conjectures, slivers of thought and fictional qualities? Isn't it true that it's not people who meet, but rather the shadows cast by their imagination?
>
> **Pascal Mercier,** *Night Train to Lisbon*

> All actual life is encounter.
>
> **Martin Buber,** *I and Thou*

Documentaries make us wonder about their meaning in numerous ways. Some films perplex: What kind of message is this? we may ask. The answer is not always clear.

- We may ask, Does this film have its facts straight? External information may convince us that a film is wrong, perhaps even riddled with errors.

- Alternatively, we may wonder, Is this film lying? We may sense the film is deliberately presenting falsehoods. In 1960, for example, the House Un-American Activities Committee produced *Operation Abolition* (HUAC,[1] 1960), a film that reversed chronology and distorted facts to make student protesters at a HUAC hearing that year at San Francisco's city hall appear to be communist agents or dupes who instigated violence. A subsequent film, produced by the regional ACLU chapter, *Operation Correction* (Northern California ACLU, 1961) demonstrated the factual distortions on a point-by-point basis, showing that the police instigated the violence against peaceful protesters.[2] Similarly, Michael Moore's *Roger & Me* (1989) reversed chronological relationships to make it appear that the decline of Flint, Michigan, was due to the closure of a General Motors factory, when the decline, in fact, had begun years earlier.[3]

- Does this film frame or label itself as something other than what it is? *Triumph of the Will* (Leni Riefenstahl, 1935) presents itself as an observational record of the 1934 Nazi propaganda rally in Nuremberg despite the fact that Riefenstahl was heavily involved in planning and orchestrating the events that she subsequently filmed. No winks or cues suggested that the filmmaker had an ironic rather than a deceptive intent. Deception is a cosmetic operation, as the Greek word, *kosmētikos*, originally indicated: adornment or allure designed to create a false impression. It is but a small step from cosmetics to spectacle and fetishism.

- Does this film mock or play with familiar conventions to amuse, disturb, or provoke us by mocking them? Films from *David Holzman's Diary* (Jim McBride, 1967) to *This Is Spinal Tap* (Rob Reiner, 1984) deploy generic conventions subversively to make us more aware of how we rely on such conventions to know what kind of film a given film is. Such films wink in various ways to cue us to their play with form. Sometimes called mockumentaries, they are, more fundamentally, ironic.

- Does this film ask us to believe two or more messages that invite contradictory responses? Films such as *Land without Bread* (Luis Buñuel, 1933), *F for Fake* (Orson Welles, 1973), and *The Act of Killing* (Joshua Oppenheimer, 2012) generate double binds that confound us. They call into question our relation to what we take to be reality and the conventions governing its representation. Such films may make us feel we are losing our footing and becoming unable to tell what kind of message a message is. Our perturbing encounter with a double bind upsets any clear sense of a stable self capable of comprehending a knowable world and acting in it judiciously. Such films call into question the very foundation stones of interpersonal encounter and whether our experience of the world can be truly understood as coherent. They befuddle us with paradox, itself a form of irony.

We can apply labels to each case. A film can be wrong, lying, deceptive, mocking (of conventions), or befuddling (to us). The first three labels lay the matter to rest. We know what errors, lies, and deceptions are. The last two belong to the realm of irony and set off reverberations that linger. We struggle to understand what kind of message a message is if it undercuts the conventions it appears to invoke or if it proposes contradictory messages. We do not readily comprehend what an ironic message, which signals it isn't what it seems, actually is. This essay focuses on these latter two categories and the issues they raise.

This is the land of irony and existential paradox or double binds. These concepts pose considerable problems for the documentary tradition and its frequent association with what I have elsewhere termed the "discourses of sobriety" such as legal, philosophic, economic, sociological, historical, anthropological, journalistic, political, and social justice discourse. Irony, paradox, and the twists of logic that they introduce have yet to be applied to the study of documentary film in any extended way. Instead, labels of reflexivity, for films that metacommunicate about the conventions of the form, and mockumentary, for films that mock or subvert these same conventions, amount to limited forays into this domain.[4] Films like *Of Great Events and Ordinary People* (Raul Ruiz, 1979) and *Reassemblage* (Trinh T. Minh-ha, 1983) represent a reflexive approach. These films reflect on their own structure and the assumptions behind other films or social processes similar to the ones they examine. They seldom negate what they say so much as metacommunicate about it, raising questions about assumptions that usually go unchallenged. Films like *No Lies* (Mitchell Block, 1973) and *Man Bites Dog* (Rémy Belvaux, André Bonzel, and Benôit Poelvoorde) represent a mockumentary approach as they adopt documentary conventions only to reveal that they do so jokingly, in the spirit of black comedy, constructing a fictive world that appears to be a representation of the historical world. Such works are seldom metacommunicative, but neither do they cover the full range of ironic possibilities. The confounding qualities of irony and paradox suggest a broader horizon for how documentary form can produce effects of an ironic, befuddling, sometimes humorous, but often unnerving and deeply destabilizing kind.[5]

Faking It and *F Is for Phony*, two important books on mockumentary, assert that such films rely on a fictional base to simulate the effects of documentary. Although fictive techniques might well play a role in mockumentary, these accounts posit a too-clear-cut demarcation. The ironic text thwarts black-and-white distinctions. Irony is not simply a category that simulates, mocks, or fakes another, distinctly different category but an activity that conveys an ostensible message only to negate this very message. The effect is internal to the structure of the message itself, not external, not a play of a work of fiction with works of nonfiction. Irony and paradox typically arise from the statement of one thing literally and the negation of that same statement figuratively. "You look great," said in an ironic tone of voice—where tone, like style, or, more broadly, like the analogical component of a statement or work, plays the figurative role—

negates the praise ostensibly conveyed by the literal statement, carried by the digital component (words). Ironic works may well mock or subvert other formal or social conventions, as satire routinely does, but that is secondary to its internal structure. Asserting one thing only to negate it at the same time expresses doubt about the adequacy of any form of representation to its task of addressing the world cogently and unambiguously. Ambiguity is irony's middle name.

Either/or distinctions miss irony's both/and quality: the ironic film both means and does not mean what it appears to mean literally. It negates an ostensible meaning without eliminating it—unlike the wave of a clarifying wand that would decisively banish an apparent documentary to the realm of fiction or expose the wrong, lying, or deceptive one for what it is. It therefore becomes possible to oscillate between two or more meanings even after the irony becomes apparent. Irony possesses what Linda Hutcheon calls an "edge" that a film that directly asserted what it, in fact, asserts ironically would not.[6] Stated ironically, "I trust you completely as a man of your word" has a very different effect from "I never know if I can honestly trust you." Being placed into a state of confusion as to how to understand a message or to grasp what kind of message a message is can have a variety of effects, salutary or distressing, that direct, constative assertions, or messages that appear to be one thing only to be subsequently identified as, in fact, another (errors, lies, deceptions, and so forth), lack.

Irony and double binds are not abstract puzzles but existential challenges. They affect recipients. Like promises, they possess a performative dimension.[7] They establish a bond between author and reader, speaker and auditor, or film and viewer, which extends beyond discourse to the lives that stand behind statements and texts even as they undermine that very bond. Additionally, undetected, irony may be mistaken for what it only appears to be saying—for its literal, denotative content—and may, therefore, produce, in retrospect, when its status is finally determined, impressions not simply of semiotic complication but of existential betrayal. To discover that someone is lying may well provoke anger at the speaker, but to discover that someone is being ironic may provoke frustration, if not anger, at the form and not simply the content of the message as well. Irony betrays the promise that language, visual or written, will speak cogently and unambiguously. It abandons us on unstable ground. But recognized for what it is, irony incorporates the recipient into its fold as a fellow participant in a play with form. It constitutes a community of fellow ironists. We have to be one to know one. Irony exposes a commonly suppressed level of doubt about the capacity of our statements to represent the world adequately.

Take Luis Buñuel's classic, and bitingly ironic, "documentary" *Land without Bread*. Already, there's the title: bread exists in this land; it's just not eaten, at least by the adults who don't know (we're told) what it is! Ostensibly a condescending, judgmental description of a remote, primitive region of Spain, Las Hurdes, the film piles winks upon winks to signal that Buñuel's target is not this allegedly backward region but the blatantly ethnocentric attitudes adopted toward such regions by their colonizers, both secular and clerical.[8] Callous references range from alluding to "barbaric customs" to discovering a "choir of idiots," and from gun smoke that pops into the frame as a goat "accidentally" falls from a cliff side, as the narrator tells us that such "accidents" are the only time the Hurdanos get to eat goat meat, to the sharply incongruous music (Brahms's Symphony no. 4) that does more to destroy any claims of authenticity than to buttress them; with all these myriad winks the film declares itself a highly unreliable and ironic work.

Unlike other films that appear to be participatory documentaries where events unfold spontaneously in front of the camera, such as *David Holzman's Diary* or *No Lies*, *Land without Bread* does not admit to any ironic play in its final credits. It simply ends. And unlike Soviet, British, and, by the later 1930s, American films that trumpet the power of government to right all social ills, Buñuel simply leaves the Hurdanos to their devices, most of which involve maddening double binds: they gather berries before they're ripe to eat them before birds do and get dysentery as a result; children bring home bread from school but then see parents destroy it because they don't know what it is (this is a land *with* bread but without the sense to consume it, it seems); inhabitants get nonfatal snakebites but then scratch and infect them so that they become lethal; they send children to Catholic schools but then see them acquire knowledge that is utterly useless; and so on. Our narrator matter-of-factly recounts these sorry predicaments and then leaves the viewer to decide whether to believe what has been said, judge the judgmental filmmaker as grossly insensitive, or consider that Buñuel's intent is to destabilize assumptions that underpin the standard travelogue and other films about struggles to survive in harsh environments such as Robert Flaherty's much praised *Nanook of the North* (1922). The Hurdanos, as Buñuel's profoundly unreliable narrator describes them, are barely better than mere savages, bereft of any cultural distinction, and incapable of taming a nature that destroys them. But given the number of winks packed into the film, it is hard not to imagine that this is a satirical attack on the literal, sober-minded, and patronizing tone of films that insist that others are somehow wholly other than our kind. As with other ironic texts, it calls into question the adequacy of our assumptions and the capacity of our communication to give coherent shape to the world around us.

Another film, No Lies, with its own form of savagery embodied in the filmmaker, gives irony's doubt about the adequacy of our representations an ethical basis, removing some of the sting that irony may produce. Structured as a raw, unscripted encounter between a male filmmaker, trying out his lightweight filmmaking equipment, and a female friend, their banter takes a sharper turn when the filmmaker begins to harass and hound his female "friend" about a recent rape.

If we miss the winks, or cues, scattered over the course of the fifteen-minute film that suggest it isn't what it appears to be,[9] feelings of betrayal may arise when we discover, in the final credits, that the film is indeed a structured, scripted fiction, with actors playing the roles of filmmaker and friend.[10] But betrayal may give way to relief when we also realize that a real woman, a social actor, has not been harassed and shamed by a callous, chauvinistic male "friend," that the real-life consequences of such brutal conduct have been given representational form but not embodied in the actual lived relation between two people going about their lives in the presence of a camera. The film intensifies what is at stake by adopting the literal form of a documentary while negating that form with multiple winks and final credits that make its ironic posture clear. A literal replication of sexist behavior shifts to a figurative, metaphorical one: this is what blaming the victim *looks and feels like* but not what it actually *is*. Just as jokes can be a more socially acceptable way of expressing hostile feelings, so irony can be a more socially acceptable, and ethical, way of expressing hurtful actions. This hints at the value it possesses even as it undermines the certainties of human communication.

Much is at stake in the moment of encounter in documentary film as in life. Knowing what kind of encounter an encounter is is vital to a sense of personal connection and social belonging. We may wish to frame face-to-face encounters within the ideal frame of Buber's I-Thou relationship as transparent, harmonious, and spiritual, where we experience self and other as of one flesh. We frequently discover, however, a more layered, densely reticulated reality of professed intentions and unconscious motivations, verbal statements and physical gestures, analog meanings and digital signification that conflict with or even contradict one another.

Doubt, puzzlement, and anxiety function as the inevitable prelude to the discovery of a suitable, though seldom fully adequate, frame in the face of irony. We confront a triangulated mix of a material work with its formal autonomy, an authorial agent with conscious and unconscious intentionalities, and receivers—with different experiences, capacities, and desires. The act of making meaning from art, as from lived encounter, involves what Clifford Geertz describes as "thick description."[11] Understanding must take account of different social and cultural contexts, varying degrees of shared values, the tactical use of prevailing conventions, and an awareness of efforts to clarify, deceive, pretend, or play as part and parcel of what *verstehen* in its fullest sense means.

When a film or message winks to undercut the very thing it's saying, or the implied frame for what it's saying, excess arises. Closure of the sort provided by our cognitive schemata falters.[12] Even though we may finally assign a film to the category of irony, the most potent effect occurs in that fleeting half-life of befuddled apprehension as we attempt to decide what kind of message we are, in fact, dealing with. Ironic and paradoxical films confound. Doubt discombobulates. Can we, let alone the films or other texts we encounter, capture the truth of things when the frames that contain "truth" loom as unreliable, manipulable forms of punctuation rather than guarantors of certainty?

Questions of interpretation are familiar enough in anthropology and literary criticism, but they also arise in systems theory. Explorations of irony and paradox in this realm stress the potent ways in which an affective, performative dimension comes to the fore. A classic description of animal play as ironic communication belongs to Gregory Bateson. The nips and growls, circlings and feigned attacks of animals at play all indicate, without overtly saying so—by analog, nonverbal, intonational, gestural, stylistic, or figurative means—that "These actions in which we now engage do not denote what those actions *for which they stand* would denote."[13]

Rather than using "not" directly, the playful dog's actions say something different from what they indirectly reference. The actions contain a wink. Like the parody of a wink, the act of nullification intrinsic to irony goes unspoken and is felt all the more. In fact, it is felt because it is unspoken: irony refuses to identify itself by identifying what it is not: instead of "This is not fighting," we simply have, literally unstated, "This is play." Recognizing and agreeing on the difference between fighting and playing is a vital act of comprehension that completely alters the animals' relation to one another. Play says, "We are going through the motions of fighting without actually fighting; instead we're playing." Play, like irony, is a form of figurative communication.

The "wink" introduces a new level of meaning distinct from the underlying level it negates. Winks—any cue telling us to take a message or film ironically—stand in contrast to the majority of signifiers that provide more of the same: other signifiers differ from one another but do not constitute a distinct level of signification. The wink introduces doubt. As Hayden White puts it, "The rhetorical figure of *aporia* (literally 'doubt'), in which the author signals in advance a real or feigned disbelief in the truth of his own statements, could be considered the favored stylistic device of Ironic language."[14] (And, as we will see, "disavowal," instead of doubt, an unconscious negation of what is otherwise expressed, comes into play for messages that constitute a double bind.)

A classic of ironic filmmaking is *David Holzman's Diary*. Like *No Lies* and *Avos* (Michael Wahrman, 2011)—a short Brazilian film that documents breakfast among a boy and his grandparents in which the grandfather reveals both his antisemitism and his status as a Holocaust survivor, only to reveal, in the credits, that it is a work of fiction—*David Holzman's Diary* withholds its decisive wink until the final credits, when we learn that the documentary-like diary that the eponymous hero creates with his Éclair camera and Nagra tape recorder is, in fact, scripted and acted. It functions as a clear rejoinder to claims of heightened authenticity made by champions of the observational and participatory modes that had burst onto the scene only a few years earlier. Unlike *No Lies*, and like *Avos*, *David Holzman's Diary* contains few if any cues to its ironic status prior to the final credits. And unlike most documentaries driven by a rhetorical or narrative aim, *David Holzman's Diary* holds out no clear trajectory from a beginning problem to a concluding resolution, or, inasmuch as it does (the film ends with a title announcing that David's camera has been stolen), does so with an ironic wink at the potentially interminable structure of a diary, a form destined to persist until or unless its very terms of existence—David as a man with a movie camera—become nullified by forces at work within the lived world inhabited by the character—the theft of his camera.

But just as it locates a pretext within the world of David's everyday life to come to a close as a film, it simultaneously nullifies its status as an authentic documentary. The end credits identify "David Holzman" as a character played by L.M. Kit Carson and the director of the film not as David Holzman but Jim McBride. Our embrace of the affective codes of human encounter and David's quest for an I-Thou relation to those close to him—from his obsession with the truth of the cinematic image in his direct-to-camera soliloquies and from his desire to capture his girlfriend Penny's beauty to his clearly uncomfortable turn as the object of a transsexual neighbor's erotic desire, spills into a confounding abyss. The film demands a process of *Nachträglichkeit* as we reexamine and reinterpret all that we have seen.[15] It may prompt feelings of betrayal if we feel less welcomed into the community of ironists at the film's conclusion than excluded from it for so much of the film's duration.

Feelings of betrayal relate to another distinct quality of the ironic and paradoxical text. Signifiers that do not signify what the signifiers for which they stand would signify invoke but do not present the signifiers for which they stand. As Bateson puts it: "Not only does the playful nip not denote what would be denoted by the bite for which it stands but, in addition, the bite itself is fictional. . . . At the human level, this leads to a vast variety of complications and inversions in the fields of play, fantasy, and art."[16] The absent signifiers—text or actions to which the text alludes—are fantasmatic. Although such signifiers may be present syntactically—David's confessions directly to the camera in *David Holzman's Diary*, for example, have all the earmarks of confessions, albeit scripted ones—they are radically altered semantically and pragmatically by the work of irony or paradox. They are *not* what *would have been* signified were it not for the ironic or paradoxical gesture—David's confessions are not those of an actual person named David Holzman but of an invented character. A "real" documentary or literally true message gets invoked but negated ("real" in quotation marks because it is, in fact, fantasmatic).

Our sense of what the "real" documentary hiding behind the ironic documentary is becomes a specter haunting the text. It enjoys a psychic reality that depends on what the spectator imagines, or fantasizes, it to be, a reality partly based on previous experience and partly invoked by the specific strategies of the film.

A desire for this familiar, idealized, and often comforting form clashes with its actual negation. In *Land without Bread, F for Fake,* and *The Act of Killing,* the imagined but negated "real" documentary would convey the moral probity, or sobriety, the clear sense of right or wrong, true or false, real or imaginary that characterizes the prototypical documentary and, in fact, the discourses of sobriety in general, and yet is utterly lacking from these films—much to the consternation of those who long for this unambiguous, but absent, alternative.

As an imaginary totality—rich in ideological implications about epistephilia, the production of knowledge, truth, falsity, and the subject-who-knows—the fantasmatic but ostensibly "real" documentary replaces a diverse and ill-defined set of real texts that constitute the actual history and tradition of documentary filmmaking.[17] This fantasmatic totality or phantom text—for which the present text stands—*would* denote, we want to believe, what the ironic or paradoxical documentary calls into question. We may know very well that there is no such actual documentary behind *Land without Bread* or *Forgotten Silver* (Costa Botes and Peter Jackson, 1995), which "discovers" a remarkable film pioneer in New Zealand who, though forgotten, foreshadowed many of the innovations later attributed to others, we may nonetheless hold to this longing for a true documentary all the same. It is a form of fetishism.[18]

I have begun to discuss paradoxical documentaries as part of the equation, but before going much further, it may be useful to contrast ironic and paradoxical films in summary-like fashion.

Both forms are embodied, temporal, and performative: "Trust me; I'm telling the truth."[19] They establish an affective relationship between message and recipient unlike statements that are disembodied, timeless, and constative: "The sun rises in the morning," for example. They do not merely report on the world but engage us while simultaneously undermining the terms of engagement we think we have or wish to have. Irony says one thing and means another: "That color really becomes you." Paradox conveys mutually contradictory imperatives: "Do not read this sentence," for example.

Irony embeds various forms of wink that let us in on the irony if we "get it." These winks or cues advise us that signifiers do not mean that for which they stand would mean. They serve as a distinct framing device of a higher logical type than that of the ostensible message.[20] Our sense of balance is upset but ultimately restored if we get the irony.

Paradox lacks a wink, making it impossible to "get it" within a coherent frame. Instead, it "gets" us. The author or filmmaker signals a disavowal of the literal meaning rather than a real or feigned disbelief in its truth. We become trapped within a frame where messages contradict each other in ways that cause us to oscillate between trusting and distrusting or obeying and disobeying. There is no exit within the established frame. Our sense of balance falters, which may induce anxiety, anger, or aporia, among other things.

Irony possesses a deictic quality: it points to something else that is only fantasmatically present and yet invokes it (usually by negating its meaning): "This is play, not fighting," for example. Paradox possesses a hermetic quality: it confines us within a frame that produces contradictory impulses, akin to what Alice felt in her ventures through Wonderland: "We are all liars here; do you believe me?" for example. Here "here" no longer points to something else for which it stands but to the statement or situation itself. It creates an existential paradox that can be neither obeyed nor disobeyed.

Irony has an "edge": it upsets the applecart; it toys with our ability to interpret or understand. Irony, therefore, calls into question the basis for our relationships with others but ultimately reaffirms them. Its half-life of disturbance, if we "get it," may be relatively brief. Paradox, on the other hand, possesses "magnitude": "a felt sense of tension between what is said or represented and our capacity to respond cogently."[21] It vivifies what lived experience outside the bounds of logical resolution feels like. "If you touch this stick, I will hit you; if you don't touch this stick, I will hit you. What will you do?" There is no viable solution within the frame as constructed. Paradox calls into question our ability to assess, frame, and interpret the world in a stable, coherent way. Its half-life can be quite considerable. It undermines our sense of self as represented by the ego.[22]

In his exploration of social causes for schizophrenia Bateson drew heavily on an encounter he witnessed in a mental hospital. Schizophrenia results from being trapped by maddening oscillations between contradictory responses created by mixed messages, or existential paradoxes. In his example denial and disavowal produce a confounding effect by mislabeling and shifting blame:

> A young man who had fairly well recovered from an acute schizophrenic episode was visited in the hospital by his [father]. He was glad to see him and impulsively put his arm around his shoulders, whereupon [his father] stiffened. He withdrew his arm and [his father] asked, "Don't you love me anymore?" He then blushed, and [his father] said, ". . . you must not be so easily embarrassed and afraid of your feelings." The patient was able to stay with him only a few minutes more and following his departure he assaulted an aide and was put in the tubs.[23]

The father says one, negating thing with his physical action (rejecting the son's expression of love by stiffening) and another, contradictory thing with his verbal statements (questioning the son's love for him and blaming him for being too embarrassed to show his feelings). The father's verbal messages disavow the validity of the son's correct interpretation of his more figurative, and honest, act of stiffening and projects his inability to express feelings of love onto his son. The father then enjoins the son to express the love he doubts he possesses even though it is the father who is incapable of expressing love. The father, like the paradoxical film, controls the frame as the "subject who knows," the one with the power to say what kind of message a message is, and yet uses that power to construct a double bind: embrace me and be told (nonverbally) "I don't love you," or withdraw and be told (verbally) "You are too easily embarrassed and afraid to love me."

These complexities, to which Bateson devotes a page and a half of close analysis, are akin to the complexities Clifford Geertz unpacks in the fraught exchanges among Cohen, a Jewish trader, marauding Berbers who kill two of his friends and steal his goods, and Captain Dumari, the local French Legionnaire commandant in 1912 Morocco in his classic essay, "Thick Description: Toward an Interpretive Theory of Culture." Geertz summarizes his interpretive efforts: "If ethnography is thick description and ethnographers those who are doing the describing, then the determining question for any given example of it, whether a field journal squib or a Malinowski-sized monograph, is whether it sorts winks from twitches and real winks from mimicked ones."[24] And, in the case of existential paradoxes, the question expands to include whether it identifies double binds and their impact when winks are nonexistent or few and far between.

The parent described by Bateson is not unlike the narrator of *Land without Bread*, who, if we recoil from his callous commentary, says, in effect, "Don't you love documentary anymore?" and if we feel chagrined at our hesitant response to an intolerable message says, "You ought not be so hesitant to believe; after all, I've been there and I know." Apart from the numerous ironic winks in an otherwise paradoxical film, the commentary remains smugly and totally in possession of a truth the images often confirm, sometimes deny, and that the viewer hesitates to believe. The gunshot, for example, at the moment a goat "accidentally" falls to its death, declares the narrator unreliable—as one commentator puts it, this moment "splits apart the contract of authenticity"—as the father's stiffened body confirms his inability to express love, but even if we get it, it may not suffice to overcome the feeling that the film has trapped us in a double bind.[25]

And even more powerfully, Joshua Oppenheimer's *The Act of Killing* reconstructs the murderous acts of government-sanctioned killers in 1960s Indonesia as if there were no external foothold from which to judge these acts as heinous. The killers remain at large, as heroes of the battle against communism (and all other enemies of the governing party and its supporters), and the viewer is left to feel she or he ought to tender sympathy for victors who also prompt revulsion. Here it is our belief in social justice and civil rights that undergoes attack: "If I believe this film, these killers are actually heroes, but if these killers are actually heroes, I can't believe this film."

The Act of Killing engenders feelings of entrapment within a double bind in an extremely affective way.[26] At the start we see men posing as gods in a sylvan setting as lovely, dancing women emerge from a gigantic fish. The mise-en-scène says, in effect, "See us as heroes and saviors worthy of admiration." These men are the killers who in large measure construct the film; they quickly go on to describe and reenact unspeakable acts of cruelty and murder. We recoil, but the film does not recoil with us. It is as if it says, "Don't you admire these men anymore?" and when we respond with consternation, the film says, through its consistent willingness to let these men explain themselves and represent their deeds just as they want them represented, "You shouldn't be embarrassed or afraid of your feelings of admiration. I know; I was there. Watch, listen, and empathize as I have done." (Oppenheimer provides outright declarations of his own critical perspective on his website for the film but withholds them from the film, with some notable exceptions, discussed below. These exceptions function like the gunshot in *Land without Bread* to rupture the paradoxical injunction created by the rest of the film.)[27]

Double binds or existential paradoxes arise when subjects, or films, convey an inherently contradictory position that "denies the usually accepted categories of truth and falsity about 'reality'—something 'inexplicable.'"[28] Elements of the inexplicable abound in *The Act of Killing*, more than any other film I can think of. Some of them can be summarized this way:

In Indonesia the rule of law does not entail civil rights, due process, trial by jury, rules of evidence, or sentencing by appointed judges but reliance on extralegal death squads made up of poorly educated gangsters like those featured in the film who rely on lists of alleged enemies to detain, torture, and kill these enemies.

State-sanctioned organizations like Permuda Pancasila may openly resort to extortion, graft, gambling, drug trafficking, and murder as part of their role in helping the existing government maintain power and be condoned for it.

Featured members of Permuda Pancasila—the heroes of this film—justify their torture and killing by showing us how brutal and sadistic communist agents are in a government-sponsored propaganda film. Not only is a blatantly propagandistic film treated as valid evidence; torture and murder are treated as valid responses to such a film.

According to Citra, the host of a nationally televised "Special Dialogue" with the film's heroes, the featured killers "developed a new, more efficient system for exterminating Communists. . . . [It was] more humane, less sadistic and avoided excessive violence." Torture, massacres, and murder are carried out, in a "more humane and efficient way" because, it seems, they imitate torture, massacres, and murder in westerns and gangster films.

Rather than providing any form of objective or independent voice, the Indonesian fifth estate provides a mechanism for fomenting hatred, identifying suspects for murder, and facilitating the implementation of this as national policy.

Seeking election to public office, as one of the killers does, involves championing the needs of businessmen and workers in public speeches and openly exalting to the camera, in private, what a fortune can be made through graft and extortion.

The best justification for the prolonged torture and gruesome murder of alleged enemies of the state and even the massacre of everyone in Kampung Kolam, a village thought to harbor enemies of the state, is for the killers to demonstrate *how* they enthusiastically tortured, murdered, and massacred by means of elaborate, stylized reenactments rather than *what* justification there can be for legitimizing such actions.

The death of innocent bystanders is of no consequence, and the rape and murder of young girls can be a source of pleasure. As one thug puts it, the rape of a fourteen-year-old girl may be hell for her "but heaven on earth for me."

This is a world upside down and inside out. Yet it is not entirely unfamiliar to members of democratic societies that legalize "harsh interrogation techniques," or torture; rely on drones to execute alleged enemies, even citizens, without trials or any other form of due process; witness extremists, pundits, talk-show hosts, and even political figures express vitriolic hatred for a variety of alleged enemies, both foreign and domestic; and heard a U.S. vice president (Dick Cheney) advocate going over to the "dark side" in dealing with terrorism. That these things all occur in a faraway country, in Oppenheimer's film, relieves some of the intensity of the paradoxes that abound. That the film seems to offer few if any winks, to take no independent perspective on its hero/killers, to refrain from providing the sober, moral frame we long for, though, hurls us into the emotional maelstrom of the double bind.

No winks, perhaps, but some gestures do occur that create an alienation effect (*verfremdungseffekt*) relative to the perspective of the killers. A notable one: Suryono, a neighbor of Anwar Congo, the featured killer, recounts to the death squad members the horrific night when he found his stepfather murdered on a nearby road while makeup artists prepare him to play the role of a victim in one of the killers' reenactments. He had to dig a hole and bury his stepfather, not in a cemetery but alongside the road, without recourse to the police or anyone else lest he, too, be suspected of being a communist sympathizer, subject to summary execution.

He hastens to reassure the killers that his tale is in no way a criticism of them but simply information so they can decide if they want to include the incident in their film. He smiles, laughs, but also tells his wrenching tale. The killers, made up to appear as the savagely tortured victims of their own actions, listen indifferently, with half smiles and limited patience, only to declare the story is "too complex" for inclusion in the film. The scene continues with a mock interrogation and the execution by garroting of Suryono, who gamely goes along. Then, as the killers pause and talk among themselves, debating whether this reenactment proves it was they who were cruel rather than the communists—as it surely does—the camera turns to Suryono, for whom this scene has been massively traumatizing. Fluids cascade down his face, a mix of profuse tears, runny mucous, and dribbling saliva. None of the killers acknowledge his distress. Oppenheimer's camera does. He holds on close-ups of Suryono as the debate about cruelty goes on in the background. Oppenheimer says, "Yes, you have proven your own cruelty in more ways than you realize," figuratively, without saying so directly.

At this moment Oppenheimer clearly breaks the paradoxical frame constructed by the killers to show us what lies beyond: pain, suffering, trauma, and crimes against humanity. That it is a nonverbal gesture, like the father's stiffening in Bateson's example, may render it less consciously perceived: we may doubt or overlook the impact and significance of what we would grasp more readily if it were spoken commentary. Nonetheless, it carries a powerful distancing effect.

Another moment: near the film's end Anwar Congo's partial sense of guilt or remorse seems to increase.[29] He describes how going through the motions of being killed in an extended, gruesome reenactment made him aware of what his victims felt. He lost his sense of dignity; he felt fear and terror. Then we hear Oppenheimer's voice, off camera, as he responds, in Indonesian, instead of simply listening: "You (Anwar) know it's only a film. They knew they were being killed." It is a powerful rejoinder to Congo's claim of empathy. Congo goes through the motions required by his fantasmatic reenactment but emerges alive and well, even if the hounds of heaven may be nipping at his heels.[30]

These moments amount to metacommunication that breaks the double binds that otherwise contain us. The relief is minimal but real. Oppenheimer's interventions remind us we need not identify with the killer's perspective exclusively nor with Congo's self-congratulatory identification with his victims; Congo deludes and flatters himself; he denies the hard reality of his guilt just as the father in Bateson's example denies his inability to express love.

There is an outside to this topsy-turvy world, and it is accessible to us. But the film does not launch its story from this perspective. It withholds the security given by a reaffirmation of our "usually accepted categories of truth and falsity"—our guardians against the inexplicable—the bread and butter, in other words, of documentaries that, no matter what their stylistic elegance or formal sophistication, uphold the tradition of a discourse of sobriety that knows right from wrong, true from false, wisdom from folly.

Hayden White states, in his discussion of why narrative is so indispensable to historical writing, "If every fully realized story ... is a kind of allegory, points to a moral, or endows events, whether real or imaginary, with a significance they do not possess as a mere sequence, then it seems possible to conclude that every historical narrative has as its latent or manifest purpose the desire to moralize the events of which it treats."[31] Here, as in most paradoxical and ironic works, such moralization seems lacking; it becomes submerged, more latent than overt, and quite possibly missed when we rely on our "usually accepted categories of truth and falsity." Feelings of betrayal may arise.[32] The signifiers and message, per Bateson's formulation, that *would have been* represented, had it not been for their ironic or paradoxical inflection, fail to appear in decisive, clear-cut form to reassure us of what we knew and believed before we encountered the film, resulting, in some, not in appreciation but anger.[33]

Ironically, this breech of categories occurs as major funding sources for documentaries put added stress on wanting films they support to have a measurable social impact.[34] Films like *Land without Bread, F for Fake, Some of These Stories Are True* (Peter Adair, 1981), *Close Up* (Abbas Kiarostami, 1990), *S21: The Khmer Rouge Killing Machine* (Rithy Panh, 2003), and *The Act of Killing*—films that disturb, provoke, challenge, and question fundamental assumptions by gesturing toward the inexplicable—would be unlikely candidates for funding compared to *An Inconvenient Truth* (Davis Guggenheim, 2006), *The Invisible War* (Kirby Dick, 2012), *Bully* (Lee Hirsh, 2011), *The Cove* (Louie Psihoyos, 2009), or *Food, Inc.* (Robert Kenner, 2008).

Sobriety prevails. And is not to be dismissed. Definitely not to be dismissed. But there are impacts beyond what the surging interest in the evaluation of measurable social impact capture, be it new legislation, hits on a website, or donations to a cause. Ironic and paradoxical films contribute to a range of work—which would include a fair portion of the avant-garde[35]—that extends beyond the liberal, or conservative, "usually accepted categories of truth and falsity" that commonly give coherence to documentaries.

These ironic and paradoxical works have an impact that lies well beyond the realm of the empirically measurable. Yet all is not lost. Despite the radical doubt about the capacity of language and consciousness that they generate, they are, fundamentally, testament to the inability of the conscious mind to get it right. Irony invites a vertiginous delirium, or despair, yet by dint of being itself communicable and comprehensible, it affirms that the sum of our psychic apparatus can attest to truths that exceed the limits of consciousness and language per se. *Le cœur a ses raisons, que la raison ne connaît point.* Like dreams and jokes, irony offers a way to speak from and listen to that part of the self that lies beyond the reach of reason.

15 **Letter to Errol Morris**

Feelings of Revulsion and the Limits of
Academic Discourse

March 20, 2010

Dear Errol,

I am writing you because I don't know what else to do. Normally
I'd write an article or give a paper, but those forms feel inadequate.
I have loved almost all your films and I try hard to avoid writing
about films I hate. It is too easy to demonize the author or the film.
I have written and talked on *The Thin Blue Line* [1988] as a land-
mark film that sent documentary filmmaking in new directions.
It remains one of the most important documentaries ever made, and
I wish I could say the same about *Standard Operating Procedure*
[2008].

So why a letter?

My body speaks the language of feelings and emotion; it is the
language of unconscious desire, as well, and is very distinct from the
signifiers of written language. I need to give expression to my bodily experience and yet fear that I will betray it in doing so, especially
with the detachment granted to the author of academic discourse.
Images are always particular and concrete, and they can pack a
punch. The particularity of an image gains clarity by contextualization, and yet as soon as it is contextualized, it loses some of its distinction as a unique slice of time and space. Translating the affect of
images into the web of signification woven by words, of which cap-
tions are a notable example, can feel like a betrayal as well.

Trauma, like images, retains its particularity by resisting contextualization; it remains incomparable. I think my feelings of revulsion on watching this one film have something to do with the way
you give form to traumatic events in an abstract, almost ethereal,

way that removes their sting on one level—as acts of torture—and reintroduces it on another—as a form of representation that seems indifferent to the horrific nature of the images it presents.

These disturbing feelings are what trouble me here. I felt confronted with atrocities—torture—in ways that throw me into the same state as seeing evidence of genocide would. Atrocities test the limits of representation. We address the unspeakable to give it form. The raw experience of encountering atrocities poses the challenge of contextualizing and determining responsibility, including perhaps our own. This challenge is what I felt your film failed to address successfully.

Instead, you take the sting from terrible images that shocked the world by decontextualizing and even fetishizing them. They line up in an aestheticized parade that has seductive power but no relation to social justice. This tactic feels at odds with their gruesome contents; and the shock of seeing them so decontextualized, in turn, became a new form of revulsion, one peculiar to the form you gave to torture at Abu Ghraib. I felt as if your film were saying to me, "When you think about it, Bill, it's not as bad as you imagine. I can fascinate you with these terrible images even if I don't attempt to fully account for them." And yet, what I could not help but say to myself was, "I feel violated. I feel I am being shown terrible crimes against humanity and getting nothing back that helps me address the issues these images raise."

You mention in your DVD commentary that we all know the photographs were a distraction, masking the responsibility of others beyond the obvious "bad apples" but then say you want to hear from the people literally behind and in the photographs to learn about their state of mind and the pressures they faced. This, to me, is a fatal error. Bertolt Brecht wrote long ago that a photograph of a Krupp's munitions factory fails to reveal the socioeconomic reality of power and hegemony that function behind this reified facade. Brecht was not concerned, certainly not exclusively concerned, with the state of mind and pressures on the photographer of that image or any other. I wish you hadn't been, either.

As I watched your film in San Francisco at a 7 p.m. show in a large auditorium with only eight or nine other patrons, strong feelings snapped through my body using faster, more primitive neural networks than those deployed by cerebral thought. I feel a fight-or-flight response at work. As your film begins and the MPs' stories unfold, my sense of discomfort increases. The speakers seemed stunned, almost expressionless, not all there, without any solid ground to stand on. Their faces possess a particularity that can vex all understanding—every face possesses such mystery—but here it's a particularity isolated from its usual density: no background, no location, not even the remainder of their bodies.

I feel as if I am watching animated portraiture, and I wonder, increasingly, as the film goes on, why these individuals are the ones sitting for their portraits and telling their stories when they are the perpetrators of horrible things, and others, ultimately responsible for what they did, are nowhere to be seen. The effect is quite remote from the catch-as-catch-can aesthetic of so many documentaries. The shooting style reminded me of paintings of religious icons with their golden halos, although you have replaced those halos with the abstract, empty "no place / any place" of a dematerialized studio backdrop. You omit any return to "les lieux de mémoires" so vital in many other documentaries, the actual scene of the crime, and substitute some clearly fabricated stage sets for moments of reenactment. And it is not confession, contrition, and the assumption of full responsibility that we hear (though full responsibility clearly lies elsewhere) but tales of rationalization, victimization, and denial. You give me perpetrators as victims, and it causes me to recoil.

An almost fetishistic quality haunts the portraits. It seems to enact a refusal to see the bigger picture on your part that parallels the blind spots of your characters. I could say you are letting the audience judge and decide, as I have done in response to your earlier films, but the MPs' excuses pile up so high that I sense an attempt to convince me to accept these self-deceptions, or to sidestep them by contemplating the photographs as free-floating signifiers, shorn of their grim particularity and geographic/historical referentiality. I feel less an invitation to decide for myself than a desire to have me accept the rationalizations and your tolerance of them as a truth in need of acknowledgment. Fight or flight is definitely taking hold of me.

My normal sense of narrative anticipation converts to a growing feeling of frustration and discomfort. The lurid photographs, no matter how many special effects surround them, remain appalling, but, like Sabrina Harmon, your response is a strangely clinical and dissociated curiosity. Where is the moral center to their testimony?

To your film? To your perspective? These lacunae leave me waiting for your moral voice to arrive.

The MPs' stories roll on with surprising monotony. My body can't find a comfortable position; I wiggle and squirm in my seat. My legs want to lift me up and carry me out of the theater, but I resolve to stay. I feel I owe it to your film; surely it will shift to a different plane before it's over.

I can clearly see that the MPs have undergone something so painful they remain traumatized by it. I wish I were a Frantz Fanon. He was capable of hearing and treating the suffering experienced by the French soldiers who tortured their Algerian prisoners, but I feel ill-equipped for the task and wonder if such a challenge is what you intended for me. What is Errol doing? I wonder; why are you subjecting me to such tortured testimony, so full of evasions and denials? You've taken me to the border zone where human action betrays inhumanity, barbarity, and the total objectification of others. Am I to follow, letting anger turn me against you just as these MPs turned against those who often angered them, sometimes for reasons that had nothing to do with terrorism and their role in "softening up" terrorist detainees?

My sense of a social order depends on accountability and responsibility of the one to the many and of the many to the one. As I watch, that web of mutual responsibility ruptures in front of me. I don't know what to do with my discomfort and anger; I need to understand it, to plunge deeper into it rather than sidestep it and see if I can discover exactly what provokes it.

Rather than shifting over to a detached mode of analysis, I focused on my feelings of revulsion and eventually came up with three reasons for these feelings. I hope I can share these reasons with you, Errol, and I hope you'll tell me if you think I am missing something vital.

The first is the painfully limited perspective of the guards. They see their past conduct through a glass darkly but are asked, and paid, to speak and are elevated to the larger-than-life proportions of the movie screen. Their images emanate from the screen like giant personages of mythic proportion, and yet they display little, if any, emotion, especially remorse. "I found myself . . . ," "I just had to . . . ," "I was told to . . . ," and other dissembling locutions deny their own agency. They "just" softened up detainees. Is the MPs' testimony meant to "just" soften us up to their unfortunate plight as scapegoats?

The MPs had nowhere to turn, they say, and found themselves doing unimaginable things. Besides, they were under fire from mortar shells, had no contact with the Iraqi population, and experienced severe stress their entire tour. They arrived at Abu Ghraib in a near hypnotic state of fear and distrust and remained so, perhaps up to the moment when you filmed them. No sense of individual responsibility emerges. Sociopaths typically lack remorse, possess no empathy, and hold the law in disregard. I hesitate to label the MPs sociopathic if that confers a mark of incorrigibility, and yet you seem to take no interest in how a specific institutional framework and a set of inhumane policies can construct sociopathic behavior. This is what *Obedience* (Stanley Milgram, 1963) explored and what *The Stanford Prison Experiment* (Kyle Alvarex, 2015), released well after your film, explores, but *SOP* takes no interest in the institutional framework that, ironically, tragically, and cleverly, blames torture solely on these poor souls.

You seem to think that, as victims, they deserve a chance to offer their rationalizations to us. But as perpetrators, they were found guilty and sentenced to jail. I understand how they were used as scapegoats by the administration, but sometimes scapegoats are also guilty. Strangely, you also don't show any particular interest in the ways in which their background and experience prior to arriving at Abu Ghraib—their family life, their educational level, their political views and social habits—contributed to their criminal conduct.

In fact, I felt that, although you knew the outcome and their clear guilt, you chose to ignore it. Your curiosity about their state of mind bore a resemblance for me to that of the press as they listened to the rationalizations and denials by public figures charged with sexual misconduct—the Mark Foleys, Eliot Spitzers, John Edwardses, and Tiger Woodses of recent infamy—even though we later learned that they had, indeed, committed the acts with which they were charged. Is denial, deception, and outright lying all that fascinating, especially when we know that is what it is? These MPs appear to be locked in that same intermediate state of denial that others confront and overcome with humility and dignity. Why you would choose to be locked into such a state with them is what I do not understand.

The second reason for my revulsion involves your reenactments of military torture. I felt the strongest visceral urge to flee the theater when you gave us tracking shots down corridors populated by ghosts as you reenacted actual interrogations and legalized torture. I felt pinned to a morally impossible space. It was like the grotesque tracking shot in *Schindler's List* [1993] when Spielberg has the camera slowly approach the door to the apparent gas chamber housing Schindler's Jews. We slip past the Nazi guards clustered around the door's peep hole to see the panic and fear inside that chamber. It's a grotesque point-of-view shot because it is literally the point of view of the death camp guards. The stakes are far higher than when I shared Norman Bates's point of view as he spied on Marion Crane in *Psycho* [1960], but you offer no moral lesson to counterbalance the pain of occupying the point of view of perpetrators of torture. The reenactments were agonizing to watch.

At Abu Ghraib we see national policy hide behind individual pathology as the lowest-level perpetrators take all the blame. We learn, in what could have been the dramatic heart of the film but feels, instead, mentioned in passing, that torture to extract useful information is fully acceptable, "standard operating procedure," in fact. At least that is what the analyst charged with examining the guards' photos and videos announces at one point. No need to prosecute the other torturers; they were doing what was deemed right and proper. These guards, unfortunately for them, did not seek to gain information and therefore engaged in criminal conduct. This distinction, though, has no apparent bearing on your reenactments where what you re-present—undocumented scenes of "standard operating procedure," aka the CIA's techniques of "enhanced interrogation"—are more aestheticized than the allegedly real torture perpetrated by the guards and captured by their own cameras. Showing this again, even and maybe especially in aestheticized form, struck me as morbid. Your response is as if you were examining a strange, unfamiliar form of conduct that you had placed inside your interrotron as if under a bell jar simply to study it.

I have always sensed a fascination and identification on your part, Errol, with people who live outside the bounds of "normal" human encounter, who become swept up in self-, or, here, small group–fashioned worlds of beliefs and behavior. This was part of the charm and strangeness of *Gates of Heaven* [1978]; *Vernon, Florida* [1981]; *Fast, Cheap and Out of Control* [1997]; and to a lesser extent *A Brief History of Time* [1991]. Your fascination achieved a perfect equilibrium between respecting outsiderness and seeking a common truth in *The Thin Blue Line* where what began as idiosyncrasy took on murderous proportions. Your commitment to untangling the Rashomon-like tales of your many witnesses to arrive at a clear and simple truth gave the film a moral center, a center that feels inexplicably missing from *SOP*.

With *Mr. Death* [1999] and *The Fog of War* [2003] you shifted from idiosyncratic behavior (peculiar but largely innocuous behavior for the society at large) to ideological behavior (individual actions that serve the needs of a given ideology). Your curiosity in these two films continues to suggest both an identification with and strong curiosity about those whose views carry them to the margins of the social order. You show a remarkable willingness to let your subjects describe and defend themselves in whatever way they wish, without prodding or challenge.

This works well with idiosyncratic and not so well with ideological behavior. The clearly self-serving testimony of Robert McNamara and the delusional claims of Fred Leuchter left me uncomfortable to the extent that I wondered if you would once again locate and occupy a moral center in these films. You didn't. That form of dialogue belonging to the I and Thou relation of mutual encounter, and honesty, remained on the horizon as you settled for relying on an expert to refute Mr. Leuchter's most outrageous claims and on limited use of special effects (a "rain" of letters and numbers instead of bombs in one clip, for example) to point to the magnitude of Mr. McNamara's war crimes, a strategy you repeat in *SOP*. I felt that you had retreated behind your interrotron and forfeited the moral ground to your subjects.

The third reason for my feelings of revulsion involves the complete absence of the voices of the Iraqi detainees. They are the living referents of these horrific photographs. What happened to them? Why did you exclude them but recycle these degrading images of them? Surely some of them, including those who were never suspected of terrorism and for whom no "softening up" or vigilante punishment could ever be justified, are readily recognizable by friends and family. Did a "higher truth" legitimize displaying these images? Did you think your film would never get to Iraq or Iraqis never see it in the U.S.?

Could you imagine making a film about American POWs held captive in Vietnam during that war that dealt exclusively with the rationalizations of Vietnamese guards for their acts of brutality and torture in violation of the Geneva Convention, and to simultaneously deny those American POWs any voice whatsoever, while recycling images of their degradation and torture?

I think of Rithy Panh's powerful film *S21* [2003] and the moral center of that film when former prisoners who survived S21 and the killing fields confront their Khmer Rouge guards. They confront one another in what is clearly a dignified and respectful encounter fostered by Mr. Panh. The encounter has enormous power as the former prisoners cut through the rationalizations offered by ex-guards and express their bewilderment at their countrymen's loss of moral compass. You are not Rithy Panh, but were you not moved to hear those absent voices, to hear how they would address these guards who lost their moral compass and who might yet regain their bearings if they could be brought to understand the full depths of what they did?

Of course you are not Ari Folman or Alain Resnais or Claude Lanzmann or Alex Gibney or Rory Kennedy either, and I am sure I will lose you if I start to discuss what these other filmmakers managed to do that your film doesn't. You are a distinct voice, one that has shone brightly when you have captured the idiosyncrasy of others nonjudgmentally. But in reflecting further on the revulsion I felt at your approach to the political complexity of torture at Abu Ghraib and the horrific images describing it, I sense that you have drifted away from your strength, despite, and, indeed, because of, a continuing curiosity with the idiosyncratic outsider and social misfit.

I continue to admire the bulk of your work enormously and hope that these comments might be of some benefit as you go on to other projects. I realize that I chose to write a letter because of what felt like the limits of academic discourse; but like others who have felt overly confined by specific forms and modalities of writing in the past, I now wonder if I have truly escaped the arena of academic discourse or in some small way, perhaps, modified it. My wish, in any case, is that it be of genuine use to you.

Sincerely,
Bill Nichols

P.S.

Why do I admire *The Act of Killing (TAOK)* and not *Standard Operating Procedure (SOP)*? Since I speak highly of Oppenheimer's film in this volume (in "Irony, Paradox, and the Documentary"), and since you were an executive producer on it, it seems worth clarifying the differences I felt in watching both.

With *TAOK* I felt dumbfounded; with *SOP* I felt appalled. *SOP* attends to the administration's scapegoats, adding to the sense that they were in some way central to the systematic torture of prisoners (detainees), when they were actually quite secondary to it and easy to condemn by everyone. You give them a voice; you listen intently; and that is certainly one of your great strengths, but it provides us with a voice that is relatively clueless about the larger picture of legalized torture and prone to rationalize their actions even though they remain unjustifiable.

As in all your films, you give people all the rope they need to spin their tale and reveal their self-deceptions, but in this case you also tend to neglect the larger context. That matters little when we dealt with pet owners and cemeteries in *Gates of Heaven* or with quirky, small-town inhabitants in *Vernon, Florida,* but it matters greatly with a man, Fred Leuchter, who denies the Holocaust in *Mr. Death* or a former secretary of defense, Robert McNamara, who wants to justify his actions in *The Fog of War*—and in those films you do find ways to offer elements of a larger, corrective picture.

Oppenheimer also gives killers a voice (they tortured and killed far more people than these guards ever did), but they remain proud of their role and continue to receive official praise for their actions. These are men who firmly believe they helped save Indonesia from communism rather than becoming caught up in a terrible nightmare of someone else's devising. Unlike the *SOP* subjects, who act more like victims than perpetrators, *TAOK*'s subjects are perpetrators through and through, and their lack of remorse, and the lack of censure for what they did, is part of what dumbfounds. It leads to the paradoxes I describe in discussing the film. Oppenheimer gives us a strong sense of what the larger context is, partly through shots that hold on victims for whom the killers have no empathy at all, and partly by omission: the absence of any reference to judicial review, due process, or criminal trial by jury. And the lack of any outcry or protest, be it from the central government to ordinary citizens, magnifies just how powerful, and terrifying, these killers are. Their brazen disregard for the law, or the effects of this film which they structure to a considerable degree, dumbfounds in a way the more conventional testimony of scapegoats cannot.

We expect victims to feel victimized, but this can hardly round the circle when they are primarily, and more fundamentally, perpetrators. The Abu Ghraib photos shocked the world because of their blatantly sadistic and sexual elements. The CIA agents who tortured as part of "standard operating procedure" may have even been appalled since no useful information could arise from merely humiliating, degrading, and torturing prisoners. It was fairly easy for everyone to feel "shocked" by what they saw, even if they knew it had been encouraged and condoned as a logical extension of the inhumane premises of the actual interrogations.

I felt you wanted to give them a chance to share their side of it, and I can't find any fault with that. It's just that it's not really an important side of it at all, but more of a thin, incomplete, deluded slice. Had you built the film around administrative leaders who approved of torture, like Vice President Dick Cheney or NSA adviser Condoleezza Rice; attorneys like John Yoo, who tortured the law to rationalize the program of "enhanced interrogation"; the two masterminds, James Mitchel and Bruce Jessen, who devised the program; or the actual perpetrators who conducted the torture, and had we heard from them what we hear from *TAOK*'s subjects—indifference to the suffering of others, smug pride, twisted doubletalk almost straight from *Alice in Wonderland*, and no doubt whatsoever about the guilt of those who were tortured and killed—we may well have been as profoundly dumbfounded by those higher up in the American chain of command as we are by these Indonesian thugs and their high-level supporters.

These low-ranked guards at Abu Ghraib, however, take no pride in what they did. They simply have rationalizations that minimize their complicity with what I have to call crimes against humanity, crimes of which they display little awareness at all. They are the wrong subject, with limited insight and self-serving stories. They do little to increase our understanding of how a society, or at least a democratically elected government, can place itself above and beyond the law it's charged to uphold. That *TAOK* reveals just what it feels like to occupy such a place, above the law, admired, feared and free from prosecution, is, in essence, what makes it a film of great paradoxical and confounding power.

16 Perpetrators, Trauma, and Film

What was a trickle of earlier works that focused on the perpetrators of war crimes—such as *Eichmann Trial* (Leo Hurwitz, 1961), *The Specialist* (Eyal Sivan, 1999), parts of *Shoah* (Claude Lanzmann, 1985), and *Hotel Terminus* (Marcel Ophüls, 1988)—approach flood level when we add *Human Weapon* (Ilan Ziv, 2002), *S21* (Rithy Panh, 2003), *Standard Operating Procedure* (Errol Morris, 2008), *Enemies of the People* (Rob Lemkin and Thet Sambath, 2009), *Duch, Master of the Forges of Hell* (Rithy Panh, 2012), *The Act of Killing* (Joshua Oppenheimer, 2012), *The Missing Picture* (Rithy Panh, 2013), and the several dozen recent Israeli films (fiction and documentary) examined by Raya Morag in her outstanding book *Waltzing with Bashir: Perpetrator Trauma and Cinema*.[1] These films are quite disparate in style and aim but also raise some general questions: what is our relationship to and responsibility for those who commit terrible deeds? How can we represent the trauma some of them experience, and what does it signify?

Such questions take us down a number of paths. A large literature and a number of films address the trauma of American soldiers who served in Vietnam and, more recently, in Iraq or Afghanistan. Most of this work centers on the events that brought on trauma, the aftermath and effects of PTSD, and efforts at recovery by various means. This work generally fits within the paradigm of what Morag describes as the psychological dimension to trauma, where she locates both psychoanalytic theory and clinical therapy. But her focus lies elsewhere. She asks what is the ethical dimension to trauma, for the perpetrator and for us, when we encounter representations of this dimension in film particularly but also literature? And what if the doer of terrible deeds—of atrocities and descent into the abject—acts in the name of the state or other institutional/organizational frameworks that recruit, indoctrinate, train, legitimate, and protect the doer? How can we understand the mechanisms related to modern warfare, or what Morag calls "new war," that increase the likelihood that "atrocity-producing situations" will occur? What responsibility must those who produce the figure of the perpetrator bear? To what extent might we, as citizens, be complicit in this process? How, primarily, do Israeli films represent these issues, knowing full well that such representations will be both specific to the Israeli situation and rich in application to many other situations as well? And how, then, even if our role is that of bystander, are we to confront the larger social context and the profoundly ethical dilemmas (as well as the political and ideological issues) that arise?

The perpetrators Morag finds in the films she examines are not the psychopaths of popular culture. Like them, they appear normal on the surface and come from familiar social milieus, but, unlike them, they do not conceal a darker shadow side of murderous impulses. They learn to commit atrocities and come to accept them as either the by-product of a broader, legitimate task, in the case of the average soldier, or as the fulfillment of their dedication and belief, in the case of the suicide bomber. Responsibility is shared with the organizational frame that makes atrocity-producing situations such as humiliation, torture, rape, and mass murder not only possible but routine, even acceptable as "standard operating procedure." The challenge then arises of how to represent this complex figure/ground, event/context relationship and our own complicity within it.

For Morag these questions and issues reach crisis proportion in response to the Second Intifada (roughly 2002–4), a crisis that engendered what she calls a "new wave" of Israeli cinema. This cinema responds not only to the military actions in the Occupied Territories (Gaza and the West Bank) during the Second Intifada but also returns to the many previous wars and the atrocities that occurred during them. She explores these situations from the perspective of the perpetrator rather than the victim. *Waltz with Bashir* (Ari Folman, 2008), for example, returns to the Lebanon War of 1982 to examine the traumatic experiences of director Ari Folman and others he knew who served in the Israeli Defense Forces and bore indirect responsibility for the massacre of thousands of civilians in the Sabra and Shatila refugee camps.

What the Second Intifada period brought home was the rise of what Morag terms "new war." Such warfare heightens the probability of atrocity-producing situations since civilians are now deemed a primary target of military action. A shift of degree more than kind, the result is nonetheless dramatic. Villages are razed and destroyed, the residents dispersed; civilians enjoying themselves in cafes or restaurants become targets, their bodies recovered in fragments, intermingled with those of their assailant. Armies, battlefields, defensive lines, offensive attacks all blur into a vaguely defined war zone for which no rules of engagement prove adequate. No longer conducted in that famous "fog of war" that accounts for mistakes, confusion, faulty communication, and miscalculation in the midst of more clear-cut and principled strategies, war now becomes a direct encounter with the abject. The body itself becomes a weapon, either in the form of the suicide bomber who passes among us undetected until that fatal instant or in the all-too-obvious form of the armed and armored soldier who looms conspicuously above those he guards or hunts as an instrument of destruction. It is, then, the body as corpse that brings us into the most direct encounter with the abject.

The litmus test for cinema is whether it, too, can confront the abject—the body, the corpse—and begin the arduous process of moving beyond trauma for victim and perpetrator alike. A number of new wave Israeli films such as *No. 17* (David Ofek, 2003) and *To See If I'm Smiling* (Tamar Yarom, 2007) do precisely this. They show how trauma revolves around the figure of the corpse, and they strive to come to terms with it.

The shift from the trauma of the victim—the backbone of trauma studies and of related theories of memory and recovery—to the trauma of the perpetrator calls for a reconsideration of many assumptions centered on the status of the victim. *Waltz with Bashir,* for example, tells us little of the suffering and pain experienced by the survivors of the massacres at the Sabra and Shatila refugee camps but a great deal of the belated guilt and enduring trauma of Ari Folman as a result of his indirect complicity. The trauma of victims opens a black hole, a tremendous lack. Victims initially don't know what hit them or how to get beyond it. Ideally, the gradual process that revolves around *Nachträglichkeit* (the retrospective act of memory and narrativization) allows them to do so. Victims struggle to find their way to shape a narrative to which they can bear witness and go on with their lives.

But the trauma of perpetrators goes largely suppressed and denied. They are, after all, chosen agents of the state or some other entity. *Nachträglichkeit* becomes deferred by a social context that treats the perpetrator as a hero, or martyr, or at least a decent person doing a difficult job to preserve the social order, for Israelis, or change it, for Palestinians. The new wave of Israeli cinema represents an awakening, as if from the nightmare so well depicted in *Waltz with Bashir,* in which former perpetrators struggle to come to terms with their own trauma and the related question of responsibility.

What strikes the victim as a sudden, traumatic blow is for the perpetrator the outcome of a process that began long before that decisive, traumatic moment. It incorporates that moment into an ongoing narrative of duty, service, and redemption. The trauma that committing atrocities produces for the perpetrator must overcome its legitimating or at least tolerant frame to generate a questioning that extends beyond the individual perpetrator to the social structure that produces him or her. It took Ari Folman twenty-six years to reach this point, and it was the Second Intifada that provided the proximate stimulus to do so for many others in Morag's view.

A large measure of what leads to atrocity-producing situations involves another shift entailed by new war. For Morag this is the shift from soldiers confronting soldiers to soldiers or cops confronting a mix of insurgents and civilians. The difficulty if not impossibility of coupling police action with military action launches an inevitable slide toward the construction of the perpetrator: the paradoxical injunction to both serve and protect and kill or be killed sets up situations in which atrocities readily occur. Soldiers do not need to be diplomats when confronting an enemy army, but they do when dealing heavily with a civilian population. Like an Escher drawing, the soldier oscillates between two conflicting figure/ground relationships: Protect the people, keep the peace / Distrust the people, upset the peace.

This key insight into the double bind produced by new war could be expanded. Once there were warriors, a discrete group whose relation and value to the larger community were well understood. Passage through the warrior stage, or others such as shaman or seer, often served as a transition to full adulthood. This figure persists primarily at an ideological or mythological level. The "detonatorg" (Morag's term for the suicide bomber as detonator and organism) and the perpetrator (the soldier who commits atrocities) belong to a different order, where the murder of civilians rather than battle with fellow warriors becomes routine. This shift and its crazy-making implications bring forth the perpetrator as a recurring and often traumatized figure.

The larger social frame that calls forth this new form of soldier/cop takes pains to deny the acts of perpetrators and the predictability of the atrocities they commit. It treats individual perpetrators as either heroes doing what they must or as bad apples and exceptions. But for some, such as the makers and subjects of new wave Israeli films, atrocity and trauma become an undeniable burden. Such subjects are haunted (as were the French torturers of Algerians treated by Frantz Fanon in his role as psychiatrist and discussed in the final part of his landmark book, *The Wretched of the Earth*).[2] The new wave films are a crucial part of an effort to get beyond trauma and guilt. Such an effort involves hearing the confession of the perpetrator, assigning responsibility at every level, and finding ways to reintegrate the traumatized perpetrator back into the social fabric that produced him or her.

What blocks this process of acknowledging perpetrator guilt and the traumatic events/atrocities that produce it? For Morag it is a "time trap" engendered by "pre-memory." Haunted by the ghosts of wars past, and that horrific ur-event, the Holocaust, subject to a seemingly endless series of chronic traumas, time takes on a new quality for Israelis. The dominant ideology, recapitulated in Israeli fiction films far more than documentaries, it seems, denies perpetrator trauma; it creates a screen memory, a state of prememory that cannot fully resolve victim trauma or address perpetrator trauma. The "persecuted perpetrator," the figure who acts as if to overturn a long history of persecution, must confront these ghosts from the past and lay them to rest. The time trap hinders this effort. Time splits between that slender, sudden, traumatic moment of destruction and the interval before it repeats. A thin sliver of now, pivoting on a fulcrum between no longer and not yet, erases duration and the time necessary for *Nachträglichkeit*. The time trap of endless trauma hurriedly cleansed, erased, and avenged stands as a barrier to the time of posttraumatic recovery. It bears kinship with the narrative fetishism I discuss in relation to the Bush administration's response to 9/11 in "The Terrorist Event." The interval, those moments of respite, possesses a "negative circularity" as it revolves around the already happened and the yet to happen again. Fear, the dark knight of modern political manipulation, takes root in the conception of time itself.

Morag's discussion of the time trap is one of the most insightful aspects of this remarkable, paradigm-shifting book. Moving beyond this trap is what the new wave films begin to do. She finds this movement in literature as well, perhaps most strikingly in Noam Chayut's *My Holocaust Thief.*[3] One day, Chayut, a member of the Israeli Defense Forces patrolling the Occupied Territories, sees a young Palestinian girl who does not see him as cop but as a (new war) soldier bringing terror and destruction. She freezes and stares at him with "black eyes." He goes on to write:

> She is the one who stole my Holocaust. . . . [This girl] took from me the belief that there is *absolute evil* in the world and the belief that I am avenging and fighting it. For this girl, I am *absolute evil*. Though I was not as cruel as the *absolute evil* I was nursed on, grew up with, and matured on. . . . The moment I internalized that I myself was the *absolute evil* in her eyes, the *absolute evil* that had governed me until then began to dissolve. And since then I have been bereft of my Holocaust.[4]

He goes on to experience a condition of profound loss at every level from his personal identity to his national allegiance. In this wrenching moment of self-discovery and the abandonment of fetishized beliefs, perpetrator trauma breaks through the time trap to make the process of recovery possible but hardly inevitable.

Interestingly, it is a set of three-minute short films that capture this movement most compellingly. Although by many standards fictions that involve imagined situations, they can also be treated as conditional documentaries in the same spirit as Peter Watkins's *The War Game* (1965). In such cases the events depicted have yet to occur but may well follow, inevitably, from the current rules of the game (nuclear deterrence as a military strategy in Watkins's case, the ramifications of the Second Intifada in Morag's case). For example, "Just Not Another Suicide Bomber" (Amit Drori, 2004) covers what we begin to believe are the final three minutes before that sudden traumatic instant on a bus when a bomb explodes. The film ends before the bomb goes off; its drama is in what we come to anticipate and fear during this lulling interval. "Three Minutes to Four" (Eliav Lilti, 2002) presents ten speakers who describe what happens to them after the explosion that occurs at four o'clock. They speak from a proleptic time and space of the already but not yet happened.

The effect of these and two other similar three-minute films is deeply unnerving. They confront the body and corpse in distinctly discomforting ways. Like the soldier/cop who must straddle demands for service to the public and assumptions that within the public lurks the enemy, these films straddle the tenuous divide between fiction and documentary and generate much of their disturbance by doing so. Although discussed in the middle of the book, they make a fitting summation of Morag's call for a prolonged look at new war, the time trap, new wave Israeli cinema, and the expansive social implications of the issues of perpetrator trauma now coming to light in any number of films. The new wave films, like this book, challenge us to acknowledge the paradigm of the perpetrator's newfound empathy for his victim, to confront our own complicity with that which makes atrocity-producing situations so common, and to find ways to overturn the narrative fetishism and time traps that perpetuate both atrocities and trauma.

PART V

Politics and the Documentary Film

PART 5 RETURNS TO THE QUESTION OF THE POLITICAL that motivated my initial attraction to documentary film. The two essays span the duration of my career, from a condensed selection on the organization and films of San Francisco Newsreel, written in 1972, drawn from my master's thesis on Newsreel more generally, to a fairly polemical response to the tendency to valorize the forms of social impact that lend themselves to empirical measurement, written in 2015. The essays therefore not only reflect on the evolving political landscape for documentary filmmaking but on my own shifting perspective on the relationship between politics and documentary filmmaking.

Writing "San Francisco Newsreel: Collectives, Politics, Films" served as part of my initial attempts to address questions relating particularly to documentary film. That meant differentiating the process of producing such films from the more familiar studio system, as well as analyzing the films themselves. San Francisco Newsreel's passage through various forms of internal organization proves an instructive reminder of what collective filmmaking can entail, albeit, in this case, with a sharply political edge in adherence to democratic centralism as a form of organization inspired by Soviet and Maoist models. The two films I discuss in detail, *Off the Pig* (aka *Black Panther*) and *San Francisco State Strike*, remain among the most widely screened Newsreel films. Meant at the time as topical reports on a vital part of the New Left movement (black militancy and campus rebellion), they now offer a striking historical perspective on political struggle in 1970s America. The essay also retains some of the original phrasings that demonstrate its temporal proximity to its subject. Newsreel was still an evolving part of the New Left, and I assessed it as such. Now it is part of the history of the American left, just as my thesis is part of the history of the rise of documentary film studies, but how that would be so was far from apparent in 1972.

The second essay, "The Political Documentary and the Question of Impact," turns from the 1970s to today. It ponders the remarkable shift from a time when San Francisco Newsreel had to devise a work-furlough program to support itself, by having some members work at full-time jobs to support the others, to a period when many individuals make a living as documentary filmmakers, often with the support of funding agencies, commissioning entities, and television outlets that were almost entirely absent in the 1970s.

The emergence of a significant base of funding support has been a great boon to the growth of documentary film generally, yet it now threatens, in my view, the fundamental need for films that combine compelling form with radical politics to see the world in fresh and revealing ways. The empirical measurement of social impact, seemingly a way to ensure that documentaries contribute to the common good, may herald the rise of more narrowly focused, less genuinely provocative bodies of work. There is an irony in comparing the radical perspective of the Newsreel films, made with no external funding support some forty-plus years ago, and the stress on "social impact" by many sources of documentary funding today. It would seem to be a dream come true, but the result is that impact becomes reduced to a diminished, tamer thing that Newsreel would never dream of. As I see it, it amounts to forms of impact that are more ameliorative than transformative; measures that can be safely championed by funders who own status as gatekeepers go unquestioned.

As a topical issue currently under debate there is no conclusion to draw, yet, but basic principles are at stake. How does a documentary, or any film or work of art, have significant impact on the culture within which it circulates? What serves to advance a radical vision of the future, and what serves to limit or control it? Do the most profound forms of social impact for any work of art, including documentaries, yield to quantifiable measurement? What might quantification capture effectively and what might it fail to grasp entirely? This essay contributes to the debate and argues that there may well be vital forms of social impact that escape the porous web constructed by any form of empirical measurement.

17 San Francisco Newsreel

Collectives, Politics, Films

THE INTERNAL STRUCTURE OF
A FILMMAKING COLLECTIVE

San Francisco Newsreel had an intimate relationship with its local environment, and one event in particular captures the electric atmosphere of protest and retaliation in which it found itself during its first year, 1968. Newsreel owned a truck from which it could project films in the street. One night several Newsreel members went to Berkeley to show a film. The film was *The Haight*—a short (six-minute) description of a police riot in the onetime center for the drug counterculture, Haight-Ashbury. While a crowd of fifty to one hundred people watched the riot footage playing against a building wall, a real riot suddenly swept around and past them. The projection site happened to be between two police barricades, and as the Newsreel members shut off the film, the sting of tear gas and cries of battle created an eerie connection between film and reality.[1]

Like much of the New Left and counterculture, Newsreel members had no great fondness for Marxism-Leninism, which still resonated with clichéd labels such as *authoritarian, dogmatic,* and *irrelevant*. There were no independent filmmakers such as those who formed the nucleus in New York. Some individuals had filmmaking skills, and others learned the fundamentals from Robert Kramer and Robert Lacativa when they came to San Francisco to help launch this major offshoot of Newsreel's New York base, but to a very large degree San Francisco Newsreel was self-taught. Ignorance is never truly bliss, however, and San Francisco's strength was not in what it did not know but in the absence of the institutional and hierarchical matrix in which that knowledge is normally lodged. The San Francisco Newsreel did not have members with independent wealth or with developed artistic sensibilities who worked uneasily within a collective mold. It did not have the manifestations of elitism, chauvinism, and some-times opportunism, which these factors can nurture. Nor was there a class difference between privileged white, male, middle-class filmmakers who expected and assumed positions of leadership and a larger body of unskilled, working-class, Third World, black and/or female followers. San Francisco Newsreel was not a pillar of the radical community without flaws or dis-sension, but from the start the membership was primarily working class in background and far more conversant with New Left activism than with radical filmmaking.

The most important Bay Area development in the early days of Newsreel was the emergence of the Black Panther Party from its national headquar-ters in Oakland. In the course of approximately one year Newsreel made three films on the Black Panthers (*Black Panther*,[2] *Mayday*, and *Interview with Bobby Seale*) and acquired a fourth (*Staggerlee*—from National Educational Television [NET], the precursor to PBS). Not only did the Panthers expose Newsreel to the black community (Newsreel was almost exclusively white) and the different strata of that community's proletariat; they also introduced Newsreel to dialectical materialism. This alone was an accomplishment almost no other group could have possibly made. On the one hand, the Black Panthers modeled the adventurist, macho, guerrilla warfare image that most Newsreel members wanted to see themselves in. They could film close-order drills and have their photos taken with armed Panthers. On the other hand, the Panther leadership had an analysis and a program founded on the principles of Marx, Lenin, and Mao Tse-Tung. When the latter program came sugarcoated with the former image, it con-stituted a delicacy Newsreel couldn't resist, despite its New Left bias against these old-school figures.

As one Newsreel member confessed, "If anyone else had said, 'Let's do some P.E. [political education] in dialectical materialism,' we'd have thrown them out the door."[3] And while the Panthers did not lead Newsreel in an abrupt about-face, they did begin a deepening of its political awareness. The political education class was brief and not very detailed. It did, though, air compelling arguments about class and class struggle that could not be ignored, especially in the face of the Panthers' power and prestige. San Francisco's orientation was already, in early 1968, turning in a direction noticeably different from New York's, where the New Left's sense that communism and its theorists were badly dated and condemned by their own checkered history remained largely in place.

The Black Panthers' strength in the Bay Area was not an isolated phe-nomenon. Ever since the days of the Industrial Workers of the World

[IWW], or "Wobblies") and the Western Federation of Miners, San Francisco has been a strongly militant union town. In the 1960s the Free Speech Movement; the hippy culture, which many mistook for a political movement or saw as an alternative to one; the Black Panther Party; the Revolutionary Union (RU, the principal Maoist group in the United States); and the most working-class, (eventually) Marxist-oriented Newsreel office all emerged here. Newsreel's proximity to these groups plus several militant unions, such as the longshoremen's and transit workers', situated it within a very different context from New York Newsreel's Manhattan base.

Even in 1968, when San Francisco Newsreel's organization and direction were not clearly oriented toward Marxism, there were noticeable differences in its ideological predilections from New York Newsreel. The *Film Quarterly* article that appeared at the end of 1968, by Robert Kramer and Norm Fruchter, also contained excerpts from interviews with two San Francisco Newsreel members, Karen Buck and Marilyn Ross.[4] The New York authors speak separately, and at greater length, than the collective voice of the two women. The men's concern is to promote confrontation— films as weapons, activism as battle, propaganda as forcing the audience to deal with where the movement is at. Militarism and highly charged emotions (hate, anger, frustration, and, above all, arrogance) dominate what they have to say. Buck and Ross, however, speak in cooler tones and a more pragmatic bent. They share the view of Newsreel as an "alternative medium," but rather than adopt an ultra-left facade to champion its potential, they analyze achievements on the basis of their own experience.

They stress two points. First, the Newsreel concept of a collective instead of a cooperative creates difficult questions of assimilation: "assimilation of the filmmaker and the radical, assimilation of the individual into the collective. In making films together which reflect a collective, a movement of ideas and actions rather than the individuality of the artist, we must develop new values, forms, new criteria for individual interaction" (44–45). They articulate what San Francisco's films realize: a dissolving of auteur theory and individual personality into a collective endeavor. Even without the entrenched nucleus of skilled filmmakers in New York Newsreel to react against, they recognized that "private political fantasies" could not suffice and that their destruction was a principal concern for the entire collective.

Second, they muted the arrogance of confronting people with Newsreel's attitudes and judgments by stressing the need to "confront people who are not motivated to go see [Newsreels]" (46). They had two proposals for achieving this end: (1) taking the films to the people on the streets and in their community and (2) evaluating audience reaction to learn what makes effective propaganda. Neither idea received systematic development in San Francisco Newsreel's subsequent history, unfortunately, but both ideas reflect an open, outward-looking, more humble spirit than the wrenching metaphor of films as "can openers" that Kramer coined.

In discussing audience response, Buck and Ross note, for example, that middle-class groups respond to the sync-sound draft-resistance films quite well, whereas young, draft-eligible Chicanos do not. Chicanos, however, become very animated when the *Haight Riot* (also known as *The Haight*) is shown. And yet, another "action" film, *Garbage*, leaves them cold and middle-class audiences befuddled.[5] These responses are not arbitrary or unfathomable (people in developing countries may have less interest in symbolic action than a counterculture group like the Motherfuckers has; this group was behind the Lincoln Center demonstration captured in *Garbage*). Buck and Ross indicate an open-minded, thoughtful perspective on audience response that seemed lost in New York Newsreel's more confrontational fervor.

The slack nature of the group's initial structure as a collective left considerable leeway for interpreting Newsreel's role within the movement. As in New York Newsreel, many felt a primary allegiance to the movement and only secondarily to film (a way, perhaps, of discounting the importance of understanding the principles of propaganda and filmmaking thoroughly). Much of the day-to-day film work was done sloppily—films shipped late or in bad condition, speakers who failed to turn up at screenings, and so forth—a situation, of course, not unique to San Francisco Newsreel or even Newsreel as a whole. Everyone acknowledged the problem, but few were prepared to face the alternative of tighter organization.

By late 1969 small factions were exploring various organizing alternatives such as running a repair garage to organize neighborhood youth and managing a movement center, a printing facility, and a health clinic. Proposals for new directions and actions came and went with alarming frequency. Film work-teams had been organized by early 1969, principally a "youth work team" and a "labor work team." They did not reflect a staunch policy of commitment to particular goals or constituencies, although the labor work team did become the germinating soil in which a Marxist orientation began to mature. Newsreel looked like a political organizing unit that happened to have some films. When this diffuseness of purpose became coupled to an absence of funds in late 1969, early 1970, San Francisco Newsreel moved into a period of crisis that only slackened many long months later.

By the beginning of 1970 San Francisco Newsreel had completed twelve films and had begun to develop a Marxist orientation within those films.

But the only film completed since that time has been *The Woman's Film* (1971). The elaboration of a Marxist orientation took place through most of 1969, and by the end of that year it had become clear that structural changes must be made. Since funds had dropped to a dangerously low level by December 1969, the group decided on two basic changes: first, a steering committee (akin to the central committees of the Communist Party) would oversee Newsreel's functioning and maintain priorities; second, resources would be restricted to the completion of two films already decided on—*The Woman's Film* and a labor history film. (The latter was never completed.)

Thus San Francisco Newsreel instituted a structure bordering on democratic centralism, where a small committee makes decisions by which the group must abide. Their tightened structure and the shearing off of some of their non-film-related activities did not resolve all the differences of opinion, however, and a deep breach was still in the making. There was sufficient solidarity and a clear enough point of view for San Francisco to take marked exception to a *Leviathan* article from New York Newsreel in October and November of 1969. In December 1969 San Francisco printed an article of its own in the *Movement* that explored some of Buck and Ross's earlier points and clarified their differences with New York.[6]

The most striking difference is in San Francisco's openly Marxist-Leninist-Maoist rhetoric. San Francisco forthrightly stated, "Our principal task is to help build a working-class movement that will address itself to the questions of imperialism, racism, women's liberation, and socialism in America."[7] The article cites the collective's working-class films *Oil Strike* and *PDM* as effective tools for striking workers to use to win support and to form their own radical organizations. It cites its student-oriented films (*High School Rising* [1969], *San Francisco State Strike* [1969]) and community-oriented film (*Los Siete* [1969]) as further examples of its Marxist orientation and dedication to Mao's principle of "from the masses, to the masses."

The film's concluding quotation from Ho Chi Minh reflects the kind of attitudes that inspired its working-class films and is a good indication of the values that New York and San Francisco still consider most important (as well as a fairly transparent attack on Kramer's sometimes self-important tone): "They [revolutionary cadres] must be kind-hearted, open-minded and sincere. Each gesture, each attitude, must conquer people's hearts. . . . Before the people, a revolutionary cadre has no right to assume a haughty and arrogant attitude as if he were a revolutionary warlord. He must be modest."[8]

San Francisco continued to operate with a steering committee (or central committee) as a cornerstone of its democratic centralism and with work teams engaged in different projects through the early part of 1970. The contradictions that had begun to emerge between lifestyle (counterculture) and working-class (Marxist) politics had already fomented the Weatherman split from SDS and the Eldridge Cleaver–Bobby Seale debate about whether the lumpen proletariat or the industrial proletariat was the principal agent of change. As Newsreel continued to experience financial hardship—a fund-raising drive failed partly because of insufficient planning—with a concomitant curtailment of film production, its own contradictions came into sharper focus. Finally, in June 1970, they came to a head.

Newsreel ran out of money. At the same time, it was committed to completing the two film projects it had already decided on. In spite of this dilemma a group of members (largely from the youth work team) proposed making a film of an Armed Forces Day rally sponsored by MDM (Movement for a Democratic Military). They argued that "it's important and the GIs need it," as well as that MDM would provide political leadership. The steering committee, however, had already decided against this project, but its advocates decided to send a film crew to the rally anyway.

During the next week or so, the group divided into two factions; each group analyzed its position and prepared a statement of how it proposed to function.[9] When the two factions met, it became clear that cooperation was not possible. Essentially, those supporting the GI film did not approve of the proposed tightening of discipline and the collective split in two. The majority of the members (about fifteen) regrouped. The dissenting minority disbanded, and although some of them made a woman's film, *Herstory*, they have not continued as a filmmaking unit.

The new structure continued to rely on democratic centralism (criticism/self-criticism sessions, the strengthening of a central committee) and a division of labor that reflected the group's economic crisis. San Francisco Newsreel envisioned three types of film: films about National Liberation struggles); "films for other classes designed to win support for the proletariat" (no completed films are given as examples), and films "aimed at the white segment of the working class because we are best equipped [being white] to serve them. . . . Our films will comment on the racism, male chauvinism and the petty bourgeois ideology of the white working class which we see as the three main obstacles that divide the working class."[10]

On one hand the decision to acknowledge its own racial composition and work primarily with the white working class is a major shift and reflects an important step away from the romantic tendency to glorify other races and other cultures from the outside. On the other hand it is perhaps a very obvious decision that blacks have been urging white radicals to make for many years. A great number of Newsreel and radical but non-Newsreel films have dealt with imperialism and the domestic colonies of black and Third World people (*The Murder of Fred Hampton* [Howard Alk, 1971], *Bushman* [David Schickele, 1971], and Newsreel's *Black Panther* are films of this type) rather than the filmmaker's almost invariably white background, where there seems to be, perhaps, a dearth of "action." Other films from the New Left itself, like New York Newsreel's *Amerika* (1969) and *The Columbia Revolt* (1968), were often about whites but seldom confronted racism as a specific, vital issue.[11]

To realize its objectives and to overcome the economic crisis that threatened to destroy it, Newsreel took a bold step into the unexplored region of a planned economy. The move advanced the collective well beyond the organizational principles of the Film and Photo League in the even more desperate 1930s and required greater discipline and dedication than less hard-pressed collectives expect today.

Economics and politics found a remarkably balanced treatment in the Newsreel economic plan. Members would divide into three groups: work furlough, film production, and distribution. Work furloughs were an innovative step that overcame several problems: the discrepancy between members who had to work and those who did not (such as occurred in New York); the desperate need for income; and the politically important need for exposure to the working-class milieu. The majority paper, written at the time of the internal split, spelled this plan out.

San Francisco Newsreel quotes Chairman Mao's remarks that the test of a revolutionary intellectual is his day-to-day association with the workers and peasants. There are three degrees of association according to Mao: looking around or "looking at the flowers while on horseback," staying a few moments or "dismounting to look at the flowers," and finally "settling down." Since members were expected to take working-class jobs, the work-furlough program allowed them to dismount "to look at the flowers."[12] Some of their earnings would be used to support those working in the other two areas, and the remainder would form a personal stipend.

The decision to submit to the discipline of a central committee and to support comrades economically, as well as politically, clearly took some of "the fun" out of revolution. And while it did not demand that members be solemn and poker-faced, it did promote a consciousness of participating in a serious endeavor, one worth doing well, with total commitment and predetermined policies. This still-burgeoning form of consciousness prompted San Francisco Newsreel to reread many political texts and to inaugurate a prolonged, carefully planned program of political education. It even (for the first time in Newsreel history) prompted the organization to begin a study of film theory and propaganda.

Since the split in the middle of 1970, San Francisco Newsreel also formalized an earlier tendency within its filmmaking procedures. Films like *Black Panther, San Francisco State Strike,* and particularly *Los Siete* were made with the advice and assistance of people directly involved in what the film depicts. Scripts and film structure were arrived at by a collective exercise that mediated between Newsreel's political analysis and the priorities that the film's subjects perceived for themselves.

As Newsreel regrouped its forces around the woman's film project and, secondarily, a labor history film, it put this principle to even greater practice. Instead of relating to its constituency through a skills training program, it chose to do it primarily through its filmmaking projects. For the woman's film months were spent talking with women and women's groups before the script and the actual subjects were chosen. Then, after the rough cut was made, the women in the film viewed it and made further suggestions. For the labor history film the procedure was intensified to the point where approximately fifty groups or individuals were asked to comment on the proposed script.

This form of preproduction consultation seems an excellent way to avoid making films that excite their makers but wind up miles away from those for whom they are made. At the same time, it flirts with several dangers. First, depending on a group's seriousness and sense of direction, it can become a way of hoping for others to provide guidance. If a group feels insecure about its own ability, it is prone to accept criticism before asking about the motives of the particular critic(s). If too much emphasis is given to what may be narrow self-interest, and it is taken at face value, the film may reflect that bias rather than correct for it.[13] Second, the criticism or suggestions may ignore important considerations for the propagandist: they may emphasize content over form.

Significantly, San Francisco Newsreel has consulted a wide range of political groups and individuals but no leftists working in the film medium themselves like Saul Landow, Haskell Wexler, or Emile de Antonio. Such individuals might be able to supply technical and aesthetic advice. Correspondingly, their political advisers will scrutinize the political analysis or "line" most thoroughly but have relatively little to say about matters such as style or pace. For a group like Newsreel, which has always tended to emphasize the political over the aesthetic, this can be a hazard.

Although a long line of critical thought (both bourgeois and Marxist) has argued for the unity of style and content, gathering suggestions from others may encourage the already manifest tendency to place the two in a hierarchical relationship. Jay Leyda comments on a similar situation in Russia when film scripts, and subsequently the completed film, were submitted to workers' committees for approval. The bureaucracy itself was one problem, but aside from that the method meant that less attention went to style, structure, technique, and so forth, since content and subject matter preoccupy the lay mind (a fact also observable in much criticism written by nonfilm specialists, whether radical or reactionary). In Russia the only anomaly was a continuing admiration for a "showy photographic manner" regardless of its purpose or effect.[14]

THREE SAN FRANCISCO NEWSREEL FILMS

San Francisco Newsreel's first film, *Black Panther,* is integral to the group's development and represents a significantly different starting point than do New York's draft-resistance and counterculture films. San Francisco Newsreel, from the start, abandoned the campus citadel for the greater community and the protagonist as street fighter for the Marxist as social analyst.

I have already discussed some of the Black Panthers' contributions to Newsreel's growth. The personal strength and spiritual vigor behind those contributions dominate *Black Panther.* The film is simply conceived: interviews with Huey P. Newton (in Alameda County Jail), Eldridge Cleaver, and Bobby Seale, intercut with each other and with shots of Black Panthers practicing close-order drills and demonstrating outside the Alameda County Courthouse. The film is spiced with sufficient cutaways to keep the interviews from creating a static impression. A particularly effective combination is a long tracking shot (from a car) of a low-income area of Oakland coupled with Bobby Seale's description of the party's "10 Point Program." The connection is oblique but not obscure. Instead of an obvious translation of Seale's description into shots of police brutality, avaricious businessmen, overcrowded jails, and welfare lines, we see only the outer shell, the general milieu, within which the struggle for black liberation must take place. The image leaves the Panther's program unfixed to specific examples, joins it with the entire black community, and unifies it through a single long take. It is one of the rare examples of superior artistry in Newsreel films.

The spokesmen who were emergent leaders then are household names today. They may not be very much better understood, however, and one of the film's great assets (evidenced by its extensive use by the Panthers for recruitment) is that *Black Panther* introduces us to these three individuals in an unobtrusive, personal manner. They are not demagogues inciting mobs or extremists mouthing absurdities. Each man conveys something of his personal reserve of humor, humility, and determination that scale the caricatures sketched by the mass media back down to human size.

The film's aesthetic appeal derives largely from a rhythmic structure. Other Newsreel films often lack a coherent rhythm for a variety of reasons, but here fifteen minutes of film time sweep past in rapid succession. Each interview presents an interviewee whose delivery is distinctive and lively. Cleaver has an assertive, parrying cadence while Newton uses a gentler, instructional intonation. Seale has a straightforward, mildly inflected rhythm that finally rips into an explosive conclusion that also ends the film. "We're gonna say to the whole damned government, 'Stick 'em up, motherfucker; this is a hold-up!'"

By cutting among the interviews regularly and by introducing cutaway material, these internal rhythms form a structural rhythm for the film as a whole. The cutaway images also contain compelling rhythms of their own, usually militaristic ones such as the parade-drilling and the Panthers chanting in front of the Alameda County Courthouse:

> The revolution has come,
> Off the Pigs!
> It's time to pick up the gun,
> Off the Pigs!

And finally by building the film's shots into a distinct rhythm (notably the concluding tracking shot joined to the static interview shots), the filmmakers create a unified, absorbing whole. There is no riot footage to spellbind the unmoved. The charisma of the men's personalities works a powerful spell of its own, and their arguments stand in clear view, not obscured by the emotional thunderstorms of confrontational rhetoric. We are invited to relate to them and the Black Panther Party not solely on the basis of our presuppositions but also by virtue of their reasoned explanations and the fresh, lively perspectives the three men share. As much as any Newsreel, it fulfills Dziga Vertov's exuberant conception of newsreel films as "fragments of actual energy (as against theatrical energy), with their intervals condensed into a cumulative whole by the great mastery of an editing technique."[15] This combination of assets has made *Black Panther* the most widely screened of all Newsreel films.

Some of San Francisco Newsreel's best films result directly from its opportunity to document a wide range of Bay Area activism. *Black Panther* and *Oil Strike* exemplify this, and so does *San Francisco State Strike*. The strike began in November 1968 and stretched into the spring of 1969. Newsreel made its film near the latter part of the strike, after contacts with the strike leaders had led to the making of *Oil Strike* (about a union-led strike in Richmond, California, against Chevron; the striking students actively supported the oil workers and manned the picket lines in considerable numbers). *San Francisco State Strike* examines the reasons for the strike—the general miseducation, racism, and tracking policies of the California "master plan" for higher education, as well as the most immediate issue: a hamstrung black studies program. Spokesmen address rallies and sometimes speak directly to the camera. President Hayakawa, who showed no patience with the demonstrators, violently rips up student petitions and throws them into a crowd of listeners, and, for a climax, the police swarm across the campus clubbing students, professors, and sympathizers from the community.

The film affords a good opportunity for a comparison of New York and San Francisco's political environment and their film response since both groups filmed college strikes. It should be clear from the start, however, that they did not film identical situations. *The Columbia Revolt* was shot a year earlier. Columbia University is an elite institution, a traditional fount of ruling-class professionals. Columbia's rebels had two goals: stopping gym construction in a predominantly poor, African American neighborhood (Harlem) and radicalizing white students to larger political issues about the class structure of higher education. Community support was relatively weak (nonmilitant, few in numbers), and the strike lasted only two months.

San Francisco State College (now University) is a working-class, commuter college whose graduates fill lower echelon bureaucratic posts, teaching jobs, and skilled labor positions. Minority groups have strong representation, and they resent their continuing proletarianization at the college level. The strike had strong community support and lasted almost an entire school year. There is no evidence that SF Newsreel considered counterculture ideology a vital force, as NY Newsreel did when it beautifully rendered the candlelight wedding of two student activists. There is ample evidence of black and Chicano leadership and of strike solidarity across student/faculty and college/community boundaries. The film's voice-over narration and the strike spokesmen stress the explicitly repressive nature of the school's role, a role that affects each student's daily life, unlike the exploitative nature of Columbia's external policies, which only affect the students with a social conscience.

San Francisco State Strike views the conflicting forces from a Marxist position and reflects little concern with issues like advocating for amnesty for strikers or celebrating confrontations as emotional release that surface throughout *The Columbia Revolt*. The film is briefer (twenty-two minutes vs. fifty minutes) with a quick pace that is something of a disadvantage in that many issues are touched on, but few receive elaboration. Whereas *The Columbia Revolt* may have less advanced politics, they are more fully developed and clearly presented than the politics in *San Francisco State Strike*.

The later film, however, contains the most graphic and provocative riot footage of any Newsreel. Rather than presenting an action montage to represent "violence" as a concept, the camera follows specific actions, firmly located in time and space, to their completion. The result is less aesthetically complex, but its very simplicity lends it a transparency that makes the violence all the more intense. We see a woman student pulled and shoved by a policeman from the street to a police van, and as she is pushed inside, another policeman appears grappling with a male student and shoving him into another van while the student bleeds profusely from the face and head. Likewise, as the police charge through a wooded area, a black student turns, blocks an officer's blow, kicks him in the groin, and wrestles him to the ground. The camera does not cut away, though, and the shot continues until four or five policemen catch the student and beat him mercilessly.

The intensely emotional quality of the riot footage, in fact, can overwhelm the film's predominantly analytical tone. When Newsreel members in Los Angeles screened the film, for example, they found that white or liberal audiences generally became uneasy over the black student's counterattack. The audience's beliefs often had a pacifist tone, and any organizer attempting to discuss self-defense would invariably find the discussion centering on that scene. Black or Third World audiences, however, generally responded with great enthusiasm, the way many cheer when the bugle sounds and the cavalry charges out against the Indians in Hollywood westerns—except that the charger and chargee have been reversed. In this context the film provides a perfect occasion for debating the necessity of self-defense.

It may not be entirely coincidental that so much of the photography of *The Strawberry Statement* (1970) resembles that of *The Columbia Revolt*. A Hollywood film about youthful maturation in the thick of campus unrest is not that far removed in theme from the lifestyle politics that *The Columbia Revolt* documents. It would be difficult to conceive of a Hollywood film, however, with as similarly consistent a cinema-verité documentation of violence or as equally great a stress on historical, material analysis as *San Francisco State Strike*. (A film that comes close is *Medium Cool* [1969], Haskell Wexler's extraordinary film set in the thick of the Chicago Democratic Convention of 1968.) It is a measure of *San Francisco*

State Strike's superiority as a propaganda weapon that it retains a currency in its examination of student issues of class, ethnicity, and opportunity, whereas *The Columbia Revolt* has largely faded into historical artifact.

By late 1969 San Francisco Newsreel had explored a variety of approaches to propaganda: recording the exemplary fusion of thought and action in the leaders of a vanguard party *(Black Panther, Mayday)*, showing the emergent buds of radical consciousness that may bring the dormant white working class to revolutionary life *(Oil Strike)*, examining the rationale for black and Third World solidarity in the face of repressive intransigence *(San Francisco State Strike)*, praising the spirit of the counterculture and connecting its suppression to the necessary requirements of ruling class ideology *(People's Park* [1969]), and, finally, mustering around San Francisco's Hispanic community, its unique problems, and the plight of those who seek to address them *(Los Siete)*.

After completing these and two other films *(Interview with Bobby Seale* and *PDM* [about a strike at Pittsburg–Des Moines Steel Company]), San Francisco Newsreel went through a nonproductive period of financial and political crisis (which included the split within the group) from which it did not emerge until the spring of 1971. During this barren stretch production inched ahead on the women's film, a Palestinian film, and a labor history film (the latter two unfinished).

The three women in charge of the women's film were supported by the remainder of the collective through the work-furlough program, but they still needed production funds. These were slow in coming. Also, their filmmaking procedure had become far more systematic and time-consuming. Many months were spent seeking out women and gaining sharpened insights into the oppressed position of many women in society. Instead of simply finding women to echo ideas already circulating in the women's movement, the filmmakers sought to discover women with an articulate consciousness of the key questions but not necessarily of the rhetorical flair of prominent leaders. Their approach was like learning what the black man on the street who had thought about black nationalism, repression, and self-defense had to say rather than presenting the coherent strategies of a vanguard party's leadership.

The completed film, *The Woman's Film*, fulfills this primary objective admirably, but a few other early goals were cast aside. The initial plans for the film envisioned a history of women's oppression with interviews to illustrate this oppression today. By the time the filmmakers had gotten to know some of the women who appear in the film, however, this idea was abandoned. Judy Smith, one of the three women filmmakers, explained:

"We saw the strength of these women, and the vitality was much more important than any kind of facts."[16]

This response may have a familiar echo when we consider how many Newsreel films have been more captivated by the heat of the moment than its historical context. What came before belongs to the lost continent of history, submerged beneath a sea of impressions and feelings, cut off from the sputtering fuse that is the moment. Basically, the film is a series of interviews like *Black Panther* coupled with occasional cutaways. The interview material is placed within a matrix that reflects a certain line of progression that illuminates contradictions, an important carryover from the historical context originally intended.

A montage of commercials idolizing women begins the film, coupled with Aretha Franklin's version of "Satisfaction." We then meet the women themselves: Florence, a white mother working with "Why Not Whites?"—a group trying to encourage white women to overcome racist biases and demand the welfare aid to which they are entitled; Vonda, a twice-married white housewife and factory worker whose first husband tied a string across the door to check on her whereabouts and whose second husband participated in the strike shown in *PDM* (where Newsreel met her); Vivian, a black welfare recipient and mother who describes the indignities of the welfare program; and several other women whom we learn less of—a publishing secretary, a telephone operator, a Chicana mother, and a migrant worker.

The interview material launches into its key themes of personal oppression in the home and economic exploitation on the job, separated by a change of pace as we plunge briefly into the past—a slave-auction song coupled with drawings of a slave marketplace and women slaves. The sequence is well timed and enlivens the overall rhythm of the film, as well as forming an effective link between the primarily personal experiences of the first half of the film with the more collective outlook of the second half. As a means of linking the present exploitation of women with its historical roots, however, it is more a token gesture than a clear analysis. After this interlude the film addresses political oppression and solutions that range from a hospital workers' strike to Vonda's conclusion that nothing will really change until the workers pick up the gun.

The overall film gives evidence of two main strengths: the warmth, humor, openness, and resilience of the women it presents, and the careful interweaving of parallel narratives toward similar conclusions, a technique that creates a sense of dialectic process and lends an organic unity to the film. The former quality is crucial to sustaining our interest and to presenting the question of women's liberation as far more than "sour grapes" complaining. The anecdotes and stories that the women tell are unique condensations of deep-felt experience into capsular time bombs that continue shaking the foundations of preconceived notions long after they have been heard. Almost every review singles out Florence's dream of mountains of Coca-Cola and candy bars after becoming married and then discovering that marriage was so far from her dreams that "I forgot all about the candy and Coca-Cola," but that is only one of several memorable accounts.

The structure of the film has received less attention, but for those concerned with merging art and propaganda, it is of no less importance. *The Woman's Film* probably comes closer than any other Newsreel to cinema-verité technique. There is no voice-over narration, and the greatest emphasis is on drawing drama and insight from the women themselves rather than imposing it. There are important differences, however, especially from the Drew Associates form of cinema verité, where interviews, music, and montage sequences built from drawings or commercials would be taboo.[17] And where a Drew film usually involved minimal research, *The Woman's Film* was extensively researched in the tradition of Flaherty.

Nonetheless, *The Woman's Film* minimizes the self-consciousness that extensive forethought often breeds. The women are in their homes: they iron, cook, or watch their children and do not simply stand before a camera. Thus there is a certain candid unguardedness about their actions that indicates their trust in the filmmakers and their lack of nervousness before the camera. Within such a context we find insights and meaning emerging slowly, from nuance and gesture more than from extreme stress or from behavior at a crisis moment. We also anticipate that the film, as a variant of cinema verité, will provide continuity to their thought and action rather than manipulate them into abstract categories through Eisensteinian montage.

The principle of Dziga Vertov—to "detect" rather than "invent" plot—becomes the virtue that preserves the integrity of the subject and liberates it from artistic manipulation. The raw material of film—life itself—unlike stone, clay, oils, or words, has form and content, values and meanings, inherent within it. While life itself can be fictionalized in film as readily as in words, it can also be captured whole or documented. There are no galvanizing incidents and no indication of which, if any, slower processes of edification or heightened awareness lead the women to their radical conclusions. Hence, the sections become like a series of stepping-stones stretched across a stream of false consciousness. But the stones lack a connecting handrail; our passage requires great leaps on a long march that, as in so many other cases, biases the film toward the predisposed if not the already convinced.

The film reflects a few other problems that impede Newsreel's progress. For example, there is one Chicano woman interviewed who speaks of her fear of gringos and her training "to not cause trouble." While she is aware of the socializing forces that shape these attitudes, her awareness has not carried her as far as the principal women in the film have gone. This leads to several nagging questions. Is the sequence meant to imply that white and black working-class women are more advanced than Chicanas, or was it tacked on simply to acknowledge Third World women in general without really examining their situation in depth? (There are no Japanese American, Chinese American, or other ethnicities represented.) The latter seems more likely from the brevity of the scene and the sense of detachment that it conveys: at one point the camera tracks past a series of migrant huts in a shot reminiscent of the tracking shots in *Black Panther* and *Oil Strike*. In this case, however, the effect is to underscore the parallel, nonmeeting lines of the camera and the Chicano community. Unlike the black women and the white women who are featured in close and medium shots, the Chicana and her problems seem more remote, somehow detached from the mainstream of Newsreel's preoccupations.

Finally, the film brushes against but never tackles what San Francisco Newsreel had defined in its position paper at the time of the major split in the group as a priority: creating propaganda for the white working class that would combat racism. Although Florence is active in "Why Not Whites?," a group that obviously must deal with racist arguments, the film never explores this issue or Florence's impressions of it. None of the other white women in the film discuss racism specifically, nor do they reflect any particular awareness of the importance of the question or their situation and objectives. The omission perhaps indicates the central dilemma that the filmmakers faced—to let the women speak for themselves and yet to present the filmmakers' own, Marxist perspective on the issues and their resolution. The omission is an egregious one that blunts the film's organizing importance and reflects a tendency toward "tailism"—following after advanced elements in one area without introducing central ideas that are available, and known, from other sectors of the same general movement. After making three films on the Panthers, which clearly establish the central importance of overcoming racism, Newsreel would seem to have a poor memory of its own history.

The weight of these criticisms may seem to relegate the film to the second rank of Newsreel's output, but, in fact, the intensity of critical engagement with the film is a measure of its strength. *The Woman's Film* repre-sents a more serious attempt at a fusion of art and propaganda than the majority of Newsreel's films, and because of this it invites more sustained criticism. The failings are relative to the scale of the project, and the scale is quite impressive. The film does not present charismatic leaders who have advanced far beyond the average viewer's consciousness. The film has coherence and a revelatory quality that, at moments, can be astounding, especially when the women relate some of their own, very personal experi-ences. Their stories, in fact, have a captivating quality similar to the anecdo-tal tales in Godard's films and far more direct political implication. The protagonists are strong, perceptive women who bear witness to the strength and self-awareness of the working class. They conquer stereotypes and demolish myths. Despite its flaws *The Woman's Film* remains one of Newsreel's most important accomplishments.

An examination of San Francisco Newsreel's entire film output leads to a few general observations. First, San Francisco appears to have taken note of the difference between agitation and propaganda. Outside of the "turn-on" films (short, music driven montages on a particular theme), San Francisco Newsreel has shied away from emotional and moral arousal, the clear clarion call to action that many hear and few heed. It seems that it has also begun to differentiate between propaganda (which draws on precon-ceptions for its effect) and education (which attempts to shape or reshape those preconceptions) in films like *Oil Strike, Los Siete,* and *The Woman's Film.* The latter distinction still lacks consistency within SF Newsreel's film work, though, suggesting the essentially intuitive level at which it corre-lates politics and art.

Language is of critical importance to the propagandist. It is a means of establishing communication and promoting dialogue. The silence pervading works expressing bourgeois stultification and decay (e.g., most of Antonioni, Roeg's *Walkabout* [1971], Pasolini's *Teorema* [1968]) yields to the sounds of a revolution in the process of construction. But *how* these sounds are communicated is also of crucial importance as San Francisco Newsreel has begun to realize. Emile de Antonio commented about Newsreel films: "What they're doing is making film for the smallest possible audience, themselves and a very tiny minority of people who share their aesthetic. The people who share their politics is a much wider audience; the people who share their aesthetics is very tiny."[18] De Antonio touches on a vital point: aesthetics can become a barrier as easily as a mediation.

Newsreel has, however, learned the importance of how sound and image are joined and has utilized two methods that seem particularly noteworthy.

Neither one is new, and the use of each reflects a policy of common sense more than aesthetic ingenuity. That they were abandoned for other, less successful techniques in many instances may be a more remarkable fact than their utilization in others. The first is counterpoint and includes music (the slave-auction song in *The Woman's Film*), words (Bobby Seale's enumeration of the 10 Point Program), and presence (the picnic sounds in the final sequence of *Los Siete*). San Francisco Newsreel has learned to skirt the easily contrived irony, as well as the disconnected parallel. These become extremes of distractingly self-conscious linkage.

In general, San Francisco Newsreel seems to have concluded that counterpoint between an offscreen voice and the image must be plausible and natural. This emphasis on the organic interconnection of image and sound also militates against balder, ironic juxtapositions, which can be a different form of "Voice of God" commentary since the juxtaposition arises solely from the filmmaker's discretion and not an event's internal integrity.

The second tendency is toward direct sound and synchronized speech, the staple of American cinema verité. Although this tendency moves away from an Eisensteinian montage of images or a Voice of God commentary as a basic pattern, it risks foundering in a sea of disconnected, inchoate voices. The resolution, though, may be a matter of proportion. Sync sound has the powerful appeal of recording testimony where charges of manipulation—within the shot—are effectively silenced. But by itself sync sound can become tiresome. The image may even restrict our range of association by tying the sound to a particular situation or individual when a contrapuntal (Eisensteinian) structure could suggest a spectrum of applicability. Newsreel has not yet settled into a comfortable pattern for itself, but films like *Black Panther, Oil Strike, Interview with Bobby Seale,* and *The Woman's Film* indicate an effort to find a balance between counterpoint and synchronization.

San Francisco Newsreel's experience has also brought it up against the aesthetics of selection. Artists like Warhol and, before him, Duchamp discovered the artist's capability to play the art object off against its context or, more precisely, to create an art object simply through context—placing a toilet bowl in a museum or painting a soup can—as the Drew films play off their subject against what society expects from a hero.[19] In a similar, but less systematic, manner San Francisco Newsreel has come to realize the importance of who or what it selects as its subject and in what context it places that subject. Mission District families in *Los Siete*, rank-and-file workers in *Oil Strike*, and nonglamorous, working-class women in *The Woman's Film* all gain an aura of importance simply by their transference to celluloid as significant film subjects. Newsreel imparts a heroic quality to those whom Hollywood films have seldom treated heroically, simply by casting them within the slot the hero normally fills. The effect is potentially an excellent synthesis of the conflict over whether the individual hero or the masses constitute the most appropriate film subject (a debate that goes back at least to the 1930s in Russia, when Eisenstein was criticized for his abstract treatment of characters).

When Newsreel chooses women like Florence or Vonda or families like the Rioses in the early scenes of *Los Siete*, it effectively transforms the masses into heroes. Most important, it does so not by singling out the exceptional or charismatic leader nor by praising the "masses" as an abstract, impersonal quantity—the choices between which the Russian film flip-flopped—Newsreel's alternative represents an important synthesis of the difficult and seldom explicated dialectic between the individual and the collective. It provides figures with whom a broad spectrum of viewers can identify in explicitly personal ways, and it places these figures within the frame customarily reserved for the hero. The result, when coupled with another Newsreel alteration of context—the formation of a "liberated zone" of discussion and debate—can mean a very important breakthrough in the creation of propaganda. Discussion allows the audience's response to be engaged more fully; it provides a means of identification that can unify historical process and personal lives, the movement of history with individual experience.

The Political Documentary and the Question of Impact

The vitality of documentary films is as indisputable as their predominantly left-of-center views. This may seem somewhat surprising given that the rightward drift of mainstream American politics after Bill Clinton not only eviscerated the Democratic Party's traditional base in working- and middle-class issues of health, education, and, most dramatically of all, welfare but also failed to foster a moral base comparable to the family values and corporate virtues of the Republican right. A right-leaning documentary surge may well be in the wings,[1] but it is also clear that there is far less onus for such a movement to manifest itself in a political climate characterized by vividly conservative mainstream news and entertainment media reporting. The right already has powerful voices and dominant outlets to such an extent that a right-leaning bias has gradually become a norm.

Where else do gays, lesbians, bisexuals, and transgendered people get to represent themselves in-depth and at length, with appreciation for the complexity and challenge of living as part of a sexual minority whose access to civil liberties and human rights cannot be taken for granted? Where else do ethnic minorities find representation that gives their voices the timbre and clarity accorded our still dominantly white, male political and business establishment? Where else do environmentalists and social activists find works that speak to their issues with passion and eloquence? And where else do women not only become subjects who can speak compellingly about harrowing experiences, unfair treatment, abuse, rape, and other crimes but also, quite often, serve as the makers of the works we see?

But are the numerous, often terrific, documentaries of recent years on the Iraq War, the Bush White House, the corporation as a psychopathic entity, the environment as an unfolding disaster, the global economy as sign of the end of the nation-state and the rise of transnational corporate hegemony, the terrors of a so-called war on terror, and the horrors of ethnic conflict and genocidal cleansings as powerful an antidote as one might think? I often wonder. For three reasons.

The first is simply that many documentaries, and most of the ones that receive theatrical play, are, indeed, genuinely documentaries and not news reports, journalistic accounts, exposés, or advocacy statements to contest those voices that defend the status quo. As such they proclaim the voice of dissent alive and well. They speak in imaginative, compelling ways. This is also a limitation. The daily barrage of conservative viewpoints easily outweighs the occasional viewing of a documentary with a contrary point of view. And the vast amount of entertainment that eschews the darker, more complex issues that lie beneath the "feel good" tone of quiz shows, comedies, Hollywood gossip, and routine news reports that pass along what politicians and businessmen want us to hear, along with the spectacle of reality TV and its clever play between contempt and fascination for eccentric characters whose lives never seem to intersect with the political and the fraught issues of the day, inevitably creates a zero degree of cultural expectations that any more trenchant work must overcome.

The machinery of entertainment, with its hands-off attitude toward the political, acts to disqualify works that take a different tack in another way as well. Although those who understand the documentary as a form to help us see the world anew understand that it is not bound by a journalistic ethics or by illusions of objectivity, this has also proven an Achilles heel. Critics cite the lack of objectivity as evidence that a given film is bad journalism and therefore unworthy of our attention. "Fair and balanced" reporting does not include Morgan Spurlock, Stephanie Black, Eugene Jarecki, Kim Longinotto, Nick Broomfield, Robert Greenwald, Heidi Ewing and Rachel Grady, or Michael Moore.

The National Rifle Association, not exactly a neutral player in these culture wars, used its website to excoriate Moore's *Bowling for Columbine* (2002) for its "factual" errors. As Dinesh D'Souza and John Sullivan did in *2016: Obama's America* (2012), the NRA strives to create an impression of genuine objectivity, clear-headed logic, and obvious conclusions, together with a touch of moral outrage at Moore's "distortions," in the one case, or Obama's secret plotting to overthrow both democracy and capitalism in favor of a pan-national Islamic state, in the other. The work of dedicated political filmmakers who captivate and provoke has its impact, but unless their provocations are taken up and carried further, unless the terms that frame debate shift to progressive ground, until there is a fierce backlash against the red tide (Republican red, that is) that would drown progressive work in its own bathwater, the long-term, systemic impact I am calling for will be lacking.

This leads to my second concern: these films, without exception, do not arise from and do not speak to any form of concerted, organized movement. They often embody the impassioned views of individuals dedicated to principles of social justice, environmental protectionism, civil liberties, equal opportunity, and human rights; but these voices and views, however widely shared, lack a common political base. The Democratic Party is no more potent—and is most often less so—as an organizing force for significant change than it was in the Johnson/Nixon/Carter/Reagan years. The Green Party has never made significant inroads on the national stage and has become, like the Peace and Freedom Party before it, and the Communist Party before that, largely irrelevant. Unions are more complicit with corporate policies than ever and attacks on them still multiply. The women's, civil rights, gay and lesbian, and other identity politics movements have not proven capable of mobilizing the type of broad coalition of progressive voices needed to counter policies that have bankrupted the federal government as a force for social change. Whether led by a Republican or Democrat, our government has essentially become a government of, by, and for the corporation. It has abandoned its role as regulator of commerce and protector of individuals, perpetuated terrorism with a new version of war that breeds the very thing it opposes, imperiled the environment, and surrendered to secrecy, deception, surveillance, and punishment for dissenters and whistleblowers rather than for the perpetrators of fundamental abuses of power.[2]

Be it *Iraq in Fragments* (James Longley, 2006) or *Fahrenheit 9/11* (Michael Moore, 2004), *An Inconvenient Truth* (Davis Guggenheim, 2006) or *The Hunting Ground* (Kirby Dick, 2015), progressive films remain eerily disconnected from the American populace except in their capacity as a significant but occasional experience. They provide an intermittent boost for many issues and causes but can hardly compete with the dominant forms of news, be it in their sanitized Yahoo or Google renditions, the local newspaper, the supermarket checkout magazines, or network and cable news. It is not the primary task of such films to build a left movement in America; that responsibility lies elsewhere. Until that responsibility is taken up, however, the triumph of the political documentary will remain a great achievement well worth celebrating but not the political victory that will turn the tide of recent events from their catastrophic direction.

A third reason for my concern about the impact of the political documentary centers, ironically, on recent efforts to systematize what is called "social impact" empirically, largely by those who provide funding for social issue / social justice documentaries. Rationalized as an effort to know what kind of results they are getting for their investment, and by a desire to make impact itself more efficient and measurable, organizations like the Ford Foundation, Working Films, the Fledgling Fund, Active Voice, BRITDOC, JustFilms, the MacArthur Foundation, and others have sought to incorporate documentary filmmaking into the conceptual arena and procedural protocols of Madison Avenue, euphemistically termed the "design thinking field."[3] Already a staple of most Hollywood studios and the MBA suits who run them, focus groups, polls, preview screenings, and audience feedback are but a few of the tools promoted within a new framework for what *social impact* means.

Buzz words like *empowerment* and *outreach* become "social impact" when good intentions join themselves to social metrics. It is essentially some of the funders of documentaries who have brought about this marriage.[4] Today, as part of the great golden age of documentary flowering, funding sources are numerous, even if not adequate, and range from the National Endowment for the Arts to national television networks across Europe, from PBS to HBO and from the Sundance Institute to crowd source websites like Indiegogo and Kickstarter. When some of these funding sources begin to dictate the terms for social impact and roll out tools to measure it, trouble begins.

What does the desire to measure social impact sound like? Not like the call to arms, or revolution, to be sure, and not like anything likely to appear in a how-to book on good writing. For example, the classic idea of a political movement no longer pertains. The idea of political movements becomes a "partisan political term" (clearly a very bad thing and no longer very progressive sounding), when what is needed is a "capacity to provide users with the option to do something as citizens" or a way to "get people to collaborate on projects" by means of a new force called "zing."[5] Of course, everything from bank accounts to election ballots, but maybe not the "Occupy Wall Street" movement, which doesn't loom as an obvious example in the zing literature, could fulfill this capacity-providing function. Projects can be of almost any kind, even if not particularly political: the example given is to get out of your car and take pictures that you post to Flickr.[6] Such projects aim to create "a networked media and advocacy landscape,"[7] something that organizing, mobilizing, and demonstrating might have done before the current crop of progressive funding entities opted to put the focus on cultivating landscape design rather than building political movements.

A vivid example of what measurable social impact amounts to is Jason Russell's YouTube video *Kony 2012*. A thirty-minute video about a terrorist insurgent in Uganda named Joseph Kony, who destroys schools and turns children into soldiers and prostitutes, or worse, it got a million hits in its first twenty-four hours.[8] Here is social impact of the highest order.

The video gives us a clear sense of just how bad this man is and proposes making him a household name—known for his notoriety rather than achievements. Although what kind of response the million visitors, or the droves of other visitors since, have to the video is not clear from the number of hits alone, other metrics can be brought to bear. At the end of the video, we're told we can take action in three ways: spread the word to bring more viewers to the site, donate funds, or ask for an "action kit." The action kit is not described and not immediately obvious. I made further inquiry and received an email explaining that I needed to click on the Kony 2012 "Store" button to order it. This is the email:

> Hey Bill,
> Thanks for reaching out and asking about our film! Here's the link to our website where you can buy the action kit you mentioned: http://shop.invisiblechildren.com/products/kony-kit
> It comes with two shirts, a bracelet, a pin, and lots of posters and stickers. If you have any other questions, feel free to ask! We'd love to hear from you![9]

What the kit does not come with is historical background on Uganda, biographical detail on Kony or his followers, information on who supports him or where his weapons come from, or how he fits into the larger picture of violence and terror worldwide. He is simply a very bad apple, and by showing support for Invisible Children, the organization behind the website, we are doing our part to put a stop to his criminal activities in a way that can be measured to show the social impact this video has had. Such is the world of social impact metrics.[10]

That much of the prose surrounding the social impact movement, if we may call it that, is jargon of the most obfuscating kind is symptomatic of the enormous challenge that established, nonprofit institutions have when they call for social change but not too much of it. Their funds come from benefactors, patrons, and endowments whose wealth derives from the system as we know it. Newly coined definitions of movements, citizen projects, and media landscapes replace actual political organizing and protest such as what Occupy Wall Street instigated. Prose such as "High impact social documentary projects stand to serve as incubators for media practices on rising platforms," which appears to mean "Great films inspire others," takes such convoluted form as a way to signal that authors and audience belong to a discreet institutional matrix that knows how to do something the average layperson, or uninformed filmmaker, does not.[11] It is impact in a fishbowl, measurable and demonstrable but safely contained at the same time. It is ameliorative rather than transformative, liberal more than radical.

What is particularly striking about this movement, apart from the jargon and the dubious notion of impact measured by hits, purchases, donations, and the like, is what is missing. Not things irrelevant but rather what might be termed structuring absences: concepts and entities that one might think central to any discussion of social change.[12] The most prominent entity that proves absent is the state. Although the state stood behind the flowering of documentary in the Soviet Union, Great Britain, Canada, and, briefly in the 1930s, the United States, as well as other countries, it seems no longer relevant. Documentary film long ago shifted from supporting or promoting state policies and actions to contesting or opposing them with the rise of the civil rights, women's, LGBT, and multiple ethnic minority movements, but such movements no longer stand at the heart of an amorphous, if not ambiguous, social impact movement. Any sense of a need to confront the state and its law, its systematic exclusion of some from equal opportunities and equal rights, recedes. If maximum social impact is to bring about needed legislation, why not spend money on lobbyists rather than films? If no change of law seems adequate to fix a dysfunctional system, why not promote a broad social movement for radical change rather than films? But funders want to continue to fund films; they just want to be sure they have measurable but not too radical an impact.

This model of social change finds graphic expression in an oft-cited diagram from Fledgling Fund (fig. 1). The diagram measures success as a series of rings or ripples spreading out from "quality film or media."[13]

Ever greater ripples spread out from a status quo "disruptive" film. It's useful, however, to remember that ripples typically die out as they spread from a central source and that no one film has ever been the cause of fundamental social change. Elegant and seductive as an image, it lacks, ironically, an empirical basis and is but a modified version of another outmoded model: the hypodermic needle. That metaphor was popular in some early debates about sex and violence in the movies. Inflammatory content would enter into the consciousness of viewers as if it had been injected directly into their nervous system, producing a proclivity to emulate the very sex and violence represented. This proved true for a very small minority of viewers and stood in direct opposition to the classic idea of catharsis.[14] The model is patently wrong for most viewers whose attitudes toward sex or

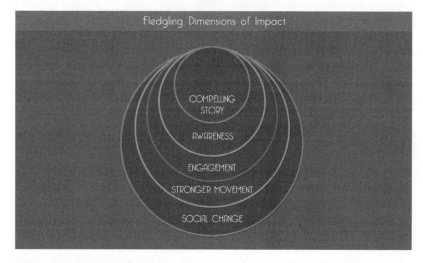

Figure 1. Fledgling Fund diagram.

violence are not so easily altered by a single exposure to suggestive content. If change could be so readily produced there would scarcely be any social cohesion and political stability left to change.

Such a model also omits any notion of resistance, any idea that viewers, or citizens, might have a deep investment in the status quo that is not so easily pried free. What happened to the work of Stuart Hall and other proponents of cultural studies with their emphasis on the complex ways in which films, television, and other cultural products are received, used, transformed, endorsed, or countered?[15] Can social impact advocates engage with viewers on a comparable level of sophistication? Or do they simply need to make films as *"components of strategic campaigns with specific agendas,"* which a report from the Center for Media and Social Impact suggests,[16] as if namby-pamby jargon could do the work previously reserved for analytic, interpretative, and organizing tools.

Another way to put this is to argue that the social impact movement acts as if ideology doesn't exist. If we consider ideology not as explicit dogma but as deeply ingrained ways of seeing, thinking, and doing that are habitual and only slowly implanted, or altered, it is clear that the Fledgling

Fund's hypodermic needle / ripple effect model, to mix metaphors, fails to take it into account. Even great, powerful social issue documentaries do not alter dominant ideologies or bolster alternative ones in a direct, measurable, lockstep way—although they may well contribute to changing how we see and understand an issue. How a progressively inclined group of individuals and institutions could demonstrate such a remarkable case of political amnesia is hard to explain apart from the obvious need to feel good about achieving measurable forms of social impact without rocking the existing ideological boat too strongly. (How might we measure the impact of a film that propelled people to revolution? Who would be left to do the measuring, and what postrevolutionary purpose could it productively serve? The entire model assumes that impact will not only be measurable but will leave the basic status quo intact.)

To see an issue in a fresh way, to feel moved by a perspective or experience that cuts against the grain of dominant ideology, is to reframe the basic rules of the game. Rather than producing ripples that lead straight to change, powerful, affective films can help reframe how we think about specific issues of social justice, global warming, the war on terror, Islamic or Christian fundamentalism, racism, sexism, corporate malfeasance, and many others. To see anew is to shift perceptual frames. To be moved to do so by works possessed of aesthetic power yields real but not necessarily empirically measurable results. This sentiment is well captured by Ty, a character in Dave Eggers's *The Circle*, a brilliant satire of the new paradigm of Internet omnipotence—at our service, of course: "Not every human activity can be measured. The ceaseless pursuit of data to quantify the value of any endeavor is catastrophic to true understanding."[17]

To be clear about one point: gaining a good feel for the way audiences respond to a given work, especially when there are opportunities to make adjustments, is not a bad thing. The problem arises when this becomes framed as an empirical, marketing problem, part and parcel of commodity culture, on the one hand, and when compliance with preestablished definitions and procedures becomes a requirement for funding in the first place, on the other.[18] Filmmakers can use all the tools they can get, but to have someone's idea of social impact measurement tools thrust upon them is a gross disservice when it narrows options, diminishes priorities, and sidesteps radical visions.

All the social impact rhetoric begins with the assumption that impact will be measured relative to a "well-made film," a "deep story," or a "high quality" film, but nothing on this entire bandwagon does more than assume this to be the case. Here is a primary mission for funders: find and support the best possible work; help the creators assess the impact of their work when that is beneficial; and abandon all hope of leading the creative horse by an empirical cart.

The empirical cart is an old familiar cart, in fact. It is the sort of outcome produced by political election campaigns and the "creatives" who fill the trenches of advertising agencies, their service conditional on the impact assessments carried out by others. Funders who truly value impact above all and yet hesitate to form political action committees, employ lobbyists, or build grassroots movements for social change might provide funding to "embed" progressive filmmakers within NGOs; offer seed money to hire in-house filmmakers at corporations eager to contribute to the public good, as companies such as Patagonia, Trader Joe's, Burt's Bees, and Odwalla have been, at least to some degree; or return to doing what they have traditionally done: fund and nurture the best possible films from the most qualified filmmakers and then let those individuals decide what tools they want to use to assess their success at reframing issues and helping see anew what we have not truly seen before.

There are voices championing this direction, such as Tabitha Jackson, the current director of the Sundance Documentary Film Program. She urges support for documentary as an art because it is art that has the greatest impact, not assessment protocols. *Filmmaker* magazine, reporting on her talk at DOC NYC in November 2014, writes, "She found a sly analog example of the current trend for data-driven, algorithmic 'curation' in Komar and Melamid's satiric 'Most Wanted Painting,' a treacly historical landscape whose style, subject matter and even color is derived from focus group findings."[19] The wisdom of her emphasis on achievement that transforms us, that helps us understand what it feels like to experience the world in a given way and to see the world anew, will be in the films that follow from her leadership.

Let's treasure, and fund, genuinely political documentaries that rely on the art and craft of filmmaking to move us in those mysterious, unfathomable ways great works do. Let's make ample room for the essay, the personal, the unique and individual, the truly independent and visionary that has its distinct impact in profound but ineffable ways, as work by Alan Berliner, Rachel Grady and Heidi Klum, Leonard Retel Helmrich, Werner Herzog, Mark Lewis, Kim Longinotto, Errol Morris, Joshua Oppenheimer, Rithy Panh, Laura Poitras, Marlon Riggs, Jean Rouch, Travis Wilkerson, Agnes Varda, and so many other outstanding filmmakers demonstrate. Would *Into the Abyss, The Fog of War, The Act of Killing, Position among the Stars, Cane Toads: The Conquest, 12th and Delaware, Nobody's*

Business, Les maître fous, Les glaneurs, Citizenfour, Hidden Faces, Tongues Untied, or *S21* only win support from a social impact funder if their makers supplied a comprehensive, empirical plan for how they would build a website—ideally with a store, comments section, and complementary Facebook page; liaise with "stakeholders" and "strategic partners" from inception to completion; produce modified versions of the same story for different users or markets; build community support through speaking engagements and discussion guides; and submit empirical proof of the measurable impact all this effort produced?

Maybe, just maybe, our successful filmmakers would have the strength and energy to go on to another project rather than find themselves trapped by their assessment labors like the hapless prisoner in *Woman in the Dunes* (Hiroshi Teshigahara, 1964). Despite the social impact metrics movement, radical, galvanizing work will continue to find its way before us but perhaps with less support and more obstacles, at least until this ill-conceived movement acknowledges that the immeasurable, incommensurate, and inexplicable are as tightly bound to the political as radical, transformative vision is to the measures taken.

Notes

INTRODUCTION

1. The full text of my thesis is available on my blog: billnichols.net.

2. Bill Nichols, *Newsreel: Documentary Filmmaking on the American Left* (New York: Arno Press, 1980).

3. "American Documentary Film History," *Screen* 13, no. 4 (1972–73): 108–15; and "Documentary: Theory and Practice," *Screen* 17, no.4 (1977): 34–48.

4. Bill Nichols, *Ideology and the Image: Social Representation in the Cinema and Other Media* (Bloomington: Indiana University Press, 1981). Portions of chapter 1, "Art and the Perceptual Process," repr. in *Semiotics: The Basics* (London: Routledge, 2001). Chapter 5, "For *The Birds*," translated into Chinese and repr. in *Contemporary Cinema* 5 (Sept. 1987). Chapter 7, on Frederick Wiseman's films, translated into German and published as "Die Dokumnetarfilme von Frederick Wiseman und in US-amerikanishen Fernsehserien," in *Frederick Wiseman: Kino des Sozialen*, ed. and trans. Eva Hohenberger (Nordhein-Westfalen: Dokumentarfilminitiative, 2009), 107–37.

5. David Bordwell, *Narration in the Fiction Film* (Madison: University of Wisconsin Press, 1985). I devoted much of the early 1980s to an ambitious history of postwar American cinema. My research involved numerous screenings at various film archives; readings of the papers of figures such as Stanley Kramer, Kirk Douglas, John Howard Lawson, Edward Dmytryk, Ben and Norma Barzman, Abe Polonsky, and many others; as well as interviews with these individuals and others, including Amos Vogel, Robert Gardner, Carlton Moss, D.A. Pennebaker, and Ricky Leacock. The intended book was never completed, but the research provided invaluable depth for some of my later writings on fiction, avant-garde, and documentary film.

6. Bill Nichols, "The Voice of Documentary," *Film Quarterly* 36, no. 3 (1983): 17–30.

7. Bill Nichols, "Form Wars: The Political Unconscious of Formalist Theory," in *Classical Hollywood Narrative: The Paradigm Wars*, ed. Jane Gaines (Durham, NC: Duke University Press, 1992): 49–77.

8. Bill Nichols, *Representing Reality: Issues and Concepts in Documentary* (Bloomington: Indiana University Press, 1991). Chap. 2, "Documentary Modes of Representation," translated and repr. in Slovenia as "Dokumentarani racini reprezentacje," *Ekran* 23, no. 35 (1998). Chap. 6, "The Fact of Realism and the Fiction of Objectivity," repr. in *Post-War Cinema and Modernity,* ed. John Orr and Olga Taxidou (Edinburgh: Edinburgh University Press, 2000), 188–207. The book was translated by Josetxo Cerdan and Eduardo Iriarte into Spanish as *La representación de la realidad* (Barcelona: Ediciones Paidós, 1997; 2nd edition, 2007).

9. Bill Nichols, *Blurred Boundaries* (Bloomington: Indiana University Press, 1994): a study of the indeterminacies between historical and fictional representation, the book undoes some of the stricter delineations of forms and modes in *Representing Reality.* Chap. 5, "Performative Documentary," translated and repr. in *Diskurs Film: Münchner Beiträge zur Filmphilologie* 7 (1995): 149–66; and in *Critical Visions in Film Theory,* ed. T. Corrigan, P. White, and M. Mazaj (New York: Bedford/St. Martin's, 2011), 672–88. Chap. 3, "At the Limits of Reality (TV)," translated and repr. in *Kwartalnik Filmowy* (Fall 1998); *Ekran* 23, no. 35 (1998); and in *Media Studies: A Reader* (1999). And Bill Nichols, *Introduction to Documentary* (Bloomington: Indiana University Press, 2001): an introductory text written on all aspects of documentary film study, it has been translated into Korean by Hanul Books (Seoul, 2005); Portuguese: *Introdução ao documentário,* trans. Mônica Saddy Martins (São Paulo: Papirus Editora, 2005); and Italian: *Introduczione al documentario* (Milan: Editrice Il Castoro, 2013); 2nd edition, trans. Alice Arecco (Milan: Editrice Il Castoro, 2014). The second edition (Bloomington: Indiana University Press, 2010) has also been translated into Czech: *Úvod do Dokumentárního Filmu* (Prague, Czech Republic: Akademie múzických umění, 2010); and Spanish: *Introducción al documental* (Coyoacán, México: Universidad Nacional Autónoma de México, 2013). *Cinema's Alchemist: The Films of Péter Forgács,* ed. Bill Nichols and Michael Renov (Minneapolis: University of Minnesota Press, 2011).

CHAPTER 1. DOCUMENTARY FILM AND
THE MODERNIST AVANT-GARDE

"Documentary Film and the Modernist Avant-Garde" originally appeared in *Critical Inquiry* 27, no. 4 (2001): 580–610. The essay grew from numerous sources of encouragement and stimulation. A commission to write on the coming of sound to documentary for vol. 6 of Historia General del Cine, *La transición del mudo al sonoro,* ed. Javier Maqua and Manuel Palacio (Madrid: Ediciones Cátedra, 1996) first caused me to wonder if the early history of documentary did not need significant revision. An invitation from Kees Bakker, director of the Joris Ivens Foundation, to deliver a keynote address at an international conference on Ivens's career in 1998 led me to take my first extended look at the relationship between early documentary and the modernist avant-garde. The conference papers were published as *Joris Ivens and the Documentary*

Context, ed. Kees Bakker (Amsterdam: Amsterdam University Press, 1999). In the fall of 1999 the acting director of the Getty Research Institute's Scholars and Seminars Program, Michael Roth, invited me to give a talk, "Documentary Film and Modernism," in a lecture series titled "The Construction of Historical Meaning," which provided the occasion for me to revisit the history of documentary in a sustained way. I am extremely grateful to the Getty Research Institute for its support during the 1999–2000 academic year, when I conducted research and prepared the present, revised version of my lecture, and, especially, to Sabine Schlosser, for editorial assistance. I benefited greatly from the comments and suggestions made during the question-and-answer session following my lecture there and from written feedback by Stefan Jonsson. Feedback from an abbreviated presentation of these arguments at Visible Evidence VIII (Utrecht, August 2000) helped me make a series of refinements to the essay. I benefited most importantly from repeated, extensive feedback and editorial assistance from Catherine M. Soussloff. This essay would not have been possible without her unstinting encouragement.

1. John Grierson, "The E.M.B. Film Unit," in *Grierson on Documentary,* ed. Forsyth Hardy (New York: Praeger, 1971), 165.

2. See Bill Nichols, "The Documentary and the Turn from Modernism," in *Joris Ivens and the Documentary Context,* ed. Kees Bakker (Amsterdam: Amsterdam University Press, 1999), 148–59.

3. See Bill Nichols, *Newsreel: Documentary Filmmaking on the American Left* (New York: Arno, 1980).

4. Paul Rotha, *Documentary Film* (London: Faber, 1935), 79.

5. Jack C. Ellis, *The Documentary Idea: A Critical History of English-Language Documentary Film and Video* (Englewood Cliffs, NJ: Prentice Hall, 1989), 9.

6. Erik Barnouw, *Documentary: A History of the Non-fiction Film* (New York: Oxford University Press, 1993), 3.

7. Among other documentary histories, Richard Meran Barsam's account distinguishes travelogues, newsreels, and other nonfiction forms from documentary proper but tends to graft his own, latter-day conception of documentary back onto this history rather than provide an origin story as such. "Documentary" simply appears, once Grierson names it in 1926, as a distinct form of nonfiction, complete with American, British, Soviet, and Continental variants. See Richard Meran Barsam, *Nonfiction Film: A Critical History* (New York: Dutton, 1973). Brian Winston prefers to begin his account with fellow Britisher John Grierson. Although he, too, notes other forms of nonfiction that precede the documentary, it is Grierson; the early and less heralded example of Edward S. Curtis, with his *In the Land of the Head Hunters* (1914); and Flaherty, with his colonial baggage and insistence of making art from life, that provide the primary moment of origin. Winston does suggest somewhat deeper roots in nineteenth-century realism after Courbet: this seems to lay the groundwork for the aesthetic principles that transfer over to film in some incompletely specified way. See Brian Winston, *Claiming the Real: The*

Documentary Film Revisited (London: BFI, 1995), 8–10, 19–23, 26–29. The sense of relatively untroubled passage from photographic realism to documentary representation remains strong in all these accounts. Kristin Thompson and David Bordwell's excellent general history of the cinema, *Film History: An Introduction* (New York: McGraw-Hill, 1994), also follows the same line but in less exaggerated form. They introduce documentary work in the 1920s in this way: "Before the 1920s, documentary filmmaking had largely been confined to newsreels and scenic shorts" (202), an assertion that smooths over any sharper distinction between early uses of photographic realism and the actual emergence of documentary proper in the 1920s. They imply that the documentary tradition traces back to early cinema, even though their own history tends to minimize the force of this myth.

8. Thompson and Bordwell, *Film History*, 352.

9. Grierson, "The E.M.B. Film Unit," 165.

10. Abigail Solomon-Godeau points out that work such as Matthew Brady's Civil War photographs and Samuel Bourne's photographs of India and Nepal in the 1860s did not produce a documentary form or tradition directly; on the contrary, it was taken for granted that such work conformed to the basic function of the photographic image to document a preexistent reality. To label such images *documentary* would produce a tautology: "Because the preponderance of photographic uses previous to the term's introduction [in the 1920s] were what we would now automatically designate as documentary, it becomes clear that the documentary concept is historical, not ontological." Even Jacob Riis's photographic illustrations for *How the Other Half Lives* (1890), though a possible progenitor for the documentary movements of the 1930s in Solomon-Godeau's account, did not spark such a movement directly or immediately. It took an extended period of symbolism and aestheticism in the form of photographic pictorialism to allow documentary to escape tautology and name a distinct form. See Abigail Solomon-Godeau, "Who Is Speaking Thus? Some Questions about Documentary Photography," in *The Event Horizon: Essays on Hope, Sexuality, Social Space, and Media(tion) in Art*, ed. Lorne Falk and Barbara Fischer (Toronto: Coach House Press, 1987), 193, 195.

11. See Maureen Turim, "The Ethics of Form: Structure and Gender in Maya Deren's Challenge to the Cinema," in *Maya Deren and the American Avant-Garde*, ed. Bill Nichols (Berkeley: University of California Press, 2001), 80.

12. The first decade of cinema produced an astonishing array of material gathered by itinerate cinematographers from around the world. To the extent that many countries, including those still yoked to Europe by colonial domination, experienced the beginnings of a motion picture industry, it was in relation to the production of actualités detailing local places and events. Early histories of cinema and of documentary, however, such as Rotha's *Documentary Film*, do not acknowledge any formative work from developing countries, only work from the Soviet Union and continental Europe. Histories devoted to Third World cinema written more recently continue this neglect. Some refer to these

early efforts but draw minimal implications for their significance to the development of national cinemas or documentary film practices as such.

It is not entirely surprising that a history of Third World documentary film production prior to World War II is sometimes acknowledged but generally discounted. Historians tend to define the emergence of a national cinema as the appearance of a sustained feature fiction mode of production. However, Catherine Benamou, in informal conversation with me, has asserted that documentary did definitely exist in Mexico in the period prior to World War II, as it probably did in other countries as well. *Mexican Cinema*, ed. Paulo Antonio Paranaguá (London: BFI, 1995) offers hints of this in an essay by Aurelio de los Eyes, "The Silent Cinema," 63–78, in which de los Eyes describes documentary work in the 1910s that "set out to inform. . . . [It] had developed its own mode of representation and carefully documented, unhindered, the major national events with complete freedom" (69). Much of the work appears to be documentation more than documentary, and the book's overview chronology claims that "the documentary is definitely put to rest" by 1917 (23) as a *film d'art* import model gains dominance, but de los Eyes's detailed account offers substantiation of Benamou's claim. Documentary remains an area of film study in need of extended investigation.

13. On the one hand documents have long been regarded as factual elements of the historical record, free of the editorializing stratagems of the orator or the interpretative leanings of the historian. Documentaries, on the other hand, are the product of a persuasive, or at least poetic, intent to have an audience see and act differently. When John Grierson praised *Moana* (Robert Flaherty, 1926) for its "documentary value" (but not its documentary form), he acknowledged its value as a document of Pacific island culture despite the fictional pretext of a coming-of-age story. The qualities of the document lurked amidst the fabrications of the fiction.

In *Documentary Expression and Thirties America* (New York: Oxford University Press, 1973) William Stott argues convincingly that the documentary tradition "carries and communicates feeling" and that "feeling comes first" (7, 8). The rhetorical tradition, of which the documentary film tradition is a specific manifestation, has always granted great importance to feeling or emotion as the means by which an audience comes to be predisposed or moved toward a set of values or course of action. The poststructural fillip that documents are themselves rhetorical constructs designed to bear greater evidentiary weight in an overall argument by dint of their apparent objectivity does not diminish the signal importance of emotion coupled with a persuasive intent that gives rhetoric, and documentary film, its social significance.

14. Tom Gunning, "The Cinema of Attractions," in *Early Cinema: Space, Frame, Narrative*, ed. Thomas Elsaesser and Adam Barker (London: BFI, 1990), 58.

15. For an extended discussion of reality TV programs and their relation to the documentary film tradition, see my "At the Limits of Reality (TV)," in *Blurred Boundaries* (Bloomington: Indiana University Press, 1994), 43–62.

16. See Lisa Cartwright, *Screening the Body: Tracing Medicine's Visual Culture* (Minneapolis: University of Minnesota Press, 1995). Cartwright offers a wide-ranging catalogue of examples that demonstrate an abuse of scientific method as well as a pseudoscientific use of medical imaging.

17. Allan Sekula, "Dismantling Modernism, Reinventing Documentary (Notes on the Politics of Representation)," in *Photography against the Grain: Essays and Photo Works, 1973–1983* (Halifax: Press of the Nova Scotia College of Art and Design, 1984), 57.

18. The written ethnography is Maurice Legendre's doctoral dissertation, "Las Jurdes: Étude de géographie humaine," School for Advanced Spanish Studies, 1927. Buñuel was also, according to John Baxter's biography, familiar with Miguel de Unamuno's description of the region in his 1922 book *Andanzas y visiones españolas.* See John Baxter, *Buñuel* (New York: Carroll and Graf, 1994), 136–46.

19. See Hayden White, "The Question of Narrative in Contemporary Historical Theory," in *The Content of the Form: Narrative Discourse and Historical Representation* (Baltimore: Johns Hopkins University Press, 1987), 26–57.

20. Character development and the centered consciousness of the individual, although a staple of classical film narrative, is something few documentarians adopted in the late 1920s and early 1930s, apart from Robert Flaherty (who completed *Nanook of the North* and *Moana* before the term *documentary* even came into common use). This form of focalization becomes far more prevalent after the appearance of cinema verité and direct or observational cinema in the late 1950s and 1960s; it continues in the wide variety of documentaries that rely on interviews as a primary aspect of their structure from the 1970s onward.

21. Peter Wollen speaks of two avant-gardes in the 1920s—(1) artist-film-makers from Europe who suppress the signified to explore the signifier in abstract or transcendental ways and (2) filmmakers from the Soviet Union, who insist on the primacy of the signified—in his "The Two Avant-Gardes," in *Readings and Writings: Semiotic Counter-Strategies* (London: Verso, 1982), 92–104. He cites as an early point of direct contact Eisenstein's meeting with Richter at the avant-garde gathering at Le Sarrazin in 1929, but this, for Wollen, marks "the end rather than the beginning of an epoch" (94). Wollen's characterization of a European, formalist avant-garde and a Soviet, political avant-garde neglects the high degree of interplay between Soviet and European artists and filmmakers through the 1920s, overlooks the elements of photographic realism in European work, and fails to trace the development of individual careers across these tenuous boundaries. Wollen omits reference to all forms of documentary expression in the 1920s and 1930s entirely and sees categories and camps where I see strategic moves to construct such categories on top of far more permeable qualities.

22. A reproduction of his graphic design and storyboard for the film exists in the catalogue compiled by the Institut Valencia d'Art Moderne, *Laszlo Moholy-Nagy* (Valencia: IVAM, 1991), 167–82.

23. Rotha, *Documentary Film,* 70.

24. Joris Ivens, "Reflections on the Avant-Garde Documentary" (1931), in *French Film Theory and Criticism: A History/Anthology,* ed. Richard Abel, 2 vols. (Princeton, NJ: Princeton University Press, 1988), 2:80.

25. Dziga Vertov, "Resolution of the Council of Three"' (1923), in *Film Culture Reader,* ed. P. Adams Sitney (New York: Praeger, 1970), 359.

26. Aleksandr Rodchenko, "Against the Synthetic Portrait, for the Snapshot" (1928), in *Russian Art of the Avant-Garde: Theory and Criticism, 1902–1934,* trans. and ed. John Bowlt (New York: Viking, 1976), 253, 251, 254.

27. Vertov, "Resolution of the Council of Three," 358.

28. Fredric Jameson, "Beyond the Cave: Demystifying the Ideology of Modernism," in *The Ideologies of Theory,* 2 vols. (Minneapolis: University of Minnesota Press, 1988), 2:121. An interestingly divergent but also Marxist assessment of modernism occurs in Arnold Hauser, *Naturalism, Impressionism, the Film Age,* vol. 4 of *The Social History of Art* (New York: Routledge, 1951). Hauser sees modernism or "post-impressionism" as an escape from reality. In the rejection of the qualities described by Jameson, Hauser sees the loss of hope in mutual understanding based on commonplaces and convention. He therefore labels, after Jean Paulhan, most modernists as "terrorists," who fight "against all externalization and institutionalization . . . against all 'culture,'" in contrast to the "'rhetoricians,' the oratorical artists . . . who know perfectly well that commonplaces and clichés are the price of mutual understanding" (232). Documentary clearly takes up this second possibility, but whether it does so in opposition to modernism or in alliance with it is what I seek to examine.

29. Jameson, "Beyond the Cave," 2:122.

30. Abel, preface to *French Film Theory and Criticism,* 2:xvi.

31. James Clifford, "On Ethnographic Surrealism," in *The Predicament of Culture: Twentieth-Century Ethnography, Literature, and Art* (Cambridge, MA: Harvard University Press, 1988), 146.

32. Slavoj Žižek, "Introduction: The Spectre of Ideology," in *Mapping Ideology,* ed. Slavoj Žižek (New York: Verso, 1994), 26.

33. Abel, "The Great Debates," in *French Film Theory and Criticism,* 1:331. Abel quotes Fernand Léger, "Peinture et cinéma," *Cahiers du mois,* nos. 16–17 (1925): 107–8.

34. Bertolt Brecht, "Theatersituation 1917–1927," in *Schriften zum Theater,* ed. Werner Hecht, 7 vols. (Frankfurt am Main: Suhrkamp, 1963–64), 1:95 (my italics; my trans.). Brecht concludes his essay: "Er [der *Regisseur*] hat die Vernflichtlung, die Versuche ständig zu erneuern, die zur Schaffung des großen epischen and dokumentarischen Theaters fiihren mussen, das unserer Zeit gemäß ist" (The director has the duty to renew, through a series of steady attempts, that which will lead to the production of a great epic and documentary theater appropriate to our times).

35. I am indebted to Paula Amad for her screening of this and other material from the Kahn archive at Visible Evidence VIII, Utrecht, August 2000.

36. See my "Eisenstein's *Strike* and the Genealogy of Documentary," in *Blurred Boundaries* (Bloomington: Indiana University Press, 1994), 107–16, for

a detailed consideration of these qualities, as well as reflections on the consequences of treating Eisenstein's work as contributing to the development of narrative cinema rather than as part of the remarkable fusion of narrative and nonnarrative, fact and fiction, document and rhetoric that characterizes this period of Soviet cinema, and art, so dramatically.

37. Margaret Olin, "'It Is Not Going to Be Easy to Look into Their Eyes': Privilege of Perception in *Let Us Now Praise Famous Men*," *Art History* 14, no. 1 (1991): 92.

38. Hubert L. Dreyfus and Paul Rabinow, *Michel Foucault: Beyond Structuralism and Hermeneutics*, 2nd ed. (Chicago: University of Chicago Press, 1983), 109.

39. On one hand the account given here diminishes Flaherty's importance. To the extent that his work stimulated others who would later adopt the name of documentary, it clearly bears significance. On the other hand Flaherty was not part of a larger movement but someone who sought to find a distinct niche within the commercial feature-film market. Indebted to Edward Curtis's 1914 film *In the Land of the Head Hunters*, Flaherty, in his first feature, *Nanook of the North*, likewise combined an ethnographic eye for the details of everyday life and social ritual with a marked propensity for the dramatic, if not melodramatic. What Flaherty lacked was the orator's sense of social suasion. He stressed story over effect, observation over amelioration. His insistence on location filmmaking, common-man heroes, and the construction of narratives that grew from a local situation bears close affinity to the neorealist impulse that took shape in postwar Japanese, American, Polish, British, and, especially, Italian cinema. His documentary affinity lies closer to the observational strategies adopted by Robert Drew, David and Albert Maysles, Richard Leacock, D.A. Pennebaker, and Frederick Wiseman in the 1960s than to the modernist mixture of oratorical and poetic practices of the 1920s and 1930s or their performative variants in the 1970s and later. Claims for Flaherty as a key paternal figure in the genealogy of documentary follow more from a desire for ancestors and lines of noble descent than from close attention to the historical circumstances that occasion the emergence of documentary film production.

40. Grierson, *Grierson on Documentary*, 181, 183.

41. Ibid., 249.

42. Ibid., 179. Rotha, Grierson's compatriot, followed the same line. He described the French avant-garde as "hypnotized by the facile tricks of the movie camera." Their films, "seldom profound, but often witty . . . were inspired by nothing more serious than kindergarten theory" (Rotha, *Documentary Film*, 85).

43. Grierson, *Grierson on Documentary*, 278–79.

44. Ibid., 327.

45. Ibid., 113.

46. Quoted in Peter Morris, "Re-thinking Grierson: The Ideology of John Grierson," in *Dialogue: Canadian and Quebec Cinema*, ed. Pierre Véronneau, Michael Dorland, and Seth Feldman (Montreal: Mediatexte, 1987), 46. This

essay presents a superb account of Grierson's ideological orientation; I am indebted to it for much of the information provided in this summary statement.

47. Quoted in ibid., 41.

48. Quoted in ibid., 45.

49. Quoted in Jay Leyda, *Kino: The History of the Russian and Soviet Film* (London: Collier, 1973), 161. Although Grierson named this new film form "documentary," Vertov had been making work that would later be labeled documentary for nearly a decade before Grierson. Vertov never gave his films a name denoting a genre or category of film. For him they were the only real cinema, plain and simple. All other forms of filmmaking were derivatives of literary, theatrical, or painterly traditions and, therefore, incapable of cinematic distinction.

50. Peter Galassi, "Rodchenko and Photography's Revolution," in *Aleksandr Rodchenko*, ed. Magdalena Dabrowski, Leah Dickerman, and Peter Galassi (New York: Museum of Modern Art, 1998), 130.

51. Hayden White, "The Modernist Event," in *The Persistence of History: Cinema, Television, and the Modern Event*, ed. Vivian Sobchack (New York: Routledge, 1996), 32.

52. Ibid., 20.

53. See William Alexander, *Film on the Left: American Documentary Film from 1931–1942* (Princeton, NJ: Princeton University Press, 1981).

54. There are several books on Ivens, but the most rigorous and comprehensive study by far is Thomas Waugh's 1981 dissertation, "Joris Ivens and the Evolution of the Radical Documentary," recently revised and published as *The Conscience of Cinema: The Works of Joris Ivens 1926–1989* (Amsterdam: Amsterdam University Press, 2016). Also see *Joris Ivens and the Documentary Context*. For biographical detail on his political leanings see Hans Schoots, *Living Dangerously: A Biography of Joris Ivens* (Amsterdam: Amsterdam University Press, 2000).

55. See Barsam, *Nonfiction Film*, which discusses nothing after *400,000,000* (1939) and mentions that film only in passing; and Ellis, *The Documentary Idea*, which discusses no films of Ivens's after *The Power and the Land* (1941). Only Barnouw's more internationally attentive *Documentary* covers Ivens's later work, but even here there is minimal sense of Ivens's overall development as a filmmaker. Barnouw provides the dates of several postwar films, for example, but fails to give their titles (see Barnouw, *Documentary*, 206). Ivens only appears in Barnouw's narrative when his films serve as one of the examples of larger tendencies Barnouw finds at work rather than as a decisive figure in his own right. Similarly, the best general film history, Thompson and Bordwell, *Film History*, mentions Ivens as one of the few 1930s documentary filmmakers to remain active after World War II but offers no discussion of his later films.

56. Some historians, like Georges Sadoul, clearly saw the impetus Soviet film provided to the constitution of a documentary form: "La révélation soviétique précipita l'évolution de l'avant-garde vers le documentaire" (Georges Sadoul, *Histoire du cinéma mondial*, 8th ed. [Paris: Denoël, 1949], 203); but

later writers like Barsam, Barnouw, and Ellis choose a myth of origins to the reality of Soviet invention.

57. See Nichols, *Maya Deren and the American Avant-Garde* for a variety of investigations into the multifaceted career of Maya Deren.

58. Maya Deren, *An Anagram of Ideas on Art, Form and Film*, in VèVè A. Clark, Millicent Hodson, and Catrina Neiman, *The Legend of Maya Deren: A Documentary Biography and Collected Works* (New York: Anthology Film Archives / Film Culture, 1988), vol. 1, pt. 2, 570.

CHAPTER 2. DOCUMENTARY REENACTMENT AND THE FANTASMATIC SUBJECT

"Documentary Reenactment and the Fantasmatic Subject" originally appeared in *Critical Inquiry* 35, no. 1 (2008): 72–89. It was published in a modified form as "Documentary Re-enactments: A Paradoxical Temporality That Is Not One," in *Given World and Time: Temporalities in Context*, ed. Tyrus Miller (Budapest: Central European University Press, 2008): 171–92.

1. Gregory Bateson's insightful essay on the difference between play and fighting among animals, where a nip no longer means exactly what a bite (to which it refers) would mean, insists that such distinctions amount to categorical shifts in comprehension. As Bateson puts it, "The playful nip denotes the bite, but it does not denote what would be denoted by the bite." See "A Theory of Play and Fantasy," in *Steps to an Ecology of Mind* (Chicago: University of Chicago Press, 2000), 180. The distinction is akin to Gilbert Ryle's discussion of the difference between an unintended blink and a fully intended wink in "The Thinking of Thoughts: What Is 'Le Penseur' Doing?" *University Lectures*, no. 18 (Saskatchewan: University of Saskatchewan, 1968).

2. Michael Renov, "Filling Up the Hole in the Real: Death and Mourning in Contemporary Documentary Film and Video," in *The Subject of Documentary* (Minneapolis: University of Minnesota Press, 2004).

3. J. Laplanche and J.-B. Pontalis, "Fantasy and the Origins of Sexuality," *International Journal of Psychoanalysis* 49, no. 1 (1968): 15n36.

4. Ibid., 16.

5. Ibid., 17.

6. See Bill Nichols, "The Voice of Documentary," *Film Quarterly* 36, no. 3 (1983): 17–30. See also Bill Nichols, *Representing Reality* (Bloomington: Indiana University Press, 1991), 128.

7. "In great moments of cinema you are hit and struck by some sort of enlightenment, by something that illuminates you, that's a deep form of truth, and I call it ecstatic truth, the ecstasy of truth, and that's what I'm after in documentaries and feature films." Werner Herzog, "Filmmaker Herzog's 'Grizzly' Tale of Life and Death," interview by Dave Davies, *Fresh Air*, NPR radio, July 28, 2005.

8. Some speak of subjectivity in documentary. This, to me, represents something of a slippery slope, slipperier than the use of subjectivity in narrative fiction, which is usually related to the perspective of characters and the voice of

the narrator. Both are different concepts from documentary subjectivity that sets out to admit that documentaries represent situated, emotionally and politically informed, views of the world. Though true, they become inevitably contrasted with an alternative idea, a different way of representing or engaging with the world: objectivity. The issue of objectivity enters, like a Trojan horse, in ways it does not do in fiction, and it causes endless trouble.

Objectivity in relation to a fictional world might seem a peculiar notion since the fiction is a subjectively endowed creation by definition, or it may seem like a way to identify a scrupulously neutral, detached mode of representing it, in the spirit of *écriture blanche,* a zero degree of style. In documentary, objectivity implies a lack or subtraction of subjectivity as if subjectivity could be put on, taken off, or stepped beyond, as if it were a bias. Unlike a fiction, the actual world, it is argued, can be viewed objectively, unless the decision is made to "add" subjectivity. In some instances, like scientific investigation, subjectivity can be subtracted to a great extent, but these instances are not the instances in which an *I* stands before a *You;* they are instances of *I*s embedded within institutional procedures and discourses that objectify or analyze, that have instrumental effects—for good or ill—but that cloak the *I* or *You* in ways the voices of these films refuse to do. Voice affirms the presence of an embodied subject who is necessarily and inescapably in possession of a subjectivity. Objectivity catapults us into another realm entirely.

9. See my *Representing Reality* for a more extended discussion of the discourse of sobriety. The tendency in much contemporary documentary is to emphasize its distance from such discourses rather than its kinship, largely through the pronounced sense of voice that characterizes so many recent films. This, in turn, locates them closer to the realm of narrative fiction film although voice, unlike style, carries with it the strong implication of address: the film sets out to address the viewer as a social subject and potential actor. The increased proximity of documentary to fiction, though, is one reason for the striking popularity of many recent documentaries.

10. See Frantz Fanon, *Black Skin, White Masks* (New York: Grove, 1967).

11. Judith Butler discusses the iterative power that lies behind any one instance of hate speech or "fighting words" in her *Excitable Speech: A Politics of the Performative* (New York: Routledge, 1997).

12. Brecht regarded social gests as physical actions that revealed social relations, or as Roland Barthes put it: "What then is a social gest? It is a gesture or set of gestures (but never a gesticulation) in which a whole social situation can be read. Not every gest is social: there is nothing social in the movements a man makes in order to brush off a fly; but if this same man, poorly dressed, is struggling against guard-dogs, the gest becomes social." Roland Barthes, "Diderot, Brecht, Eisenstein," in *Image, Music, Text* (New York: Hill and Wang, 1977), 73–74.

13. Vivian Sobchack, *Carnal Thoughts: Embodiment and Moving Image Culture* (Berkeley: University of California Press, 2004), 281.

14. Sobchack develops this point in relation to fiction film and moments when the image ceases to function as a typical particular and takes on the full

force of a singular moment, such as the image of a real rabbit shot during the fictional hunting scene in Jean Renoir's 1939 classic, *The Rules of the Game* (Sobchack, *Carnal Thoughts,* 283). This attitude seems a default value for documentary film in general.

15. Images of illustration constitute those images utilized to support a typically verbal argument or perspective. They offer particular instantiations of points that may imply broader application or offer what appears to be evidence in support of a specific assertion.

CHAPTER 4. *BREAKING THE FRAME*

"Breaking the Frame: Gender, Violation, and the Avant-Garde" was originally posted August 30, 2013, on billnichols.net.

1. See www.theguardian.com/artanddesign/2014/mar/10/carole-schneemann-naked-art-performance.

PART 2. THE AUDIO IN *AUDIOVISUAL*

1. See Bill Nichols, "The Voice of Documentary," *Film Quarterly* 36, no. 3 (1983): 17–30.

2. See Bill Nichols, preface to *Music and Sound in the Documentary Film,* ed. Holly Rogers (London: Routledge, 2014).

CHAPTER 5. DOCUMENTARY FILM AND THE COMING OF SOUND

An earlier version of this essay appeared in vol. 6 of the series Historia General del Cine, *La transición del mudo al sonoro,* ed. Javier Maqua and Manuel Palacio (Madrid: Ediciones Cátedra, 1996), 273–95; and in *Documentary Box,* no. 6 (1995): 1–8. The version here has undergone substantial revision.

1. I provide extended discussion of the modes and models for documentary filmmaking in my *Introduction to Documentary,* 2nd ed. (Bloomington: Indiana University Press, 2010). A 3rd edition is forthcoming from Indiana University Press in 2017.

2. *Housing Problems* (Edgar Anstey and Arthur Elton, 1935) was a pioneering exception. Part of the British documentary film movement of the 1930s, it featured on-location sync interviews with slum inhabitants who recounted their problems in their own words. Much more typical were British documentaries like *Song of Ceylon* (Basil Wright, 1935) and *Coal Face* (Alberto Cavalcanti, 1935) or American ones like *The Plow That Broke the Plains* (Pare Lorentz, 1936) and *The City* (Ralph Steiner and Willard van Dyke, 1939). They all feature musical scores, often of a lively, experimental nature, and voice-over commentary with no sync sound at all.

3. I discuss the linkage of documentary and the avant-garde in "Documentary Film and the Modernist Avant-Garde," *Critical Inquiry* 27, no.

4 (2001): 580–610, included here. I later elaborated on this argument in the second edition of my *Introduction to Documentary*. The use of studio recording occurred on occasion, such as in *Night Mail* (Harry Watt and Basil Wright, 1936), but for the most part documentary filmmakers favored filming without sound, building a collage of images and adding a musical sound track and voice-over commentary of a poetic or rhetorical bent.

4. Jack C. Ellis, *The Documentary Idea: A Critical History of English-Language Documentary Film and Video* (Englewood Cliffs, NJ: Prentice Hall, 1989), 27–28, 44, 56–57.

5. Lewis Jacobs, ed., *The Documentary Tradition*, 2nd ed. (New York: Norton, 1979), 70.

6. Erik Barnouw, *A Documentary History of the Non-fiction Film* (New York: Oxford University Press, 1974), 7.

7. I discuss these levels of recognition in Bill Nichols, *Representing Reality: Issues and Concepts in Documentary* (Bloomington: Indiana University Press, 1991), 160–64.

8. This phrase is featured on many of the contemporary posters for the film's initial release. See, e.g., www.impawards.com/1922/nanook_of_the_north.html.

9. See my "Documentary Film and the Modernist Avant-Garde" for more on the intermingling of documentary and experimental impulses in the 1920s and 1930s. Innovative storytelling would include the montage-driven work in the Soviet Union during the 1920s and early 1930s and the Italian neorealist movement of the 1940s.

10. Nichols, *Representing Reality*, 41.

11. For demonstrations of how vividly music can serve as a form of authorial perspective, or voice, see Holly Rogers, ed., *Music and Sound in the Documentary Film* (London: Routledge, 2014). The next essay here, "To See the World Anew," elaborates substantially on the idea of voice.

12. James Clifford, *The Predicament of Culture: Twentieth-Century Ethnography, Literature, and Art* (Cambridge, MA: Harvard University Press, 1988), 145.

13. Barnouw, *Documentary History*, 24–26, 38.

14. Emilie de Brigard, "The History of Ethnographic Film," in *Principles of Visual Anthropology*, ed. Paul Hockings (The Hague: Mouton, 1975), 19.

CHAPTER 6. TO SEE THE WORLD ANEW

This essay expands on my previous writing on voice in documentary. I first used the term in "The Voice of Documentary," *Film Quarterly* 36, no. 3 (1983): 17–30. I elaborate on it in my *Introduction to Documentary*, 2nd ed. (Bloomington: Indiana University Press, 2010).

1. Louis Althusser, "Ideology and Ideological State Apparatuses," in *"Lenin and Philosophy" and Other Essays*, trans. Ben Brewster (New York: Monthly Review Press, 1971).

2. A prescient and insightful discussion of how we can interpret the speech of the body in a cross-cultural context is Marcel Mauss's "Les techniques du corps," originally published in *Journal de psychologie* 32, no. 3–4 (1936): www.philo-online.com/TEXTES/MAUSS%20Marcel%20Les%20techniques%20 du%20corps.pdf.

3. See my "Documentary Film and the Modernist Avant-Garde" (reprinted in part 1 here) for further discussion of this period and its very fluid boundaries. I regard the 1920s and early 1930s as the origin of the modern documentary.

4. These different forms of truth are discussed in Stephanie Marlin-Curiel, "Re-collecting the Collective: Mediatised Memory and the South African Truth and Reconciliation Commission," in *The Image and the Witness: Trauma, Memory and Visual Culture*, ed. Frances Guerin and Roger Hallas (London: Wallflower, 2007), 69–81, esp. 80n12.

5. These films move us toward the essay film, or personal documentary. Although I do not see the essay film as a sharply distinct category, it is discussed well in Timothy Corrigan, *The Essay Film* (New York: Oxford University Press, 2011).

6. A fifth emphasis involves political engagement and social impact; I take this topic up in a separate essay (see "The Political Documentary and the Question of Impact" in part 5 below).

7. Louis Marcorelles, *Living Cinema: New Directions in Contemporary Film-Making* (New York: Praeger, 1973).

8. Forgács has extended his film work into a remarkable installation piece, *Letters from Afar* (2014). The work assembles home movies made by Polish American Jews who return to their homeland in the 1920s and film the cities and shtetls from which they came. Shown on multiple screens and in multiple arrangements (three streams of images stacked vertically in one case, arranged horizontally in another, on large diaphanous screens that can be seen from either side and on monitors mounted on the walls, some with sound and some without), the work achieves an extreme intensity within which we can wander and discover a lost world brought back to life. For more discussion of his work see Bill Nichols and Michael Renov, eds., *Cinema's Alchemist* (Minneapolis: University of Minnesota Press, 2011).

9. My essay "Irony, Paradox, and the Documentary" (reprinted in part 4 here) also discusses this film from a somewhat different point of view.

CHAPTER 7. THE SOUND OF MUSIC

"The Sound of Music" originally appeared, in quite different form, as the preface to *Music and Sound in the Documentary Film*, ed. Holly Rogers (London: Routledge, 2014). Reprinted courtesy of Routledge.

1. Bill Nichols, "A Fiction (Un)like Any Other," in *Representing Reality* (Bloomington: Indiana University Press, 1991), 107–98.

CHAPTER 8. THE QUESTION OF EVIDENCE

"The Question of Evidence" first appeared in German in *Die Listen der Evidenz* (The cunning of evidence), ed. Michael Cuntz (Cologne: DuMont, 2006), 86–106.

1. R.G. Collingwood, *The Idea of History* (Oxford: Oxford University Press, 1946), 280.

2. Ibid., 275.

3. Ludwig Wittgenstein, *Tractatus Logico-Philosophicus* [1922], trans. C.K. Ogden (London: Routledge and Kegan Paul, 1985), 5.634.

4. Roland Barthes, "The Rhetoric of the Image," in *Image-Music-Text*, trans. Stephen Heath (New York: Hill and Wang, 1977), 49.

5. See Robin Jackson, Kimon Lycos, Harold Tarrant, trans., *Olympiodorus: Commentary on Plato's Gorgias* (Leiden: The Netherlands, 1998), 131.

6. Quintilian, *Institutio oratoria*, trans. H.E. Butler (Cambridge, MA: Harvard University Press, 1966–69).

7. This discussion of Quintilian's correction of Plato's apparent condemnation of rhetoric draws heavily on Jacqueline Lichtenstein's discussion in her *The Eloquence of Color: Rhetoric and Painting in the French Classical Age* (Berkeley: University of California Press, 1993), 86–88.

8. Lichtenstein, *The Eloquence of Color*, 88–89.

9. Werner Herzog, "Filmmaker Herzog's 'Grizzly' Tale of Life and Death," interview by Dave Davies, *Fresh Air*, NPR, July 28, 2005.

10. See Göran Therborn, *The Ideology of Power and the Power of Ideology* (London: Verso, 1980) for a lucid discussion of the various forms of ideology that operate in any given social formation. Therborn's treatment of ideology dissolves the Althusserian notion of ideology-in-general, akin to the "general ideology" adopted by Barthes in "The Rhetoric of the Image," into its component parts in a given historical moment. A general ideology that constitutes the subject may remain operative, but concrete class ideologies and counterideologies are the more common sites of political struggle, unless redesigning the subject is our singular goal.

11. Martin Jay's *Downcast Eyes: The Denigration of Vision in Twentieth-Century French Thought* (Berkeley: University of California Press, 1993) traces the history of a profound distrust of vision and the visible among French theorists such as Michel Foucault, Jacques Lacan, Guy Debord, Jacques Derrida, and Louis Althusser. It provides a superb account of the general trend and its implications for film theory.

12. Barthes, "Rhetoric of the Image," 51.

13. For a full discussion of the Rodney King footage, and its use in the trials of the police officers charged with beating Mr. King, see Bill Nichols, "The Trials and Tribulations of Rodney King," in *Blurred Boundaries: Questions of Meaning in Contemporary Culture* (Bloomington: Indiana University Press, 1994), 17–42.

CHAPTER 9. THE TERRORIST EVENT

Epigraphs: The Stahl and Morton quotes are cited in Dan Hallin, "Network News: 'We Keep America on Top of the World,'" in *Watching Television: A Pantheon Guide to Popular Culture,* ed. Todd Gitlin (New York: Pantheon, 1986), 12, 10.

"The Terrorist Event" was originally published in *Ritual Transformations,* ed. Mark Franko (New York: Routledge, 2006): 94–108; also published in "Representing Humanity in an Age of Terror," ed. Sophia A. McClennen and Henry James Morello, special issue, *CLCWeb: Comparative Literature and Culture* 9, no. 1 (2007): http://clcwebjournal.lib.purdue.edu/vol9/iss1/14; also in *O cinema do real,* ed. Maria Dora Maurão and Amir Labaki (Ediciones Colihue: Buenos Aires, 2005): 174–95; also in *Representing Humanity in an Age of Terror,* ed. Sophia A. McClennen and Henry James Morello (West Lafayette, IN: Purdue University Press, 2010).

  1. In some ways the live coverage on September 11 reproduced the conventions of morning television talk shows, which promise to cover "news you can use": stories that explore the backdrop of everyday life to cover "perversions, exaltations, interruptions and crises" (Hallin, "Network News," 17). Such coverage presents most crises as unexplained events similar to natural disasters, and they focus on the disruption caused in the lives of ordinary people. Courage and heroism provide thematic content more than background information or explanatory detail. See Hallin, "Network News," 15–23.

  2. Maurice Blanchot, *The Writing of the Disaster,* trans. Ann Smock (Lincoln: University of Nebraska Press, 1995), 28.

  3. I am indebted to my fellow panelist Stella Senra at the "Images of Conflict" conference in São Paulo, Brazil, April 18–19, 2002, for these observations about the kidnapping of the media by the terrorists.

  4. A notable exception, pointed out in the *One Day in September* documentary, was the coverage of the Arab terrorists who held the Israeli Olympic team captive, coverage that was shot by the East German television crew. This crew placed itself in an apartment building opposite from the Israeli teams and had a clear view of the rooftop just above the apartment. It was on this roof that the German government positioned a team of agents with the idea of storming into the apartment and overpowering the terrorists. The terrorists, however, were able to see these events unfold by tuning in the East German coverage on the television in the Israeli apartment and thwart the plan. The documentary notes this bizarre incident without investigating how the East German TV crew gained access to such a convenient apartment or how they were allowed to broadcast such compromising footage.

  5. A useful discussion of real-time events and interactions occurs in Lev Manovich, "To Lie and to Act: Cinema and Telepresence," in *Cinema Futures: Cain, Abel or Cable?* ed. Thomas Elsaesser and Kay Hoffmann (Amsterdam: Amsterdam University Press, 1998).

6. The World Trade Center towers themselves played a similar, tragic role as index of the magnitude of the disaster when they were judged by observers in hovering police helicopters to be in danger of imminent collapse. The helicopter crews neither landed on the rooftops to evacuate survivors, nor were their messages relayed to fire department coordinators, who still had hundreds of men inside the towers, unaware of the immediate danger.

7. A flexible sense of technology in relation to the modernist event allows for both high-tech devastation, such as the deployment of atomic bombs against the civilian populations of Hiroshima and Nagasaki, and low-tech devastation, such as the genocide of hundreds of thousands of Hutus in Rwanda by means of little more than machetes, clubs, and, sometimes, handguns and rifles. This latter example clearly implicated institutions such as the Catholic Church and technologies such as those of the mass media, but it relied for its efficacy on a Malthusian technology of populations: a large segment of the Hutu population itself acted as an instrument of terror.

8. Hayden White, "The Modernist Event," in *The Persistence of History*, ed. Vivian Sobchack (New York: Routledge, 1996), 20–21. I have rearranged the order of White's comments the better to fit their adaptation here.

9. For a fuller treatment of "discourses of sobriety" see my *Representing Reality: Issues and Concepts in Documentary* (Bloomington: Indiana University Press, 1991).

10. In relativity theory an event is an observable physical entity that can be located within a four-dimensional grid of space and time.

11. The best-known articulation of this infidelity or betrayal of experience by expression is Theodore Adorno's "*Nach Auschwitz ein Gedicht zu schreiben ist barbarisch*" (Writing poetry after Auschwitz is barbaric). Adorno, "Kulturkritik und Gesellschaft," *Gesammelte Schriften*, vol. 10 (Frankfurt: Suhrkamp, 1974), 30. Another perspective that takes account of Adorno's reconsiderations is Berel Lang's. Lang acknowledges the challenge that art, and historical narrative, face: "The denial of individuality and personhood in the act of genocide; the abstract bureaucracy that empowered the 'Final Solution,' moved by an almost indistinguishable combination of corporate and individual will and blindness to evil, constitute a subject that in its elements seems at odds with the insulation of figurative discourse and the individuation of character and motivation that literary 'making' tends to impose on its subjects." Lang goes on to consider silence as an inevitable limit rather than necessary prohibition. See Berel Lang, "The Representation of Limits," in *Probing the Limits of Representation: Nazism and the "Final Solution,"* ed. Saul Friedlander (Cambridge, MA: Harvard University Press, 1992), 316–17. Whether Adorno and Lang remain within the grips of a traditional, realist aesthetic or acknowledge the potential for representation of modernist and postmodern strategies may be an important question to pursue. Whether the act of writing poetry must be counterbalanced against the act of forgetting the Holocaust also deserves consideration of the sort Lang's comments make possible. My own account of September 11, in its focus on the mass media and popular response,

also addresses realist strategies and attempts to demonstrate how they are both adequate and inadequate to the experience of the event.

12. The theory of logical types derives from Bertrand Russell, but communication and systems theorists like Gregory Bateson extended its application to a wide range of ecological and cultural phenomena. The dictum "A class cannot be a member of itself" stipulates that a radical separation distinguishes the category that frames or encapsulates a group of related items from the items themselves. The distinction can be violated in discourse, but this typically leads to paradox, double binds, and those forms of resolution made available by fantasy. See Gregory Bateson, "The Logical Categories of Learning and Communication," in *Steps to an Ecology of Mind* (Chicago: University of Chicago Press, 2000).

13. In a more poststructural vein that accounts for the activity of the reader, viewer, or participant/observer of historical events, Barthes describes *functions* as "actions (terms of the proairetic code). . . . The proairetic sequence is never more than the result of an artifice of reading: whoever reads the text [Barthes is referring to Balzac's novella *Sarrasine,* but the *process* he describes seems readily applicable to historical interpretation as well] amasses certain data under some generic titles for actions *(stroll, murder, rendezvous),* and this title embodies the sequence; the sequence exists when and because it can be given a name." Roland Barthes, *S/Z* (New York: Farrar, Strauss and Giroux, 1974), 19.

14. Gregory Bateson, "A Theory of Play and Fantasy," in *Steps to an Ecology of Mind* (Chicago: University of Chicago Press, 2000), 186–87.

15. "This recognition [by the child of his own image] is indicated in the illuminative mimicry of the *Aha-Erlebnis,* which Köhler sees as the expression of situational apperception, an essential stage of the act of intelligence." Jacques Lacan, "The Mirror Stage as Formative of the Function of the I as Revealed in Psychoanalytic Experience," in *Écrits: A Selection,* trans. Alan Sheridan (New York: Norton, 1977), 1.

16. The temporal form provided by narrative grants entry to the apperception of what Paul Ricoeur calls "historicality" and "deep temporality." Narrative form, of a higher logical type than the events recounted, and of an order different from the verifiably factual or wholly imaginary status of the events, gives material embodiment to the experience of historical time itself as a quality of consciousness distinct from mere chronology or duration. See Paul Ricoeur, *Time and Narrative,* vols. 1–3 (Chicago: University of Chicago Press, 1984–88); see also Hayden White's commentary, "The Metaphysics of Narrativity: Time and Symbol in Ricoeur's *Philosophy of History,*" in *The Content of the Form* (Baltimore: Johns Hopkins University Press, 1987).

17. Lacan adopts the term *gestalt* as well as that of the "aha experience" in his discussion of the mirror stage: "The fact is that the total form of the body by which the subject anticipates in a mirage the maturation of his power is given to him only as *Gestalt,* that is to say, in an exteriority in which this form is certainly more constituent than constituted" (Lacan, *Écrits,* 2). As I understand him, Lacan is acknowledging the role of misrecognition or fantasy that

comes into play when the child imagines its body to have the wholeness and integrity it "sees" in the gestalt that the child assigns to the image reflected back to him.

18. This is the term used by Laplanche and Pontalis to describe fantasy. See J. Laplanche and J.-B. Pontalis, *The Language of Psychoanalysis* (New York: Norton, 1973), 318.

19. Eric L. Santner, "History beyond the Pleasure Principle: Some Thoughts on the Representation of Trauma," in *Probing the Limits of Representation: Nazism and the "Final Solution,"* ed. Saul Friedlander (Cambridge, MA: Harvard University Press, 1992), 143–54, 144.

20. Already, a distortion in this concept of terrorism has become apparent in the tendency of some governments to label any armed or revolutionary opposition terrorist. Whether such an opposition engages in more classically defined terrorist acts such as murderous attacks on an unsuspecting civilian population receives less consideration than the fact that the opposition refuses to play by the rules of the game as defined by those who hold power. These historically specific and politically conceived rules come to be regarded as synonymous with civilization itself. Repressive regimes whose own actions tend to foment violent insurrection, if not revolution, are particularly prone to make use of the term in this way. The act of constituting the specter that is then said to haunt the body politic remains at work but in a way that intensifies the legitimization of the erosion of liberties and rights often said to characterize civilized, or at least bourgeois, democratic society. If, as former secretary of defense John Ashcroft once remarked, terrorists "use America's freedom as a weapon against us," then the only recourse Ashcroft can suggest is to deprive them of this weapon, even if that means depriving Americans of it as well.

21. Sigmund Freud, "Beyond the Pleasure Principle," in *The Standard Edition of the Complete Psychological Works,* ed. James Strachey (London: Hogarth, 1953–74), 18:30.

22. Fantasy, as the staging of desire, occupies a complex position in relation to reality. The idea that fantasy and imaginary gratification eventually yield to a reality principle and delayed gratification may oversimplify. As Laplanche and Pontalis note in their commentary on fantasy, the psychoanalyst seeks to unearth fantasies on multiple levels. "As the [psychoanalytic] investigation progresses, even aspects of behavior that are far removed from imaginative activity, and which appear at first glance to be governed solely by the demands of reality, emerge as emanations, as 'derivatives' of unconscious phantasy. In the light of this evidence, it is the subject's life as a whole which is seen to be shaped and ordered by what might be called, in order to stress this structuring action, 'a phantasmatic' *(une fantasmatique)."* Laplanche and Pontalis, *The Language of Psychoanalysis,* 317.

23. Freud uses a striking analogy: "We may compare them with individuals of mixed race who, taken all round, resemble white men, but who betray their coloured descent by some striking feature or other, and on that account are excluded from society and enjoy none of the privileges of white people" (quoted in Laplanche and Pontalis, *The Language of Psychoanalysis,* 317).

24. Hayden White carries this thought to its logical extreme when he argues that historiography devotes itself to masking the sublime in order to celebrate the beautiful, all at the expense of a ruthless honesty "that history may be as meaningless 'in itself' as the theorists of the historical sublime thought it to be." "The Politics of Historical Interpretation: Discipline and De-sublimation," in *The Content of the Form*, 82. For White the assignment of meaningfulness to history comes as a result of a "reaction-formation" to the recognition of history's intrinsic meaninglessness (72).

25. Victor Burgin, James Donald, and Cora Kaplan, preface to *Formations of Fantasy*, ed. Victor Burgin, James Donald, and Cora Kaplan (London: Methuen, 1986), 1.

26. Judith Butler, *Excitable Speech: A Politics of the Performative* (New York: Routledge, 1997), 45–46. Butler is paraphrasing Nietzsche, on whom she bases much of her argument.

27. Slavoj Žižek, "Are We in a War? Do We Have an Enemy?" *London Review of Books* 24, no. 10 (May 23, 2002): 5–6.

28. Subjects, of course, retain the "fantastic" ability to contest their very status and to institute those forms of transformation that alter the institutional frame that necessitates their initial appearance as the one accountable. Such actions transgress by turning accountability against those who judge the judged.

The discussion here often has the ring of the paradoxical about it. It is this quality that *The Act of Killing* (Joshua Oppenheimer, 2012) elaborates so powerfully in its representation of death squad leaders who killed thousands of Indonesians. It is discussed in greater detail in my essay "Irony, Paradox, and the Documentary: Double Meanings and Double Binds" (reprinted here in part 4).

29. The films of Rithy Panh (*S21: The Khmer Rouge Killing Machine* [2003], *Duch, Master of the Forges of Hell* [2011], and *The Missing Picture* [2013], among others) and those of Joshua Oppenheimer (*The Act of Killing* and *The Look of Silence* [2014]) explore some of the massive crimes against humanity committed in Cambodia and Indonesia respectively in organized purges of perceived opponents to the rule of the dominant party.

30. The filmmakers actually worked in video, using a lightweight digital camera. This technology afforded them access and mobility to an extraordinary degree. It also posed issues of tact. In being able to see so much of what there was to see, they constantly had to decide whether to include such sights as the plummeting bodies of workers who jumped from the upper floors of the towers or the sundered remains of those caught in the debris. One cannot know from the program itself if the filmmakers consistently refused to record such sights or they were removed in the course of editing. The sound of bodies striking canopies and the ground, however, is quite apparent, once the viewer assigns a cause to this unexplained effect.

CHAPTER 10. REMAKING HISTORY

"Remaking History: Jay Leyda and the Compilation Film" first appeared as a book review in *Film History* 26, no. 4 (2015): 146–56. It launched a new series of essays on older, neglected works of continuing importance and is reprinted here, in revised form, with permission from Indiana University Press.

1. Jay Leyda, *Films Beget Films: A Study of the Compilation Film* (1964; New York: Hill and Wang, 1971). The original paperback edition now sells for $38 used.

2. Paul Rotha, *Documentary Film* (New York: Norton, 1939), 269. Rotha mentions compilation films in a single paragraph devoted to the work of Esther Schub, but he had not yet seen any of her films. Of far greater concern was the use of recent newsreel footage that could be combined into various treatments of a theme or subject. Leyda, by contrast, devotes his entire second chapter, "Bridge," to the work of Schub. The chapter's subtitle is "Esther Schub Shapes a New Art."

3. Throughout this review I have retained spellings and titles used by Jay Leyda (Esther Schub rather than Esfir Shub, for example).

4. Louis Marcorelles, *Living Cinema: New Directions in Contemporary Filmmaking* (New York: Praeger, 1973). First published as *Éléments pour un nouveau cinéma* (Paris: UNESCO, 1970).

5. A. William Bluem, *Documentary in American Television* (New York: Hastings House, 1965); Eric Barnouw, *Documentary: A History of the Nonfiction Film* (New York: Oxford University Press, 1974).

6. Jamie Baron, *The Archive Effect: Found Footage and the Audiovisual Experience of History* (New York: Routledge, 2014).

7. Bill Nichols, *Representing Reality* (Bloomington: Indiana University Press, 1991), 133.

8. Jay Leyda, *Kino: A History of the Russian and Soviet Film* (London: George Allen and Unwin, 1960).

9. Walter Benjamin, "The Work of Art in the Age of Mechanical Reproduction," in *Illuminations*, ed. Hannah Arendt, trans. Harry Zohn (New York: Schocken, 1968), 238.

10. Leyda, *Films Beget Films*, 48.

11. Victor Shklovsky, "Art as Technique," in *Russian Formalist Criticism: Four Essays*, trans. Lee T. Lemon and Marion J. Reis (Lincoln: University of Nebraska Press, 1965), 12.

12. Leyda, *Films Beget Films*, 100.

13. An insightful application of this concept is Leyda's discussion of fiction films. It is quite possible to find a documentary dimension to otherwise purely fiction films in location shooting or in the physical appearance of actors at a given point in their careers. As Leyda goes on to note, such material can readily migrate into compilation films, where it may take on the aura of documentary authenticity directly—if the original source is not noted. Leyda also considers the degree of authenticity required of footage that illustrates spoken commentary, where reference to an event may be served by footage from a fictional representation or authentic archival footage but is culled, perhaps, from a different but similar event. This issue remains a lively one, and I discuss it further here in relation to Leyda's views on the reuse of staged documentary footage.

14. See Raymond Williams, *Marxism and Literature* (New York: Oxford University Press, 1977) for a discussion of "structures of feeling" as those nascent states in which ideology is felt more than conceived as one fruitful way to explore the degree to which documentaries can be compelling as well as convincing.

15. Cited in Bluem, *Documentary in American Television,* 148 (italics in original).

16. Roland Barthes, *Mythologies* (London: Jonathan Cape, 1972), 102.

17. Leyda, *Films Beget Films,* 108.

18. The expository mode is one of six modes, or cinematically specific forms of documentary filmmaking, that I discuss in my *Introduction to Documentary,* 2nd ed. (Bloomington: Indiana University Press, 2011).

19. Leyda, *Films Beget Films,* 109.

20. Pat Aufderheide, ed., *Honest Truths: Documentary Filmmakers on Ethical Challenges in Their Work,* www.cmsimpact.org/making-your-media-matter/documents/best-practices/honest-truths-documentary-filmmakers-ethical-chall. I served as a consultant for this project.

21. See Nichols, *Representing Reality,* 249–54, for a discussion of "a body too many" in relation to the representation of historical events in documentary.

22. Leyda, *Films Beget Films,* 131.

23. Many of these films are not available for rental or sale, but some do exist on the Internet. The British Film Institute offers a few clips from *Yellow Caesar* at www.screenonline.org.uk/film/id/1423861/index.html. *The Song of the Rivers* is listed as available at www.ovguide.com/the-song-of-the-rivers-9202a8c04000641f800000000af1724d#, although it may not be truly available. (This site links to Amazon and a subscription viewing plan I do not have.) *Description d'un combat,* with a mediocre voice-over commentary in English, resides at www.veoh.com/watch/v20609472P3KKqwJC?h1=siberia%2Fisrael-Description+of+a+Struggle-1957–1960-Chris+Marker+Description+d'un+combat+. Others, however, are yet to be found anywhere, a somewhat rash statement, perhaps, in these days of proliferating Internet content.

24. Among these published but scarcely reviewed novels are Albert Maltz, *The Journey of Simon McKeever* (Boston: Little, Brown, 1949); Albert Maltz, *A Long Day in a Short Life* (New York: International Publishers, 1951); Ring Lardner Jr., *The Ecstasy of Owen Muir* (London: Jonathan Cape, 1954); Abe Polonsky, *The World Above* (Boston: Little, Brown, 1951); Abe Polonsky, *A Season of Fear* (New York: Cameron and Associates, 1956). None received significant reviews although they possess considerable merit and, in retrospect, offer another revealing window on the activities of blacklisted writers.

CHAPTER 11. *RESTREPO*

1. The current *Army/Marine Corps Field Manual* on counterinsurgency, updated in 2014, is available at http://fas.org/irp/doddir/army/fm3–24.pdf. It replaces but does not reject General Petraeus's "Counterinsurgency Field

Manual," which appeared in 2006 and is available at http://usacac.army.mil/cac2/Repository/Materials/COIN-FM3–24.pdf.

2. *Army/Marine Corps Field Manual*, 2.

3. It can be argued that the attacks of 9/11 called for a police action more than a military one, but this argument has even stronger claims when it comes to building democracy in foreign lands. A military occupation suspends many civil liberties and imposes top-down law and order, as the U.S. occupation of Japan did after World War II. An indigenous police force, by contrast, functions to "serve and protect," to uphold the rule of law, not suspend it, and to provide for public safety, not imperil it. The use of force is much more tightly circumscribed and is rarely, if ever, legitimately used with the degree of indifference to "collateral damage" that military power can be. The war on terror, however, has not made building a democratic, civil society as great a priority as rooting out, by any means necessary, an insurgent enemy that only grows in number as a result of the terror, oppression, and anger that military occupation breeds.

PART 4. ETHICS AND IRONY IN DOCUMENTARY

1. Challenge for Change was a major initiative that spanned some thirteen years and dozens of films in which local citizens had a large say, if not control, over what was produced. It is thoroughly described in Thomas Waugh, Michael Brendan Baker, and Ezra Winton, eds., *Challenge for Change: Activist Documentary at the National Film Board of Canada* (Montréal: McGill-Queens University Press, 2010).

CHAPTER 13. DOCUMENTARY ETHICS

A significantly different version of this essay appeared in the English-language magazine *Documentary;* see Bill Nichols, "What to Do about Documentary Distortion," *Documentary,* March-April 2006, 28–33.

1. For a summary of the controversy see Irene Lacher, "Documentary Criticized for Re-enacted Scenes," *New York Times,* March 29, 2005, www.nytimes.com/2005/03/29/movies/documentary-criticized-for-reenacted-scenes.html.

2. This is not to say that scholars have ignored the issue. A classic text on ethics and documentary is Larry Gross, John Katz, and Jay Ruby, eds., *Image Ethics: The Moral Rights of Subjects in Photographs, Film, and Television* (New York: Oxford University Press, 1988). The same editors have also assembled *Image Ethics in the Digital Age* (Minneapolis: University of Minnesota Press, 2003).

3. See Brian Winston, "The Tradition of the Victim in Griersonian Documentary," in *New Challenges for Documentary,* ed. Alan Rosenthal (Berkeley: University of California Press, 1988), 269–87.

4. Frank Manchel, *Film Study: An Analytic Bibliography* (Teaneck, NJ: Fairleigh Dickenson Press, 1990), 1:245.

5. Lisa Leeman, "How Close Is Too Close? A Consideration of the Filmmaker-Subject Relationship," *International Documentary*, June 2003, www.documentary.org/magazine/how-close-too-close-consideration-film-maker-subject-relationship.

6. For Jill Godmilow's harsh critique of the film's ethics and politics see www.indiewire.com/article/killing-the-documentary-an-oscar-nominated-filmmaker-takes-issue-with-the-act-of-killing.

CHAPTER 14. IRONY, PARADOX, AND THE DOCUMENTARY

1. Fulton Lewis III received directing credit for HUAC and J. Edgar Hoover a screenwriting credit.

2. The two films are a classic example of the deliberate lie and its refutation. In addition, the program note for a screening at Princeton University in 2010 states, "*Operation Correction* was not the only film released that tried to debunk or criticize *Operation Abolition*. A Jesuit group called Impact Films produced *Autopsy on Operation Abolition*, which presented a debate over the truthfulness of the HUAC's account while California students Michael and Philip Burton produced *Wasn't That a Time*, which examined the cases of three people called to testify before the HUAC" (http://blogs.princeton.edu/reelmudd/2010/10/operation-abolition-and-operation-correction/).

3. Harlan Jacobson, "Michael and Me," *Film Comment* 25 (Nov.-Dec., 1989): 16–26. Moore's film raised much debate about the obligation of a personal or essay-type documentary to adhere to historical fact. See, e.g., Roger Ebert's commentary on the controversy at www.rogerebert.com/rogers-journal/attacks-on-roger-and-me-completely-miss-point-of-film.

4. For an extended discussion of reflexivity see my *Representing Reality* (Bloomington: Indiana University Press, 1991), 69–75, 240–43. For explorations of the many variations of the mockumentary see Jane Roscoe and Craig Hight, *Faking It: Mock-Documentary and the Subversion of Factuality* (Manchester: Manchester University Press, 2001); and Alexandra Juhasz and Jesse Lerner, eds., *F Is for Phony: Fake Documentaries and Truth's Undoing* (Minneapolis: University of Minnesota Press, 2006).

5. This quality of adding a new meaning that confounds the literal or apparent meaning stands at the heart of irony in general. The principle of collage and the compilation film add a fresh layer of meaning to what the recruited material originally meant. They complicate more than they wink. Something new emerges (and forms the basis for copyright protection for a compilation film as an original work of art). These examples also remind us that the ironic or parodic work need not be of a different type from what it ironizes or parodies: a mockumentary need not be a fiction film. Look no further than Buñuel's *Land without Bread*, Jayne Loader, Kevin Rafferty, and Pierce Rafferty's *Atomic Café* (1982), Trinh T. Minh-ha's *Surname Viet Given Name Nam* (1989), or Péter Forgács's *Free Fall* (1996). Irony abounds in works that are decidedly not fictions in any useful sense but not fully documentaries in the conventional sense either.

6. See Linda Hutcheon, *Irony's Edge: The Theory and Politics of Irony* (New York: Routledge, 1995). Hutcheon discusses such phenomena as Beauvais Lyon's traveling exhibition, "Reconstruction of an Aazudian Temple," a fake anthropological exhibit, and the Royal Ontario Museum's display of its collection of African artifacts in a way that was meant to challenge the colonialist assumptions behind their acquisition rather than celebrate them as the treasures of conquest. These and other examples generated an edge by confounding viewers: were they saying one thing and meaning another, or was it a genuine exhibit, in the one case, and a show complicit with colonialism in the other? Attendees did not merely respond to this question as an abstract puzzle but as something that struck a nerve involving trust, belief, and whether irony's edge was applied appropriately or not.

Interestingly, neither *Faking It* nor *F Is for Phony* addresses irony in any detail, and although *F Is for Phony* makes reference to Hutcheon's earlier book *The Theory of Parody* (New York: Methuen, 1985), neither book refers to her yet more germane *Irony's Edge*.

7. For extended discussions of this topic see J.L. Austin, *How to Do Things with Words*, 2nd ed. (New York: Oxford University Press, 1975); and Paul Watzlawick, Janet Bavelas, and Don Jackson, *Pragmatics of Human Communication: A Study of Interactional Patterns, Pathologies, and Paradoxes* (New York: Norton, 2011).

8. The film has been heavily discussed ever since it was first screened. An excellent historical contextualization of its strategies and reception is Jeffrey Ruoff's "An Ethnographic Surrealist Film: Luis Buñuel's *Land without Bread*," *Visual Anthropology Review* 14, no. 1 (1998): 45–57. Other valuable analyses of the film are Vivian Sobchack, "Synthetic Vision: The Dialectical Imperative of Buñuel's *Las Hurdes*," *Millennium Film Journal* 7–9 (Fall/Winter 1981): 140–50; and Catherine Russell, "Surrealist Ethnography," in *Experimental Ethnography* (Durham, NC: Duke University Press, 1999).

9. Examples include the filmmaker saying, near the start of the film, "You're in the movies," to his friend. The comment can be understood as a playful quip or an honest admission of the scripted fabrication taking place in the guise of a documentary, especially on re-viewing the film. Likewise, when the female subject of the film (neither character is named) turns on the light in her bedroom, she flinches and says, "I feel like I'm in a spotlight." She is: it's a spotlight needed for the movie, rather than a standard lightbulb, that illuminates the room.

10. Vivian Sobchack addresses the complex ethical issues raised by this particular film in "*No Lies*: Direct Cinema as Rape," *Journal of the University Film Association* 29, no. 4 (1997): 13–18.

11. Here is one of Geertz's many apt formulations of this complexity: "The thing to ask about a burlesqued wink or a mock sheep raid is not what their ontological status is. . . . The thing to ask is what their import is: what it is, ridicule or challenge, irony or anger, snobbery or pride, that, in their occurrence and through their agency, is getting said." Geertz, "Thick Description: Toward

an Interpretive Theory of Culture," in *The Interpretation of Cultures* (New York: Basic Books, 1973), 10.

12. David Bordwell, in his useful but literal-minded book *Narration in the Fiction Film*, gives schemata a central place in the comprehension of fiction films. He does not discuss irony. It is as if film language were all *schema* and no *figura*. *Figura* opens onto the world of metaphor, metonymy, synecdoche, irony, and all the other rhetorical figures of speech so aptly catalogued by the Greeks. A language without the irrational leaps *figurae* provide would be a quite impoverished one, like Morse code. In complex systems of *schema* and *figura* we enter the terrain Geertz describes as thick description or that Gilbert Ryle identifies when someone attempts to parody a wink. See Gilbert Ryle, "The Thinker of Thoughts: What Is 'Le Penseur' Doing?" at http://lucy.ukc.ac.uk/csacsia/vol14/papers/ryle_1.html.

13. Gregory Bateson, "A Theory of Play and Fantasy," in *Steps to an Ecology of Mind* (Chicago: University of Chicago Press, 2000), 180 (Bateson's italics).

14. Hayden White, *Metahistory: The Historical Imagination in Nineteenth-Century Europe* (Baltimore: Johns Hopkins University Press, 1973), 37.

15. *Nachträglichkeit*, as described by Freud, involves the attempt to forge a new interpretation based on oscillating shifts between a relationship sustained in the present moment with a past moment and with past iterations of this relationship. Memory must be rearranged to allow us to go forward with a continuing sense of a stable, functional relationship to the world rather than to succumb to a paralyzing sense of paradoxical injunctions.

16. Bateson, "Theory of Play and Fantasy," 182.

17. I treat epistephilia more fully, comparing it to scopophilia in fiction films, in my *Representing Reality* (Bloomington: Indiana University Press, 1991).

18. Octave Mannoni, "Je sais bien, mais quand-même," *Clefs pour l'imaginaire ou l'autre scène* (Paris: Éditions de Seuil, 1969), 9–33.

19. For an extended discussion of embodiment in documentary see Bill Nichols, "Embodied Knowledge and the Politics of Location," in *Blurred Boundaries: Questions of Meaning in Contemporary Culture* (Bloomington: Indiana University Press, 1994), 1–16

20. For a discussion of logical typing see Gregory Bateson, "The Logical Categories of Learning and Communication," in *Steps to an Ecology of Mind* (Chicago: University of Chicago Press, 2000), 279–308.

21. Nichols, *Representing Reality*, 232. The final chapter of that book, "Representing the Body: Questions of Meaning and Magnitude," addresses the ways documentary film can vivify lived experience. "What is needed beyond [reflexivity as a strategy] is a vivification of existential paradox, lived contradiction itself, those tensions and conflicts that exist between the text and the world, that give form to its content and also in-form the text in ways that can be apprehended" (241).

22. As Paul de Man puts it, and I believe his comment can refer to paradox as well as irony, "It is a question of whether it is possible to understand or not

understand." Paul de Man, "The Concept of Irony," in *Aesthetic Ideology* (Minneapolis: University of Minnesota Press, 1996), 166. He also speaks of irony as a "dialectics of the self" (ibid., 169–70). Hayden White puts it differently but with a similar emphasis on radical aporia: "In irony, figurative language folds back upon itself and brings its own potentialities for distorting perception under question" (White, *Metahistory*, 37).

23. Bateson, "Toward a Theory of Schizophrenia," *Steps to an Ecology of Mind* (Chicago: University of Chicago Press, 2000), 217. I have changed the parent from "mother" to "father" since Bateson drew false conclusions from his quite perceptive research. He assigned responsibility for schizophrenogenesis to the mother exclusively. It does a disservice to his insightful description of a communicative double bind to couple it with his erroneous idea about its etiological relation to schizophrenia and the role of mothers. What matters here is that this type of interaction creates an existential double bind.

A film version of this sort of double bind as a schizophrenogenic form of communication is Ken Loach's *Family Life* (1971), which, like Bateson, blames the mother for a child's mental illness. Linda Hutcheon takes up similar dire effects in her discussion of the "Into the Heart of Africa" exhibition at the Royal Ontario Museum in 1990: many members of the African-Canadian community missed the ironic markers and reacted angrily at what appeared to them as a straight-faced celebration of colonial conquest.

24. Geertz, *Interpretation of Cultures*, 16.

25. Catherine Russell, "*Las Hurdes:* Surreal Ethnography and the Documentary Unconscious," in *F Is for Phony: Fake Documentaries and Truth's Undoing*, ed. Alexandra Juhasz and Jesse Lerner (Minneapolis: University of Minnesota Press, 2006), 111.

26. Widely discussed and nominated for an Oscar as Best Documentary in 2013, the film is the subject of a dossier of eight short essays and an interview with the director in *Film Quarterly* 67, no. 2 (2014) to which I contributed "Irony, Cruelty, Evil (and a Wink) in *The Act of Killing*," 25–29.

27. Documentaries such as *Night and Fog* (Alain Resnais, 1955)—where Jean Cayrol's voice-over commentary speaks from the interior position of a Holocaust survivor—and *S21: The Khmer Rouge Killing Machine* (Rithy Panh, 2003)—where a former prisoner from this notorious prison righteously but patiently confronts a former guard from the same prison and witnesses guards reenacting aspects of their brutal conduct—provide a definite moral perspective on the heinous act of genocide. They are close to what the film *The Act of Killing would have been* were it not so fundamentally paradoxical.

Rithy Panh's films and a number of others, including Oppenheimer's *The Act of Killing*, usher in what Raya Morag aptly calls "perpetrator trauma." Her book closely scrutinizes the subjectivity of the perpetrators of atrocities in a wide range of films. See Raya Morag, *Waltzing with Bashir: Perpetrator Trauma and Cinema* (New York: I.B. Taurus, 2013).

28. Anthony Wilden, *System and Structure: Essays in Communication and Exchange*, 2nd ed. (London: Tavistock, 1980), 103.

29. See my "Irony, Cruelty, Evil," where I argue that his remorse may be what he feels his screen character ought to experience in a reenactment of his real-life role as a killer to provide a narrative arc to his tale. Jill Godmilow also argues for this possibility in "Killing the Documentary: An Oscar-Nominated Filmmaker Takes Issue with 'The Act of Killing,'" *Indiewire*, March 5, 2014, www.indiewire.com/article/killing-the-documentary-an-oscar-nominated-filmmaker-takes-issue-with-the-act-of-killing.

30. Congo's final scene at a rooftop execution site has him attempting to vomit but only retching, and then, as he picks up and handles the wire he previously used to demonstrate his garroting technique, he soliloquizes about his role as executioner. The soliloquy is a massive shift from any feelings of remorse: it propels him back to the *how* of it all rather than the why or the incalculable consequences. He shifts from noting that his conscience dictated that he had to kill his victims—already a move from remorse to rationalization—to the ease with which the wire he holds in his hands can kill and the secrecy with which bodies could be hauled away inside burlap bags like the one he picks up. His dry retching and dim awareness of what a loss of dignity, and life, entails contrast massively with the immense trauma expressed by Suryono after he is "executed" by garroting in a reenactment and his bodily fluids pour off his anguished face.

31. Hayden White, "The Value of Narrativity in the Representation of Reality," *The Content of the Form* (Baltimore: Johns Hopkins University Press, 1987), 14.

32. Some of the most intense feelings of betrayal may relate to the apparent failure of what Kristeva sees as "our ultimate and inseparable fetish": language. We know very well that the signifier is not the referent, the map not the territory, but all the same we will act as if it is, as if it at least gestures faithfully and truly. As she puts it, "the fetish becomes a life preserver, temporary and slippery, but nonetheless indispensable." Julia Kristeva, *Powers of Horror: An Essay on Abjection* (New York: Columbia University Press, 1982), 37. Irony and paradox unmask the fetish.

33. A vivid example of such anger, directed at *The Act of Killing*, is Jill Godmilow's "Killing the Documentary." Godmilow makes a number of good points about what a more sober documentary should do, but that is to ask for a film that orients us to atrocities within a clear-cut moral frame, the very thing that Oppenheimer's film undermines. My position is that *The Act of Killing* has a powerful and salutary effect but one that is different from reinforcing our preexisting moral and political beliefs or pointing us toward the neglected scene of a crime.

34. I explore this issue at greater length in the final essay here, "The Political Documentary and the Question of Impact." Two reports that capture the overall tenor of this development come from the Center for Social Media: Jessica Clark and Barbara Abrash, "Designing for Impact," www.cmsimpact.org/sites/default/files/documents/pages/designing_for_impact.pdf; and Jessica Clark and Sue Schardt, "Spreading the Zing: Reimagining Public Media

through the Makers Quest 2.0," www.cmsimpact.org/sites/default/files/documents/pages/AIRPerspective2010.pdf. The Ford Foundation's JustFilms, a category for work intended to have measurable social impact, cites the evaluation guidelines developed by the Bill and Melinda Gates Foundation as a model. See www.gatesfoundation.org/How-We-Work. Meanwhile, Patricia Finneran's "Documentary Impact: Social Change through Storytelling," written for HotDocs, a Canadian documentary film festival, identifies numerous efforts to quantify more precisely the evaluation of impact, including the work at the Lear Center, part of USC's Media Impact Project, an initiative partly sponsored by the Bill and Melinda Gates Foundation, which is developing the Participant Index, "a platform and approach to examining the power of storytelling to inspire social change," 10, http://s3.amazonaws.com/assets.hotdocs.ca/doc/HD14_Documentary_Impact_Report.PDF. Additionally, a number of individuals, groups, and organizations like Firelight Media and Working Films ("Linking non-fiction film with cutting edge activism") now specialize in the task of developing engagement strategies across multiple platforms to help filmmakers achieve empirically measurable social impact.

35. See, e.g., the avant-garde works discussed by Jeffrey Skoller, *Shadows, Specters, Shards: Making History in Avant-Garde Film* (Minneapolis: University of Minnesota Press, 2005).

CHAPTER 15. LETTER TO ERROL MORRIS

"Letter to Errol Morris: Feelings of Revulsion and the Limits of Academic Discourse" was first a paper presented at the Society for Cinema and Media Studies in 2010 and then an article in *Jump Cut*, no. 52 (Summer 2010): www.ejumpcut.org/archive/jc52.2010/index.html. It has been modified for inclusion here.

CHAPTER 16. PERPETRATORS, TRAUMA, AND FILM

"Perpetrators, Trauma, and Film" is derived in part from a review of Raya Morag's book *Waltzing with Bashir: Perpetrator Trauma and Cinema*, in *Studies in Documentary Film* 8, no. 1 (2014): 81–85.

1. Raya Morag, *Waltzing with Bashir: Perpetrator Trauma and Cinema* (New York: I.B. Tauris, 2013).

2. Frantz Fanon, *The Wretched of the Earth* (New York: Grove, 1963).

3. Noam Chayut, *My Holocaust Thief* (London: Verso, 2013).

4. Ibid., 205 (Chayut's italics).

CHAPTER 17. SAN FRANCISCO NEWSREEL

1. Interview with San Francisco Newsreel by the author. I conducted numerous interviews in New York and San Francisco for the thesis. The bulk of the information about Newsreel's internal structure, debates, and divisions stems

from these interviews, which were tape-recorded and transcribed. Newsreel members insisted on anonymity, and in what was probably excess deference, I did not include any names, not even first names, nor did I indicate dates. I have therefore reduced the number of notes somewhat since they are, in their minimalist form, basically redundant. The original research material is now on deposit in the university archive at the University of Wisconsin at Madison.

2. *Black Panther* was originally given the more inflammatory title *Off the Pig*, taken from a line in one of the Black Panthers' chants used in public demonstrations and aimed at the police who were inevitably present in force. At some point the title was changed to *Black Panther*.

3. San Francisco Newsreel, interview by the author.

4. See "Newsreel," *Film Quarterly* 22, no. 2 (1968–69): 43–48.

5. Ibid., 46–47.

6. San Francisco Newsreel, "Newsreel," *Movement* 5, no. 11 (1969).

7. Ibid., 4.

8. Ibid., 5.

9. The two groups' position papers are included in the full thesis and are available on my blog, billnichols.net.

10. San Francisco Newsreel, "Majority Position Paper" (unpublished, 1970), 5.

11. Sexism and racism are undoubtedly fundamental obstacles to working-class unity, and this point allowed Newsreel to maintain a classic Marxist perspective while also acknowledging that its own mission lay within the predominantly white sector of the working class. See Shulamith Firestone's book *The Dialectic of Sex: The Case for Feminist Revolution* (New York: Morrow, 1970); see also two Radical Education Project publications: "White Blindspot," by Noel Ignatin; and "Can White ~~Workers~~ Radicals Be Radicalized," by Ted Allen for cogent arguments on the nature of each (both articles are housed in box 1 of the Radical Education Project publications collection, Bentley Historical Library, University of Michigan).

12. Mao Tse Tung, *Literature and Art* (Beijing: Foreign Language Press, 1967), 148.

13. This is the concern that my "The Voice of Documentary" article took up later: how to ensure that the filmmaker's voice does not become submerged beneath the voices of those invited to tell their stories for the film. See Bill Nichols, "The Voice of Documentary," *Film Quarterly* 36, no. 3 (1983): 17–30.

14. Jay Leyda, *Kino: A History of the Russian and Soviet Film* (New York: Macmillan, 1960), 247.

15. Dziga Vertov, "The Writings of Dziga Vertov," in *Film Culture Reader*, ed. P. Adams Sitney (New York: Praeger, 1970), 361.

16. Judy Smith, interview by the author.

17. Robert Drew spearheaded a team of filmmakers working for ABC who made a number of pioneering observational documentaries such as *Primary* (1960), which followed John F. Kennedy and Hubert Humphrey as they competed for the Democratic nomination in the Wisconsin primary.

18. Emile de Antonio, interview by the author, New York, April 1971.

19. Stephen Mamber, *Cinema Verite in America: Studies in Uncontrolled Documentary* (Cambridge, MA: MIT Press, 1974), 209.

CHAPTER 18. THE POLITICAL DOCUMENTARY AND
THE QUESTION OF IMPACT

This chapter was originally published in very different, briefer form as "What Current Documentaries Do and Can't Do," *Velvet Light Trap* 60 (Fall 2007): 85–86.

1. The most striking example of such a trend is Dinesh D'Souza and John Sullivan's *2016: Obama's America*, ranked second out of the top ten political documentaries in box-office revenue, according to http://www.boxofficemojo. com/genres/chart/?id=politicaldoc.htm. Its success is primarily due to its promotion among conservative groups. The top ten films are:

Fahrenheit 9/11	$119,194,771.00
2016: Obama's America	$33,449,086.00
Sicko	$24,540,079.00
An Inconvenient Truth	$24,146,161.00
Bowling for Columbine	$21,576,018.00
America (2014)	$14,444,502.00
Capitalism: A Love Story	$14,363,397.00
Expelled: No Intelligence Allowed	$7,720,487.00
Roger and Me	$6,706,368.00
Inside Job	$4,312,735.00

The website does not describe how the figures were determined, and the films are quite diverse in subject and potential audience.

2. A striking example of the task at hand for documentary is the impact, the negligible impact, of PBS's Frontline broadcast of *The Rise of ISIS* (Martin Smith) in November 2014 on the seemingly sudden emergence of the Islamic State (ISIS or ISIL). The film is a standard journalistic report but well researched and quite convincing. ISIL arose from the failure of Nouri al-Malicki to build a central government in Iraq that honored multiculturalism, especially between his own Shiite faction and Sunni Iraqis. Instead, he mounted a campaign of terror, with tacit consent from the United States. Our complicity and his folly bred the fear, frustration, anger, and hatred that propelled Sunni militants to take arms against a government that refused to incorporate them within a democratic process. Just as our own drone strikes and special forces operations, detailed in an Oscar-nominated documentary, *Dirty Wars* (Richard Rowley and Jeremy Scahill, 2013), have bred as many terrorists as they have killed, if not more, Malicki created his own monster, one that has driven him from power

and now threatens to destroy the nation and government the Bush administration's initial invasion sought to implant.

3. Jessica Clark and Barbara Abrash, "Designing for Impact," Center for Media and Social Impact, Sept. 2011, www.cmsimpact.org/sites/default/files/documents/pages/designing_for_impact.pdf, 5.

4. The Center for Media and Social Impact, American University (originally known as the Center for Social Media), came early to the game, but its contribution has been more to champion this shift than to fund it. As such its role differs considerably from that of actual funding sources.

5. Jessica Clark and Sue Schardt, "Spreading the Zing: Reimagining Public Media through the Makers Quest 2.0," www.airmedia.org/PDFs/AIRPerspective2010.pdf, 9, 1. *Zing* belongs to the new jargon. It "marries an older set of production practices designed to move audiences intellectually or emotionally to the new capacity to involve, engage, and collaborate with them directly in constructing public media projects" (1), as if art, the "old" production practice, could not have involved, engaged, or collaborated with its viewers until Internet 2.0 arrived.

6. Ibid., 2.

7. Clark and Abrash, "Designing for Impact," 20.

8. See www.businessinsider.com/the-guy-behind-the-kony-2012-video-finally-explains-how-everything-went-so-weird-2013-3.

9. Email to author, Nov. 11, 2014, from info@invisiblechildren.com.

10. A *New Yorker* article on Emerson Spartz, a young man skilled at creating viral websites, paints a skeptical portrait of his achievements and mentions, as an analogy, the Kony phenomenon: "[*Kony 2012*] has been viewed on YouTube more than a hundred million times, but it did not achieve its ultimate goal: Kony remains at large, as does his militia, The Lord's Resistance Army." Andrew Marantz, "The Virologist," *New Yorker*, Jan. 5, 2015, 21.

11. Clark and Abrash, "Designing for Impact," 13.

12. The notion of structuring absences comes from Louis Althusser. It refers to how we identify large conceptual entities like ideology, faith, or the universe but only experience their impact in specific instances or effects. In relation to media culture and art, ideology may be a force that affects the actions of characters but is rarely identified or directly named. This idea underpins Althusser's general theory of ideology, most fully elaborated in his "Ideology and Ideological State Apparatuses," in *"Lenin and Philosophy" and Other Essays,* trans. Ben Brewster (New York: Monthly Review Press, 1971).

13. Fledgling Fund, www.thefledglingfund.org/resources/impact.

14. Research continues and has become more in accord with models of ideology as a broad, long-term, pervasive, and gradual process in which exposure to sex and violence can play a contributory role, often by desensitizing some individuals to the real-life effects of disrespectful and harmful actions toward others. See, e.g., Neil Malamuth and John Briere, "Sexual Violence in the Media: Indirect Effects on Aggression against Women," *Journal of Social Issues* 42, no. 3 (1986): 75–92.

15. Hall wrote numerous papers, but a good introduction to some of his key ideas is "Encoding/Decoding," in *Culture, Media, Language: Working Papers in Cultural Studies, 1972–79,* ed. Stuart Hall, Dorothy Hobson, Andrew Lowe, and Paul Willis (London: Hutchinson, 1980), 128–38.

16. Clark and Abrash, "Designing for Impact," 6.

17. Dave Eggers, *The Circle* (New York: Random House, 2013), 490.

18. A useful, though jargon-riddled, survey of the social impact field is Caty Borum Chattoo, "Assessing the Social Impact of Social Issue Documentaries: Research Methods and Future Considerations," Center for Media and Social Impact, Oct. 2014, www.cmsimpact.org/media-impact/related-materials/documents/assessing-social-impact-issues-focused-documentaries.

19. Scott Macaulay, "The Lingua Franca of Non-fiction Filmmaking Should Be the Language of Cinema, Not Grant Applications," *Filmmaker,* http://filmmaker-magazine.com/88344-the-lingua-franca-of-non-fiction-filmmaking-should-be-the-language-of-cinema-not-grant-applications-sundance-documentary-film-program-director-tabitha-jackson-at-doc-nyc/#.

Index